BE THE GO-TO

BE THE
GO-TO

How to Own Your Competitive
Market, Charge More, and
HAVE CUSTOMERS LOVE YOU FOR IT

Theresa M. Līna

LIONCREST
PUBLISHING

BE THE GO-TO
How to Own Your Competitive Market,
Charge More, and Have Customers Love You For It

Library of Congress Cataloging-in-Publication Data has been applied for.

ISBN   978-1-5445-1436-9   *Hardcover*
       978-1-5445-1435-2   *Paperback*
       978-1-5445-1434-5   *Ebook*

To my career-long mentor, friend, and role model,
Al Burgess, who gave me limitless opportunities as a young
executive and taught me what it takes to be the Go-To.

To my husband and daughters, who are the loves
of my life and make it all worthwhile.

To my parents, who made it all possible.

CONTENTS

I. WHY

II. WHAT

III. HOW

PART I

WHY

PROLOGUE

While at a reception hosted by the Soviet Union's embassy in Washington, DC, *New York Times* reporter Walter Sullivan received a panic-stricken phone call from his Washington Bureau chief. It was October 4, 1957. Meant to cap off a week of international scientific meetings among prestigious rocket and satellite researchers from seven countries, the reception proved to be an intentionally timed public relations and propaganda coup for the Soviets and a complete humiliation for the US. What had the bureau chief relayed to Sullivan? Soviet news sources had just announced the launch of the first Earth-orbiting artificial satellite, *Sputnik 1*.

The Soviet Union had beaten the United States into space.

Sputnik 1 was simply a twenty-two-inch metal sphere weighing less than 200 pounds, orbited the earth in ninety-six minutes, and stayed up for three months. But it had officially kicked off the Space Race.

In what would come to be known as the "Sputnik Crisis," this event set off alarm bells. NASA archives say it had a "Pearl Harbor" effect on American public opinion. In NASA's own words:

It was a shock, introducing the average citizen to the space age in a crisis setting...In the Cold War environment of the late 1950s, [with the looming threat of nuclear war hanging in the air] this disparity of capability portended menacing implications.

Just a month later, *Sputnik 2* carried a living creature, a dog, into space in an even larger vehicle that orbited for almost 200 days.

Over the next several years, the United States (representing the free world at that time) made only occasional incremental gains in the space race against its Cold War opponent. US space exploration then consisted of a hodgepodge of initiatives. There were numerous independent projects in progress, spread among multiple government agencies and contractors, involving thousands of people and investments of billions of dollars per year. And with little to show for it all.

According to *Apollo* astronaut Dick Gordon, in looking back:

The only driving theme was speed, to be the first at something, anything. All of that time and money was being expended while the Soviets kicked our butts with one historical achievement after another.

By 1961, newly elected president John F. Kennedy realized the US space mission needed focus. He said:

I believe that this nation should commit itself to achieving the goal, before this decade is out, of landing a man on the Moon and returning him safely to the Earth.

He didn't set this goal quietly either. He branded the initiative as the Apollo Space Program and **launched** it with a grand gesture in the most public way possible: a historic speech to Congress on May 25,

1961, that the entire world heard. He put a stake in the ground with a proud declaration of a singular goal. No one knew at the time how to do it, but if achieved, this feat clearly would establish the US and the rest of the free world as the dominant force in space.

(Image: NASA)

Requiring unprecedented funding and public support in order to keep the program alive over such an extended period, Apollo Space Program leaders continuously **ignited** engagement and support from politicians, the general public and influential scientists, and researchers inside and outside of NASA on how to make it work. *Apollo* astronauts became the faces of the program, even visiting schools and civic meetings to drum up support. Some regard the program as the "most successful public relations campaign in history."

But the Apollo Space Program had to walk the talk—it had to deliver. To do this, it **navigated** an eight-year, multi-mission journey from inception to successful Moon landing involving thousands of people inside and outside of NASA, including academics, defense contractors, and other partners who helped bring myriad pieces together.

And despite a declaration of success with a Moon landing on July 20, 1969, the Apollo Space Program didn't stop. It **accelerated** its efforts with continued Moon landings and additional accomplishments over the course of six more missions in order to maintain US dominance in space, until an easing of tensions led to an era of US-Soviet cooperation in space endeavors.

The Apollo Space Program has gone down in history as a shining example of what can happen when an organization decides to become the Go-To for a specific problem and takes a methodical four-phased approach toward achieving it.

INTRODUCTION

"How in the world is that person making $50,000 a day?"
This is the question that started it all.

A few years into my consulting business, one of my colleagues told me about her close friend who had less hands-on client experience than either of us and was personally commanding $50,000 a day to provide expertise to top executives. I was at once terribly envious and incredibly inspired.

This conversation occurred while I was in the midst of a reevaluation of my firm's strategy, because we, on the other hand, were being forced to *lower* our prices. Somewhere along the way, our consulting services had come to be viewed as commodities, even by loyal clients who knew our capabilities well, understood how deep our expertise was, and had been engaging us for years. They were starting to put pressure on us to lower our fees and talk about replacing us with less expensive, less experienced consultants as though we were interchangeable parts. We were also getting pushed further down into our clients' organizations, with less and less influence.

Meanwhile, and quite ironically, we were finding it increasingly difficult to convince our clients that they didn't look, sound, or act any different from the competition; that it wasn't clear as to whom they were trying to serve; and that they didn't have a clear message that resonated with prospects. Even leading technology companies were beginning to face the same challenges as competitors started matching them on functions, features, and price.

These experiences were in stark contrast to my earlier experience in helping to launch and grow what was then called the Communications Industry Group (CIG) at Accenture. Starting from ground zero and operating much like a venture-backed startup, we had lots of market forces working against us and still managed organic growth to revenues of over $850 million in less than a decade...in the midst of a recession. This despite the fact that, at the time, if you weren't a telecommunications company, you had no credibility in that industry; no one knew who we were or what we did; there was no existing market for what we were selling; the industry was already dominated by a few gigantic, well-entrenched providers; and we didn't start out as experts. Nonetheless, we managed huge and very profitable year-over-year revenue growth, became the dominant player in our target markets, and laid the groundwork for what is today a multi*billion*-dollar business unit.

What did my colleague's friend and CIG do right? What did my firm and most other companies need to do to achieve this kind of *sustainable* differentiation in order to ensure ongoing, profitable growth? Somehow, certain companies were each succeeding at becoming *and remaining* the dominant Go-To brand, able to command high prices relative to the competition, while everyone else languished as me-too providers. I became obsessed with figuring out the recipe, embarking on an intensive research and analysis effort.

One day, on a plane to Chicago to meet with clients, I sketched out a strategy for my company. With so many years of Accenture's methodology and project management training ingrained in me, it was a step-by-step framework in the form of a flow diagram. I looked at it for a few minutes and said to myself, "This is what *all* of our clients need to be doing! *This* is how companies dominate a market space and become the Go-To."

Somehow, certain companies were each succeeding at becoming and remaining the dominant Go-To brand, able to command high prices relative to the competition, while everyone else languished as me-too providers.

Having grown up in NASA territory where many people in the neighborhood had once worked on the Apollo Space Program, I immediately saw parallels between this approach and how the United States put a human on the Moon when that seemed an utterly impossible task. The US had been losing the space race in the midst of the Cold War with the Soviet Union, and Kennedy finally decided to skip incremental achievements and go for broke by landing a person on the Moon.

What's useful about the Apollo Space Program as a metaphor is that the fundamental circumstances were very similar to what many companies are facing, but the stakes were infinitely higher and the challenge infinitely greater at a time when technological superiority represented the power of liberty over oppression. You'll read throughout the book about how the Apollo Space Program leaders had to rally all the necessary players around the goal; manage the program, projects, and business processes; build and motivate numerous organizations and engage partners; demonstrate milestone successes along the way and continuously make the case to both the public and Congress for continued funding; and the list goes on. There were many ups and downs, including a devastating tragedy you'll read about later. It was not an easy journey, but it was immensely rewarding and made history. If the Apollo team could accomplish its seemingly unachievable task in less than ten years, anything is possible in the corporate realm.

Now let me be clear. As with any metaphor or case study, there is not a 100 percent, precise parallel of the Apollo Space Program with circumstances facing corporations, startups, and individuals. Some of the many differences will cross your mind as you read. However, if you fixate on those, you'll miss the opportunity to learn some excellent lessons and apply them to your situation. The intent is to give you a vivid point of reference that helps you easily visualize the general path you need to take. The collective Apollo team's ability to overcome adversity in the face of so much uncertainty, so much complexity, and so many obstacles is as impressive as its ultimate achievement. The Apollo Space Program is an incredibly inspirational story and serves as a useful model for companies to follow in pursuing market dominance, as I hope you'll see throughout this book.

When I sketched out my plan that day on the plane, it was immediately apparent that the framework should be called the Apollo Method for Market Dominance.

That was many years ago. Since then, I have been seeking out the method's weaknesses. I've gone inside companies as a full-time strategy and marketing executive to find out what's hard about implementing it in practice. I've looked for better alternatives. I've continued to research it, conducting over 500 executive interviews. I've lived through the "dot-com boom" and "bust" of the 1990s and the Great Recession circa 2008–11. And I've watched hundreds of companies go out of business because they didn't implement one or more of the key elements.

Through all this, it became clear that the approach works, especially now that enterprise customers and even consumers are demanding full *solutions* to their problems and not just generic products or services, which is a key underpinning of the Apollo Method.

This means they want to buy *results*—they want offerings that take them all the way to the outcome and not just buy functions or features. You'll learn more about what this means and how to do that.

Through all this, it became clear that the approach works, especially now that enterprise customers and even consumers are demanding full solutions to their problems and not just generic products or services, which is a key underpinning of the Apollo Method.

My research and experiences have resulted in some fascinating stories, examples, and analogies, which I share in this book. Beyond Apollo Space Program lessons, you'll learn how to build momentum in the marketplace around your point of view and solutions the way successful companies have done it; the way political campaigns build awareness and support for their candidates; and the way musicians build a following. You will read inspirational stories about how companies like Disney, REI, Google, Facebook, Amazon, Tesla, and many others each became the Go-To in a relatively specific area of focus and then built from there. And you will find out about spectacular failures and lessons learned, including some of my own.

One company you will hear a lot of inspirational stories about is Salesforce, which provides cloud-based customer relationship management (CRM) software to companies. Salesforce was a David versus Goliath story upon its founding in an apartment in 1999, taking on huge players and enduring a market crash just as it was finding its legs. At that time, CRM was jokingly referred to as "consultants raking in millions," because a CRM implementation required hundreds of people and millions of dollars to accomplish. As you'll read, Salesforce founder Marc Benioff believed this was ridiculous. He declared his own moonshot and led a movement to change the entire industry: he wanted to eliminate corporate dependence upon expensive, complex, installed software by offering "software-as-a-service" based in the cloud. Within three years, Salesforce revenues were $24 million. By year seven, they were $175 million. Now, twenty years later, the company has grown revenues every single year and dominates the crowded CRM space with 16.8 percent market share (the next closest competitor has a mere 5.7 percent share). In 2019, the company posted revenues of $13.3 *billion* (26 percent year-over-year growth), with another $25.7 billion in bookings (revenues under contract but not yet recognized) and $3.4 billion in operating cash flow, an increase of 24 percent over the prior year. According to eTrade, its gross margin (cash available to spend on operations) is 75 percent. It's also number two on the *Fortune* list of "Best Companies to Work For" and is fourteenth on the list of "Most Admired Companies in the World" across all industries. And indeed, the company did spark a revolution in its own industry, given that KBV Research expects global spending on software-as-a-service to reach a whopping $185.8 billion by 2024. You'll read about how Salesforce achieved all of this by instinctively implementing each of the four key strategies that we'll talk about in the coming chapters (the four phases of the Apollo Method for Market Dominance).

WHO THIS BOOK IS FOR

This book is for you if your company operates in a highly competitive market full of me-toos. It's for you if your company is having trouble differentiating from the competition and is competing on price. It's especially for you if your company sells some kind of *intangible* product or service—the kind of product or service that is difficult for customers to hold in their hands, evaluate, or compare to others until they have bought and are using it. These concepts even apply to individuals seeking to build a personal brand. Regardless of the sector, you will find that many, if not all, of these principles apply and can improve your margins and prospects for growth. This book is for you if your work has a direct or indirect bearing on revenue and/or margins. This includes direct or support roles in business unit operations and management; sales, business development, and partner relationships; marketing; product, service, and/or solution development and maintenance; client delivery and support activity; human resources and training; infrastructure and information systems; and financial management.

WHAT YOU'LL GET FROM THIS BOOK

In short, this book will give you an *actionable* path to higher revenues and gross margins that will then provide the money to invest in innovation and growth.

A pile of bricks is nothing but an obstacle, but organize those bricks and add some mortar, and you have sturdy walls that serve many powerful purposes—a structure within which to operate or live, protection from outside threats, and much more. Take a pile of LEGO bricks, and you can organize them into countless functional structures and sculptures, including an operational car—which has been done!

One of my frustrations as a strategy and marketing practitioner is the dearth of books or even articles that lay out a step-by-step rationale and approach for achieving market dominance. Many discuss concepts but not the precise tasks, start to finish. I have written or created generic strategic planning and marketing methodologies, but they are templates—they don't explain how to achieve a particular business outcome. There are plenty of methodologies for systems development, project management, process improvement, product development, and even generic marketing plan development and digital marketing initiatives. But the weakness with most marketing plans is that there is a terrific analysis of the situation, the market, the competition, the strategy, and so forth and then one big giant bucket of tactics you may as well call "Stuff."

I've never found anything that tells you, step by step, how to win in your market. Neither have I seen anything that shows a methodology for deciding which strategy or marketing tactics to choose and how to best implement them. Shockingly, no leadership executive or board member I've ever worked with has asked for one. In presenting a plan, I've always expected questions like, "Of the thousands of options to choose from, how did you decide on those specific tactics? How do the pieces fit together and build on one another? How are these going to develop the market? How will they lead us to market dominance and attract clients? What's the long-term roadmap—how do these build on each other over the next few years to build our brand and entrench us? How do these investments tie to business outcomes, and how are you going to measure them?"

There is no reason why any business should have to languish as a thin-margin, me-too player when there is the option to become a Go-To. The key is figuring out how to deliver such superior business impact that your clients will not fixate on price but rather on the value you deliver. This book will show you how to do that.

This book will give you answers. Chapter 1 talks about your commoditization challenge and why that is a serious problem for your business. Chapter 2 talks about the advantages of being the Go-To. Chapter 3 shares what a Go-To brand does differently from other companies. Chapters 4–8 take you through the Apollo Method for Market Dominance step by step in guiding you to becoming the Go-To in your own market. In addition to a conceptual overview, you'll get practical advice on how to execute key components. You'll also see examples of how the Apollo Space Program and other companies have successfully implemented them. At the end of each chapter, there are action items and worksheets to help you immediately apply the Apollo Method to your business. Chapter 9 helps you assemble all of that work into a simple but profoundly powerful one-page flight plan to focus your early efforts. You'll walk away with actions that you can start implementing immediately and refine as you go.

If you implement this plan, you should see immediate improvements in competitive differentiation, your brand image, and your ability to deliver more powerful results to customers at healthy prices.

Because you're working on a strategy that will impact all aspects of your business, I recommend your entire leadership team and other key stakeholders all read the book and complete the action items and worksheets together. This gives you a common lexicon, keeps all of you in sync, and ensures buy-in throughout the process. All of this leads to more effective implementation and better results.

There is no reason why any business should have to languish as a thin-margin, me-too player when there is the option to become a Go-To. The key is figuring out how to deliver such superior business impact that your clients will not fixate on price but rather on the value you deliver. This book will show you how to do that.

CHAPTER 1

COMMODITIZATION IS ENEMY #1

I once spent a Saturday night in Atlanta's Fulton County jail with renowned actress Candice Bergen. We had both been arrested.

When the guy on the other side of the bars yelled, "Cut!" it was a relief to step out of that nasty, smelly cell. The outcome of that evening was a really bad, low-budget movie, but I learned some things.

You see, by day I was a buttoned-up young management consultant working for Accenture, but by night, I fed my creative side with acting and improvisation lessons. It was in this offbeat world among my eccentric acting friends that I was exposed to some of my most powerful lessons about differentiation when marketing something intangible—why it's hard to achieve, why it's even harder to sustain, and most importantly, why it's so crucial to survival in a competitive environment.

Let's start with acting auditions offering no way to obviously stand out. I remember the irony of one in particular. It was for a television commercial. The character was a young corporate type exactly my age, and those auditioning were to wear formal business attire. Easy for me. I'd just wear a suit and heels to work. Everyone would assume I was giving a client presentation that day, and I'd slip out at lunch to audition. I thought, "How hard is it going to be to play myself?"

Silly me.

Once there, I received a script with just one line of dialogue. They provided no story or other context about this person or situation except this: I was to run from one corner of the room to another carrying a football like a running back, while shouting, "Get out of my way!!!!!!"

The worst of it was that at least forty other actresses showed up looking just like me. We all wanted to think we were different, but we weren't. Yes, we all had relevant experience, training, and talent, but those were our tickets to entry really. You didn't get invited to the party if you didn't have the requisite credentials. We were complete commodities with zero control over our destinies. There was no way to be memorable or offer more value than someone else. It was a crapshoot. I'd have had better odds playing the lottery.

We all wanted to think we were different, but we weren't.

I found that aspect of the acting world to be completely absurd. Half the time, judging from the array of people at a given audition, the directors didn't even know what they were looking for—they'd "know it when they saw it." I understood that it was just how the game was played, but I quickly figured out that going from one cattle call to the next wasn't for me. There was no going-in advantage, no control, no sure way to distinguish yourself in advance or afterward, no way to get your distinctive qualities across (as if they mattered), and low odds of success relative to the investment of time, energy, and ego required.

As it turns out, things aren't that different when competing for business.

It was around that time that my employer, Accenture, kept losing proposals to what it felt were inferior competitors, so it decided to dig into what was happening. It hired an outside firm to conduct a win-loss analysis and prepare a report called, "A Primer on How to Beat Accenture." The outside firm interviewed buyers, and this response from one summed up the problem:

> Our evaluation of a variety of things that all the vendors threw up was that they were pretty much equal on them. For example, when you talk about tools, software development methods, development centers, client lists, the pace of your approach, and even things Accenture would consider proprietary...we found that all the responses were the same. And we awarded zero points to those.

When your business looks and sounds like everyone else, you're effectively at a cattle-call audition. Like 99 percent of the companies out there, you are failing to differentiate in a way that's blatantly obvious to customers, which makes you a me-too commodity forced to compete on price when competition increases and/or demand ebbs.

DIFFERENCES NO ONE CAN SEE

When you're a me-too in a crowded space, prospects can no more tell the difference between you and the competition than a wine novice can distinguish a zinfandel from a merlot. As non-connoisseurs of your business category, the differences are not just subtle; they're impossible to detect.

Let's take just one example of how quickly a brand can disappear into the crowd. Every year or two since 2011, Scott Brinker has been publishing the "Marketing Technology Landscape Supergraphic" showing every company in the space. In 2011, there were roughly 150 companies on the list. In 2019, there were over 7,000. The progression has looked like this:

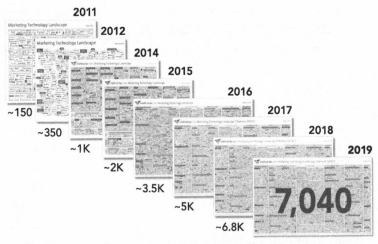

The Marketing Technology Landscape: an example of how quickly brands can disappear into the crowd, even in a relatively new market. *(Image: Scott Brinker, chiefmartec.com)*

Imagine what it takes to compete in that morass. Imagine how much harder it's gotten every year.

As a prospective buyer trying to figure out who to call, you'd basically have to roll the dice. As a company trying to stand out, you have the same odds I did in that acting audition. Getting selected becomes a matter of dumb luck, and that's no way to run or market a business.

Chances are that you can strip the names off the boilerplate paragraphs for companies within a category, mix them up, and find it impossible to know which paragraph belongs to which firm.

Intangible products and services are especially susceptible. Buyers can't easily touch or experience them before making a purchase. Almost any professional service category is a great example. Go out to the websites of various doctors, lawyers, graphic designers, advertising or graphic design agencies, Silicon Valley venture capital firms, architecture firms, information technology service providers, communications service providers, and so on, and try to figure out what makes each unique. Chances are that you can strip the names off the boilerplate paragraphs for companies within a category, mix them up, and find it impossible to know which paragraph belongs to which firm.

ARE YOU A ME-TOO?

If you can't instantly convey what makes you unique and of particular value to a particular market, you are a me-too copycat in the eyes of the market, which is the only place where it matters. If a prospect, a market influencer, a prospective employee, a supplier, or someone who could potentially refer you to a possible buyer can't quickly figure out what makes you special, you're sunk.

Take the test on the next page to see how you stack up. (It's also available as a tool on apollomethod.com if you want to have others in your organization take it just to see what happens.)

If you answered, "No," to *any* of the questions, you have a problem. If you answered, "No," to *more than half*, you are a me-too commodity and in dire need of a course correction.

Are You Indeed a Me-Too?

Take this little test to find out.

	No	Yes
Are most of your sales opportunities noncompetitive?		
Are you able to charge premium prices, regardless of what the competition is charging?		
Is it easy for prospective customers to quickly grasp what your product or service does?		
Is it easy for them to quickly see what makes your offering unique?		
Is it crystal clear as to why a prospective customer should turn to you instead of someone else?		
Is it difficult for a buyer to do an apples-to-apples comparison of your offering vs. a competitor's?		
In one sentence, can you state what you stand for?		
Can you state it in one brief phrase?		
Can you capture it in one to two words?		
Would we get the same answer from each of your employees? Customers?		
Can you make claims about the results you deliver that no competitive alternative can say?		
Do your proposals, marketing materials, website, etc., have a unique voice?		
Do you have such a strong market position that customers actively seek you out?		
Do talented recruits actively seek to work for you vs. your top competitors?		
Is the market willing to pay a premium for your stock?		

And if you're feeling a little beat up right now, don't, because it's really tough to stand out in a market like yours. Let's find out why.

THE COMMODITIZATION NIGHTMARE: CAN YOU RELATE?

In thousands of conversations with senior executives across sectors, when I've asked for one sentence or phrase that sums up their biggest business problem, the refrain has remained the same. Note the theme.

"How to avoid becoming a commodity—it's very difficult to differentiate ourselves from the competition."

"How to protect our margins—we have to be competitive, and clients are pressuring us to reduce our prices."

"How to establish awareness in the marketplace—we are a well-kept secret, and it's been hard to stand out from the crowd."

"How to get prospects to understand what we do and what makes us different."

"How to improve our business model so we can leverage our experience and reduce service delivery costs."

"How to attract and retain the right people—we're competing against other employers for the same, limited skillset."

"How to get the *right* business—we have a lot of business, but it's not of the quality that will build our future."

When you boil down all the problems and challenges affecting the health of these companies in the past, present, and future (anomalies like a global financial meltdown aside), the fundamental problem is a lack of adequate differentiation, *as perceived and valued by the buyer.* **Commoditization is the single biggest competitive threat they face.**

This is a massive issue that plagues executives everywhere, and almost no one worldwide is immune in today's global economy. Amazon has transformed retail in the US and is now out to dominate in Australia and other countries. On a personal level for many people, you know you're a commodity when your job is handed to a robot or a computer with artificial intelligence capabilities. In a study of forty-six countries and *800 occupations* (we're not just talking factory jobs here), the McKinsey Global Institute found that by 2030, robotic automation will replace as many as 800 million global workers—one-fifth of the global workforce. This means it's probably not hard to be like you (whether a company, product/service, or individual) or be cheaper. Here's why.

WHY MARKET FORCES ARE ALWAYS PUSHING YOU TOWARD COMMODITY STATUS

Even if you are in the fortunate position of being unique in some way, me-too copycats will always come after you.

Let's look at how this happens. Let's suppose that you've entered a relatively new market with a unique or proprietary (e.g., patent-protected) offering, whether it's a product or service. Initially, your customers have few options to choose from. You enjoy reasonable market share, are able to charge a healthy price, and earn nice margins.

Inevitably, competitors emerge with their own proprietary offerings or copycats of yours. Or perhaps your patent expires. Suddenly, customers have more choices, and providers have increasing difficulty standing apart. The differences between offerings become less and less discernable to the naked eye. At 50,000 feet, customers can no longer distinguish one provider from another. Each sale starts to take longer and cost you more time, effort, and money. You start cutting your prices to close deals.

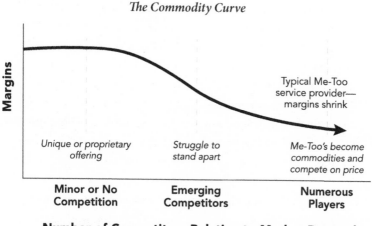

The Commodity Curve

As the market fills with competitors, pricing pressure tends to push margins down. *(Source: Apollo Method for Market Dominance)*

Then the market matures even more and completely fills up with competition. Supply has grown faster than demand, and the market is full of me-toos. Everyone looks and sounds the same. It takes a lot of time on the part of a prospect to even begin to understand what makes one provider different from another—more time than they are usually willing to invest. Customers now have their pick of who to work with. They start to put minimal effort into coming up with a shortlist and begin to operate under the assumption that the offerings are basically all at parity; they start shopping completely on price.

You're really in trouble when the procurement department gets involved. Edward Bond, Jr., CEO of Bond Brothers, a fourth-generation construction and construction management company, describes a classic scenario:

> When I first started in the construction industry, I had one energy client that provided 90 percent of my revenue. It wasn't long before I heard Death knocking at my door. The icy-cold purchasing agent stated that my price was too high and that, if I wanted to work with them, I'd have to drop my price. "Purchasing" was clearly not interested in understanding why my fee was what it was; rather, Purchasing's job was to get the lowest price from vendors and professionals alike. I was cornered without an informed economic decision maker to whom to appeal about value versus cost.

Meanwhile, your costs have gone way up—you're having to invest and scramble to develop the next generation of your offering; your sales costs have skyrocketed, as sales cycles get longer; your pipeline of work is spotty, leaving lots of your people underutilized; and industry advancements are pressuring you to invest in skill enhancement for your client delivery people. In short, your margins are sinking like a stone.

This is the cycle you can expect. It's Economics 101. Without making any fundamental changes to your business, there are only three realistic forces that will allow your margins to temporarily (and only temporarily) go up again without changing anything else: a bunch of competitors disappear (bow out or go out of business), a disruptive technology or trend suddenly removes significant cost (e.g., outsourcing software engineering work to India and China), or demand surges.

WE'RE TALKING ABOUT GROSS PROFIT AND MARGIN HERE

To keep the discussions simple throughout the book, my references to "profit" and "margin" are primarily to *gross profit* (an amount) and *gross margin* (a percentage). These measure the difference in the revenue you generate (driven by your pricing) versus what it cost you to produce or provide the offering. This is in contrast to net profit and net profit margin, which also include discretionary expenditures and investments like R&D.

A healthy gross profit is critical, because it is the rocket fuel that lets you invest in innovation and growth. Just to be clear, it is the *fundamental* reason you are pursuing a Go-To market leadership position.

For example, a company like Amazon can have extremely healthy gross profits and be in great shape, even though it's posting a net loss on the bottom line.

(Another relevant metric is *contribution margin*: the difference between revenue and the variable costs associated with generating that revenue, which tells you which products and customers are most profitable.)

The commodity problem spans nearly every sector in the business-to-business world, most professional services sectors, nearly all technology companies, and even many consumer-oriented companies and individuals seeking jobs or freelance contract work. It also spans nonbusiness sectors, such as education (e.g., institutions trying to attract quality applicants and donations), not-for-profit, and government. Anytime you're competing internally or externally for dollars, other resources, and/or mindshare, you are in trouble if you are a me-too.

I was on the buyer's side of this when looking for a literary agent. One of the big complaints a lot of agents have is that they get inundated with author submissions in genres they don't represent and material not packaged in the manner they prefer. And it's no wonder. Of the hundreds of agents I researched, only a handful distinguished themselves at all or stated exactly what they are interested in. A good 99 percent all looked and sounded exactly the same. For a group of people so flooded with bad material, you would be amazed at how few agents took the opportunity to be extremely specific as to the content they like to represent.

This me-too trap is something very few executives understand or appreciate. I've been "watching déjà vu all over again" for many years.

TEST: PICK US OUT OF A LINEUP

WILL YOU PASS?

Try this in your own competitive sector. Enlist the help of someone not associated with your company but who knows the industry. Give them the names of five to ten of your closest competitors. Have that person pull from the company websites and also your website the one to three sentences that best summarize what each company does, remove the names, shuffle them around, and give them to another objective third party. Can they pick you out? Do they feel you sound different? Can they tell what you offer? Take a look yourself through your market's eyes. Are you as unique as you think?

WHY IT'S ONLY GOING TO GET WORSE

In addition to price-based competition, several trends are forcing companies to reevaluate their competitive strategies, what they offer, and the way in which they approach marketing. First, customers often start their buyer journey on the web. This immediately commoditizes any company that can't quickly demonstrate its uniqueness. And that's *if* the customer runs across the company in the first place. Customers can easily shop around and find a cheaper, identical alternative to what you sell.

Second, it used to be that the distinctions between market categories were very clear. Today, it's different. As the customer who needs social media help, do I contact a PR agency, a digital marketing firm, a social selling company, a branding agency, or what? Maybe I'll need media help later, so it should be the PR firm. But wait. I'm going to need a customer relationship management system (database) and email campaigns, so maybe it should be a digital marketing firm instead. Then who will help me with graphic design? Do I need a separate company for that? ARGHHH! I'm so confused!

Customers often start their buyer journey on the web. This immediately commoditizes any company that can't quickly demonstrate its uniqueness.

A related trend is today's vanishing barriers to entry. In many industries, especially those that are technology driven, your competitors need almost no capital to threaten you with cheaper or better alternatives. Anyone in the world can start a company, build a website, and be selling in minutes. With a 3D printer, they can build sophisticated prototypes and even products at the kitchen table.

With Alibaba, Amazon, eBay, and other online support, they can quickly produce, sell, and ship products globally. As a result, new entrants jump into any given market every single day.

On the enterprise front, business problems, processes, and technology infrastructure have become so complex and interdependent that customers often want vendors to provide complete, integrated business solutions, which are a combination of products and services. Sometimes these solutions are composed of elements provided by several companies partnering together. This requires a business model that's very different from what most companies have.

For emerging sectors such as sustainable products or the "Internet of Things," there is a significant market development challenge. Providers are rapidly introducing new technology or new ways of doing business; they are asking customers to buy an entirely new type of product, such as solar technology; they are asking customers to use familiar products in new ways, like controlling one's home security system from a mobile phone app; or they are somehow changing the customer's business processes. This calls for positioning and marketing practices that go beyond traditional approaches.

Another challenging trend is the speed at which some markets and competitors move. Providers of your favorite apps and online tools can match one another on functions and features in a matter of hours or days. Even highly specialized products such as optical technology, medical devices, or telecommunications routers and switches quickly become commodities. These companies are so accustomed to operating in fiercely competitive environments that they are very nimble and responsive to market changes. As soon as one competitor adds a new product or set of features, others match it.

Many products are software driven, meaning what used to be physical features are now software. A simple and very familiar example is smartphones, but it's happening to devices and products anywhere and everywhere, including the cars we drive. Before, a change in a product feature set meant a change to the manufacturing process and possibly even the supply chain. Changes were not easy to make, so competitors couldn't match one another quickly or easily. Even if they could, they still had to get customers to buy the new version of the device. Now the competitor just modifies software code in one place and pushes it out to customers' devices. Function and feature barriers have almost evaporated.

THE ME-TOO DEATH SPIRAL

The Me-Too Death Spiral is a matter of simple arithmetic and economics. Revenue minus costs equals profits. If revenues are increasing at a greater rate than costs, profits are rising. If revenues are decreasing at a greater rate than you can decrease costs, then profits are shrinking. We all know this, but here is the rub. The cost of running a business rarely decreases and usually increases over time.

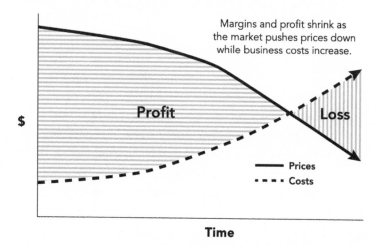

Margins and profit shrink as the market pushes prices down while business costs increase.

If you provide any kind of service; if you have a product that is at all variable from customer to customer; if your product requires customer support; if you are in a fast-changing or competitive sector requiring ongoing product improvement and innovation; if you need to invest heavily in brand building; if human expertise is a big portion of your value proposition, your costs will always rise.

You will need to continually be training and developing people in order to keep up with industry and market trends. Your people will need, at a minimum, cost-of-living raises. If you want to keep them motivated, they'll need more than that. Employment overhead such as taxes, healthcare, insurance, and so forth rise over time.

In addition, growth costs money and requires investment in R&D. Whether you sell robotic surgical devices or cosmetics, you must invest to keep up with industry and market advancements if you want to remain relevant. Factors such as facilities, support infrastructure, and other operations costs also creep up over time. In any highly competitive environment, you need to invest properly in marketing and sales support unless you want to rob your future. While you may be able to find ways to cut in the short run, long-term costs will only rise.

Bottom line: Since your costs are always going to rise at least linearly, if not exponentially, you had better be doing two things: figuring out how to raise the value of your offerings in order to raise your prices at least proportionally to rising costs, and figuring out how to get the most leverage and efficiency possible out of your operations in order to reduce costs.

Meanwhile, cost-plus pricing doesn't work. Customers will revolt if you try to raise prices every time costs go up. They only pay higher prices when receiving higher value. Sure, they may accept it to a point, but a comparable provider has only to swoop in and offer a slightly lower price for the same value, and you're sunk.

I experienced this when I moved my company from Atlanta to Silicon Valley. Do you think existing clients were willing to absorb a 100 percent increase in prices just because some of our costs suddenly increased 100 percent? Of course not. It sounds like an absurd question, but businesses try to do this to their customers all the time, even if the methods and messaging are more subtle.

Bottom line: Since your costs are always going to rise at least linearly, if not exponentially, you had better be doing two things: figuring out how to raise the value of your offerings in order to raise your prices at least proportionally to rising costs, and figuring out how to get the most leverage and efficiency possible out of your operations in order to reduce costs.

If you don't figure out a way to justify higher prices and/or reduce what it costs you to deliver your products and services, you are slowly, if not quickly, on your way out of business.

RECAP AND ACTION ITEMS

The most critical competitive threat to most companies is commoditization in the eyes of customers and the market as a whole, which then puts downward pressure on prices customers are willing to pay. This causes margins to shrink, which then reduces the money available to invest back into the business to fund growth, R&D, continued training and development of people, marketing, and other important investments.

ACTION ITEMS

You can access tools or download worksheets for each of these action items at apollomethod.com. Have some colleagues join you in doing these exercises. It will be interesting to compare notes.

1. **Assess:** Take the "Are You a Me-Too?" test shown earlier in the chapter.
2. **Assess:** Take the "Pick Us Out of a Lineup" test shown earlier in the chapter.
3. **Measure:** Determine the current gross margin and gross contribution margin for the parts of your business that drive most of your revenue. How do they compare to the rest of the industry? Are they sufficient to drive future growth and investment? (If you are a startup, project what these are likely to be once you have traction.)
4. **Write:** What financial difference would it make for your business to be able to double your gross margins? What would you be able to do that you can't do today?

By now, I doubt you want to continue to look and sound like everyone else, compete on price, and scrape by for each dollar of declining profit you earn until you finally go out of business. The good news is that there is an exciting alternative: be absolutely unique in a particular market, offer something of very high value that is in high and urgent demand, and charge high prices while prospects line up at the door.

In case there is any hesitation, let's look at what the latter offers. It's pretty awesome and will change your life.

PART II

WHAT

CHAPTER 2

REMEDY

Be the Go-To for a Solution to a Market Problem

A t 3:41 a.m. on Sunday, April 29, 2007, James Mosqueda was driving a tanker carrying 8,600 gallons of unleaded gasoline to Oakland, California. He ascended the ramp onto one portion of the MacArthur Maze a little too fast and clipped the guardrail. What seemed like an innocuous bump proved too much for the truck to take at that velocity, and over it went. Within twenty-one minutes, not only had the truck become a fireball, but the concrete and rebar overpass upon which it rested had completely melted and collapsed onto the freeway under it. Poof. A major commuting artery serving 80,000 cars a day in the San Francisco Bay Area was gone. This was an economic and logistical disaster.

The MacArthur Maze in the San Francisco Bay Area is a complex set of interchanges where several major freeways come together.

On a daily basis, it is central to the movement of 280,000 vehicles passing east, west, north, and south. The damaged portion was what formerly took cars off the Bay Bridge from San Francisco or allowed them to move southbound through Oakland. Even without traffic anomalies, gridlock and slowdowns are a way of life in this area. Construction projects of this magnitude are usually measured in years, but in this case, California Department of Transportation (Caltrans) officials knew that every day would count.

They needed to find a construction company with incredibly deep expertise. It needed to have done this exact project so many times before that it could walk onto the job with an extraordinarily efficient delivery mechanism—people with the right skills, established suppliers who were willing to ship as soon as possible, and a proven approach to rapid but safe freeway construction. In short, they needed the Go-To.

In this case, speed and quality mattered more than money, so Caltrans was willing to pay the winning contractor a whopping $200,000 completion bonus for each *day* it could shave off the already-aggressive deadline. C. C. Myers Inc., a Sacramento-based contractor with a reputation for making rapid emergency highway repairs stepped up to the plate. Caltrans required a completion time of fifty days. To collect the maximum bonus of $5 million, the firm would have to deliver in twenty-five days. C. C. Myers Inc. had crews on the job site within an hour of signing the contract and delivered in seventeen days, not for money (there was no financial incentive to beat twenty-five days) but for pride and reputation. Even still, its profit margin on the project was 50 percent plus millions in public relations value. The entire Bay Area bowed on its knees in gratitude as C. C. Myers executives opened the new road in time for Memorial Day weekend. They were heroes.

In contrast to commodity players fighting to preserve their margins, why is it that certain firms seem to command more margin, more attention, and more respect than others? And why is it that they rarely find themselves in competitive situations, clients usually seek them out, and clients will pay almost any price for the privilege of working with them?

In contrast to commodity players fighting to preserve their margins, why is it that certain firms seem to command more margin, more attention, and more respect than others?...It's because they own their markets.

It's because they own their markets. Amazon. Facebook. LEGO. They dominate their spaces. They are Go-To brands in their domains. McKinsey & Co. is not the largest in its category, but it owns "boardroom strategy." Accenture owns "large-scale, high-risk systems implementation projects for large enterprises." Gartner owns "IT market analysis." Heidrick & Struggles owns "CEO executive search." SAP owns "integrated enterprise resource planning (ERP) software." Those firms have defined, committed to, and established a unique market position. They are regarded as the de facto standards in their respective spaces. Anyone else in that space becomes an also-ran.

WHAT IT'S LIKE TO BE THE GO-TO

A Go-To sometimes turns work away. It names its terms. Prospects may even compete for its business, not the other way around.

It's one thing to differentiate and focus. But taken a step further, it's incredibly powerful and profitable to become the Go-To brand in your chosen markets. In addition to obtaining sustainable differentiation, your firm will maintain healthy margins and grow revenues over time.

Market dominance simply means becoming the Go-To brand for a particular market need and being so unique and superior at filling that need that you are able to command premium prices, work with premium customers, and hire premium people. Any company, no matter its size, can pursue it. Your goal is to get people to seek you out and believe so firmly in your ability to make a unique contribution that they will pay you whatever it takes.

What does it really mean to be the "Go-To" for something? Go-to status sits on a continuum, but here's the ultimate ideal. You know you are the Go-To when:

- ☑ You are the first name that comes to mind when buyers think of _____ (insert your specialty area).
- ☑ You are the first one people turn to for solving a particular problem.
- ☑ No one can deliver on this problem like you can.
- ☑ There is wide recognition and respect for your brand.
- ☑ Your stellar reputation precedes you.
- ☑ Prospects hope you'll be willing to work with them.
- ☑ You rarely, if ever, compete for business or develop proposals.
- ☑ You never have to give anything away.
- ☑ You actually turn some business away, because it's not the right business.
- ☑ You name your price, often receiving success-sharing premiums.
- ☑ You work with the most progressive, successful companies or people in your market.
- ☑ You are viewed as the Harvard Business School of employers in your space—candidates vie to work for you.

Google has certainly achieved market dominance as the Go-To brand for sponsored search. At present, Google is on the far end of the market dominance spectrum, as witnessed by the fact that people clamor to work for Google. Buyers don't haggle over pricing because, well, no other provider even comes close.

IDEO is the Go-To for "design thinking" and innovative industrial design. People travel from all over the world to tour IDEO's offices, and its design methodology is the basis for an entire design institute at Stanford University.

Apple is the Go-To for "elegant, user-friendly technology." In an industry of almost complete commoditization, Apple has continued to charge more for its products than category competitors. Apple stands alone. There are Apple products, and then there is "everything else."

TED. There are thousands of conferences, podcasts, video lectures, and other thought-provoking content out there. Yet TED conferences command premium prices and always sell out, even though they offer the talks online for free!

THE ADVANTAGES OF BEING A GO-TO

We believe that a fundamental measure of our success will be the shareholder value we create over the long term. This value will be a direct result of our ability to extend and solidify our current market leadership position. The stronger our market leadership, the more powerful our economic model. Market leadership can translate directly to higher revenue, higher profitability, greater capital velocity, and correspondingly stronger returns on invested capital.

—Jeff Bezos, in his first letter to shareholders
after going public in 1997

Bain & Company says that the "ultimate point of a brand is not to create emotional appeal or to generate buzz. The point is to shift customer demand" in terms of a higher price, more volume, or a combination of the two.

The greatest advantage of being the Go-To is financial. Many academic and industry studies have demonstrated that being the preferred brand in a competitive market leads to higher enterprise value by driving increased profits, pricing, cash flow, and market share. The Marketing Accountability Standards Board (MASB) has found that brand stature provides an average of 19.5 percent and often as much as 50 percent of enterprise value. Frank Findley, director of MASB, summarizes decades of research in this way:

> Over the last 40 years an array of brand-tracking studies by academics and independent research houses have proven again and again that brand preference is a primary driver of customer choice, business outcomes, market share, and cash flow.

As the Go-To brand, you will likely compete less on price, if at all. Usually, you can command much higher prices than the competition because the buyer considers the benefits you offer to far outweigh your cost. A study by the Marketing Science Institute found that brand reputation can lead to pricing premiums of 26 percent on average for similar quality. A study of consumer product categories by Bain & Company found that a leading brand can sometimes double its price and still maintain market share equal to the second most esteemed brand. Of course, many of us have paid (or watched others pay) premiums far higher than this for a Go-To brand.

If you think of Amazon, mentioned earlier, as an antithetical example, think again. Although Amazon may offer low prices to the consumer on certain products and books, it charges nonnegotiable, healthy prices at healthy margins to suppliers and publishers wishing to leverage its uniquely ubiquitous distribution channel and its fulfillment service. And its high-margin businesses are also its high-est-growth businesses: Amazon Web Services (AWS), Amazon Prime, and advertising. In the first quarter of 2018, Amazon's gross profit hit a whopping 40 percent. Its *growth* in gross profit in the first quarter of that year exceeded that of the *next five largest retailers combined.*

The Go-To Grows While Others Struggle

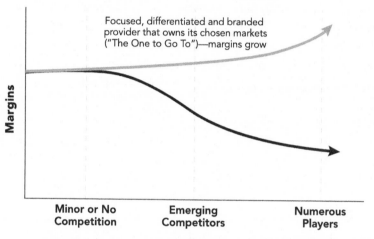

Number of Competitors Relative to Market Demand

When a company clearly differentiates as the Go-To in its market, it can escape the Commodity Curve and actually increase gross margins over time. *(Source: The Apollo Method for Market Dominance)*

Another big advantage as a Go-To brand is that you are no longer part of the pack—you stand out. As the top-of-mind solution to a particular problem, buyers often will proactively reach out, particularly when time is of the essence, as in the case of C. C. Myers when the freeway melted. Many publishers *only* sell through Amazon. They design and market their books purely through an Amazon lens, as if it's the only game in town.

Often, selling costs for a Go-To are much lower, because you're not starting from ground zero in a sales situation. Your reputation precedes you, so you don't have to work as hard as a lesser-known competitor to establish your credibility. You don't have to prove yourself as much. You can cut right to the situation at hand and how you can help. AWS (Amazon's innovative and rapidly growing cloud platform) has customers beating down its doors. Or let's take Google. Advertising sales is usually a high-touch, relationship-intensive activity involving legions of sales reps and lots of negotiating, but Google is so dominant in paid search that it doesn't have to provide any human involvement at all. Customers seek it out and serve themselves. Everything is done via an online tool with no haggling.

As the Go-To, you are in a position to fundamentally alter the direction of the market.

As the Go-To brand in a particular field, you wield great power and influence in the marketplace. You aren't just part of the fabric of the industry; you sit at the top of the pyramid à la Amazon. You help set the direction of the industry. You have a vision others want to follow. As the Go-To, you are in a position to fundamentally alter the direction of the market.

A lesser-known but equally apt example is McMahon Group in Saint Louis, the Go-To for private-club strategic planning and consulting. I experienced the power of their Go-To status while playing the role of buyer.

I am an avid sailor and belong to a yacht club that was once falling prey to the same tough trends impacting private clubs across the US, if not the world—an aging membership, flat membership numbers that would decline if we didn't change, and less-than-optimal utilization of club facilities and programs—despite this being a club that's highly respected throughout the yachting community. I was on a committee tasked with addressing this problem. One of our first steps was to seek out a firm that could help us conduct a member survey and determine a plan of action based on the results. In this situation, you can imagine how price sensitive the club was. However, results were more important. We could have sought out a generic market research firm. After all, how hard is it to put together a bunch of questions about how and why members use club facilities and what they wish they were getting that they weren't? Heck, we could have done it with a free online survey tool.

We weren't after just a survey, though. We were after a long-term plan that would improve our future. We needed expertise. As it happens, there is an entire subspecialty of private-club market researchers and consultants we could turn to. Who knew? The club leadership decided that it made perfect sense to hire a firm that understands the unique issues and trends impacting private clubs, even if it was going to cost a little more. We knew that member feedback and input was just one piece of what we ultimately needed, and we wanted a firm that could help us ask the right questions, interpret the feedback appropriately, and guide us toward best actions.

Then it became a matter of selecting the firm. The private club sector, like most industries, is a tight community at the upper leadership levels. Just like any industry, club managers all belong to one leading professional association, see each other at meetings, read the same publications, network with each other, and progress from club to club as they climb their career ladders. As a result, our general manager already knew of the top three consultants in the business, telling us that one in particular was the Go-To; so we interviewed each. Two were impressive—they had great credentials, stellar reputations, and "trusted partner" status with their clients; had done many similar projects; obviously had deep expertise in this specific area; and offered strong teams. The cost of their services was also extremely reasonable and competitive. We knew they could each do a great job.

The third firm, McMahon Group, was all of that and much more. In addition to the above, it was *the* thought leader in the field. McMahon didn't just serve the industry; it *led* the industry by proactively investing in, conducting, and sharing trends research, not just on where the industry had been and where it currently was, but also on where it was going. When we had lunch to interview their president, Frank Vain, he humored us by listening to our litany of challenges and problems; however, he could have told them to us himself, because they were no different from what he saw at every club they work with. He was finishing our sentences. And further, he laid out the trajectory we were on. Most of all, he prescribed the solutions right then and there—told us exactly what we needed to do.

In talking to Frank, it was clear that McMahon Group lived, ate, and breathed private club trends and operational excellence best practices. This is all they do. They know everything going on in the industry. They know all of the key players. They study and watch the trends on everyone's behalf and warn the industry of what's coming on the horizon. They've taken "spiritual ownership" for understanding and solving the industry's most pressing problems.

We hired them, even though they were about *twice* as expensive as the other options. The reason is that we felt we would get great value—we knew they would not just execute a survey to tell us what the members wanted but would also help us take the optimal actions as a result. We weren't buying market research services; we were buying a treasure trove of expertise, experience, and wisdom. They would help us solve our problem.

And that's exactly what happened. We did the survey. It told us precisely what Frank had told us it would at lunch that day (yes, looking back, we could have saved a lot of money by letting him just give us the answers, but we needed to hear it from our members). The action plan ended up being exactly what he had prescribed during that same conversation. As a result, membership growth and club utilization have soared. The club has been thriving and doing better than ever, even through a major financial downturn.

The private club sector might sound like a small, limited market for a company like McMahon Group to target, but it's about a $26 billion market. McMahon doesn't have to capture much of that market to have a great business. And by capturing the top end of that market and charging a premium price for their premium value, they have built quite a profitable business with a reputation that precedes them. They are, indeed, the Go-To.

RECAP AND ACTION ITEMS

There are tremendous economic, operating, and long-term shareholder value advantages in being the Go-To brand in a given market. By having a reputation that precedes you, being able to name your price, and having customers seek you out, you stand above competitive jockeying as an also-ran. You earn healthy margins that fuel growth and investment in your future. And life is just easier.

ACTION ITEMS

You can access tools or download worksheets for each of these action items at apollomethod.com. Again, it will be useful to have coworkers do these with you.

1. **List:** Identify at least three companies in your sector that currently meet most or all of the checklist criteria for a Go-To brand provided earlier in the chapter.
2. **Analyze:** What are some of the things they're doing differently from others in the space?

3. **Visualize:** How would it change things if your company was the Go-To in your chosen market? What would it be like to have business flooding in? How would it feel to have customers asking you to name your price in order to solve their problems?

CHAPTER 3

WHAT A GO-TO BRAND DOES DIFFERENTLY

Companies that achieve Go-To status in their chosen markets follow a particular set of strategies that me-toos typically don't. Let's look at eight things a Go-To brand does differently.

A GO-TO HAS MANIACAL FOCUS

The first and most critical strategy a Go-To brand employs in its early days is to focus on a singular strategic goal. *Apollo* astronaut Dick Gordon reinforced this when telling me the most significant lesson learned from the Apollo Space Program:

> The power of focus. Anything is possible when you have a very clear desired outcome shared by everyone and around which all action revolves. In our case, it was the Moon.

President John F. Kennedy delivering his historic "Moon Shot" speech to a joint session of Congress on May 25, 1961. *(Image: NASA)*

With four words, "man on the Moon," John F. Kennedy instantly focused everyone involved in the space program on one specific goal, one specific domain. Just land a guy on the Moon and bring him home. That's it.

The book *Focus: The Future of Your Company Depends on It*, by legendary marketer Al Ries, is considered a marketing classic and makes a strong case for focus. Bill Gross, the famed serial entrepreneur and founder of startup incubator IdeaLab, has raved about how this book turned around his thinking, strategic approach, and fortunes. This excerpt from the book's introduction sums it up:

The sun is a powerful source of energy. Every hour the sun washes the earth with billions of kilowatts of energy. Yet with a hat and some sunscreen you can bathe in the light of the sun for hours at a time with few ill effects.

A laser is a weak source of energy. A laser takes a few watts of energy and focuses them in a coherent stream of light. But with a laser you can drill a hole in a diamond or wipe out a cancer.

When you focus a company, you create the same effect. You create a powerful, laser-like ability to dominate a market. That's what focusing is all about.

When a company becomes unfocused, it loses its power. It becomes a sun that dissipates its energy over too many products and too many markets.

From 2003 to 2004, LEGO was in a state of crisis, with falling revenues following a long period of stagnation. When new CEO Jørgen Vig Knudstorp came in, he declared LEGO would go "back to the brick" by concentrating on core products and core customers. As detailed in the book *Brick by Brick*, the company cut back on many of its brand extensions, cut the number of brick designs by 46 percent, and re-narrowed its market focus to kids ages five to nine. The next year, sales increased 12 percent, and LEGO had come back from a $292 million loss in 2004 to a pretax profit of $117 million in 2005. In fact, as stated by the *Financial Times*, LEGO enjoyed twelve more straight years of revenue growth and "long defied gravity as other toymakers succumbed to the trend of children spending more time playing digitally." In time, the company briefly lost focus, and revenues took a hit in 2017, though LEGO still dominated with a two-thirds share of the "construction toy" market. After a quick course correction, however, growth resumed in 2018.

Focus lets you concentrate your resources. It lets you concentrate your message so that it speaks directly to your targets' pain points and needs in their own language. It helps unqualified prospects self-select out before they waste your precious selling energies. It tells employees what you *don't* do so that they stay focused on the right priorities.

A GO-TO STARTS WITH A BEACHHEAD MARKET AND CENTRAL THEME BEFORE IT BROADENS

Closely related to focus, another thing a Go-To does differently is to build from a base of strength. It does this by initially concentrating on a specific market that is large enough to provide opportunity but specific enough to allow the company to concentrate its finite resources in order to capitalize on synergies.

Only after being able to declare undisputed success with Moon exploration did NASA broaden into exploration of other planets such as Jupiter, Saturn, and Mars and the exploration of other galaxies.

Rather than a mishmash of messages, products, services, and activities, a Go-To builds its brand around a central theme/market, and every aspect of its being revolves around that theme until the company has enough of a dominant position to broaden from there into adjacent markets.

Oracle gained its footing as the Go-To for relational database technology before broadening into applications a full ten years after it was founded. Salesforce (the company) built its foundation as a salesforce automation application before broadening into other sales and marketing applications and growing to annual revenues in excess of $13 billion.

Accenture is a $30 billion company today but started in the early 1950s as a tiny consulting division of the accounting firm Arthur Andersen to meet audit client demand for financial and manufacturing process automation. The bulk of this division's business was focused on these two areas well into the 1970s.

Facebook was initially only available to Harvard students; once strong there, it allowed students from just eight other universities to join. Not until it had a firm foothold in those markets, with others asking to join, did it open itself to most universities and corporations before finally allowing anyone thirteen and older to sign up. Even with Facebook's lightning-speed growth trajectory, this progression took two and a half years.

Geoffrey Moore discusses the importance of a beachhead in market dominance strategy in his seminal strategic marketing book *Crossing the Chasm*. Using a D-Day analogy, he explains the importance of focusing your scant resources to secure a stronghold from which to expand. One of the metaphors he references is the use of kindling to start a fire:

> The bunched-up paper represents your promotional budget, and the log, a major market opportunity. No matter how much paper you put under that log, if you don't have any target market segments to act as kindling, sooner or later, the paper will be all used up, and the log still won't be burning…[this] isn't rocket science, but it does represent a kind of discipline.

The key, then, is to figure out a beachhead.

A GO-TO IS OBSESSED WITH ITS AREA OF EXPERTISE

Clearly, the Apollo Space Program and every member of its team was obsessed with its core mission. A Go-To doesn't just specialize. A Go-To is a passionate aficionado, a devotee. A Go-To obsesses. And a Go-To is very opinionated when it comes to a particular market issue.

I used to have an ancient Mercedes diesel sedan and would take it to the San Francisco Go-To for these cars: Fred at Silver Star Motor Services. Fred didn't just work on old Mercedes diesels. He *loved* them. He was an aficionado. He was constantly thinking about them, reading about them, learning more about them. And he had strong opinions about them. He could bend your ear for hours talking about the ins and outs of these cars. He wasn't showing off; he was waxing poetic about something he was passionate about. He would just light up at the thought of these cars. It wasn't a business or job for him—it was his life.

Steve Jobs was obsessed with distinctive design. He insisted that Apple's mantra be simplicity. In his mind, consumer technology was too complex, hard to use, and ugly. As a result, the company has always been obsessed with creating innovative, easy-to-use technology that people have an emotional connection with. When Apple started to work on the iPhone, Steve Jobs didn't instruct the development team to create a device that would put a computer in your pocket. His directive was: "Create the first phone that people [will] fall in love with."

According to former Apple product manager Bob Borchers, "The idea was, he wanted to create something that was so instrumental and integrated in peoples' lives that you'd rather leave your wallet at home than your iPhone."

Steve Jobs was clearly passionate, obsessive, and strongly opinionated about how people should interact with technology, and these qualities have informed everything Apple has created, even after his passing.

When Marc Benioff founded Salesforce in 1999, he was absolutely passionate about the need for companies to move away from installed software and to adopt the software-as-a-service (SaaS or "cloud") model. On stage at a conference in 2006, he relentlessly and completely unapologetically pounded on his primary thesis that installed enterprise software was on its way to extinction. At the time, it was still an emerging idea, but Salesforce was so passionate about the idea that it put a "stamp" of the word *software* in a red circle with a slash through it on every ad, on its website, and any other bit of material associated with the company. Benioff wore a trademarked pin of the image everywhere he went, including on the stage that day.

A GO-TO HAS A HIGHER PURPOSE: IT TAKES MARKET OWNERSHIP OF A PROBLEM

A Go-To says, "I'll take this one. I'll own this problem." And that problem becomes its purpose in life. For Apollo, it was, "How do you land a tiny object on a celestial body while they're both hurtling through space and then bring that tiny object back to Earth, while keeping the humans in that object alive?"

Companies basically exist to (profitably) solve problems, especially in the business-to-business world. But a Go-To declares intellectual ownership for it, effectively becoming the ringleader, the primary thought leader, for related discussions and market activity.

RSA Security took ownership for "encryption" early on and is a driving force in the cybersecurity industry. It conducts a major conference series regarded as "where the world talks security," publishes respected research, and spearheads industry groups like the Security for Business Innovation Council.

Kaiser Permanente, the large health maintenance organization, doesn't just offer an integrated delivery system, where you and your family can get all of your healthcare in one place, with a single set of medical records, and a multidisciplinary team devoted to your well-being; it believes this model is the way of the future. Kaiser has been running its "Thrive" campaign for fifteen years, offering tips for healthy living. Many of its ads don't talk about Kaiser at all. They address Kaiser's higher purpose.

For example, one print ad showed an image of a jump rope curled into the shape of a human brain, with the copy, "Exercise doesn't just make you feel better, offering a good defense against depression and anxiety. It helps you stay more alert and focused. Something you can think clearly about as you knock out just one last set. To learn more, go to kp.org/thrive."

According to Diane Gage Lofgren, a former senior vice president, brand strategy, communications, and public relations at Kaiser, and Debbie Cantu, a former Kaiser vice president, brand marketing, and advertising, the company aims to play the role of health advocate "completely dedicated to health and well-being with the fact that no matter what their stages of life, people want to be as healthy as they can be."

Apple created iTunes to make it easy for iPod owners to legally download music instead of relying on illegal options in wide use at the time.

According to Amazon's first employee, Shel Kaphan, the company's initial, singular goal was to "make [books] available to everyone in the world."

As part of owning the problem (or challenge, as some might state it), a Go-To brand engages the market. It creates forums for interaction and stands at the center of those as the ringleader—not to put itself front and center but to drive the conversation toward continuous innovation and results.

Discovery Education wants to "ignite student curiosity and inspire educators to reimagine learning." To that end, it offers community and engagement programs like Siemens STEM Day and a partnership with the Tiger Woods Foundation.

So it's not just about solving a market problem. It's also about keeping the conversation alive and working with the market to make continuing, collective progress against the problem.

A GO-TO EVANGELIZES A PRESCRIPTIVE POINT OF VIEW ON THE PROBLEM WITH CONVICTION AND BUILDS A FOLLOWING

NASA could never have achieved the Moon landing on its own. It had to have many partners, the support of the general public, and continuous funding from Congress. To obtain and retain all of that support, it evangelized its point of view on what it would take to achieve the goal, turned skeptics into believers, and rallied people around the approach, all of which we'll explore more deeply later in the book.

For a company, the point of view is a genuine perspective on what needs to be done, with or without the Go-To's help. Investor and startup advisor Guy Kawasaki would describe it as a "cause." This is not a sales pitch.

The Stanford Technology Ventures Program (STVP), which is part of the Department of Management Science and Engineering in the School of Engineering at Stanford University, has become the Go-To for technology entrepreneurship education, as evidenced by (among other things) the fact that the National Science Foundation chose it over numerous other institutions vying for a rare $10 million grant to help engineering students across the United States become more entrepreneurial and innovative. STVP firmly believes that all students can benefit from learning entrepreneurial leadership skills regardless of their major or intended career.

STVP faculty, staff, and affiliates travel extensively and maintain close relationships with other leaders and influencers in technology entrepreneurship education and research. Most key people in entrepreneurship education around the globe know or know of STVP professors Kathy Eisenhardt, Tom Byers, and Tina Seelig, who are fervent evangelists of STVP's point of view. They are so prolific in their "market" that all of them have won numerous awards for their work and impact. Kathy Eisenhardt's research is so influential that she was noted in 2008 as the most-cited research author in strategy and organization studies for the past twenty-five years, ahead of renowned Harvard Business School professor and author Michael Porter. Byers and Seelig won the prestigious Bernard M. Gordon Prize for Innovation in Engineering and Technology Education for their influence in this area. It is presented by the National Academy of Engineering (NAE). Then-president William Wulf said the NAE created the award as "essentially the 'Nobel Prize' for engineering educators." And all three of these professors have written books sharing STVP practices and insights.

A Go-To understands the value and power of engaging audiences' emotions with storytelling and drama. The problem provides dramatic tension as the villain, and the prescriptive point of view saves the day as hero.

In the early days of Salesforce, Marc Benioff positioned software as a villain and software-as-a-service as the hero that could come to the rescue.

A Go-To brand understands the soft-sell power of thought leadership.

When Frank Vain of McMahon Group stands up in front of an audience of private club general managers, he doesn't talk at all about McMahon Group. He educates the audience on the core problem facing the private club sector and McMahon's research-based point of view on what club leadership teams can do to solve this problem. By the time he's done openly and freely sharing his expertise, he's essentially given a credentials presentation while keeping the audience hanging on his every word. It's like standing outside a restaurant giving free samples of your most delicious dishes. Customers can't help but want more.

A Go-To brand also understands the power of building a following so that others in the marketplace start doing your selling for you.

Apple has an entire army of rabid fans who spread the Apple gospel on its behalf. Mozilla, proud provider of internet browser Firefox, actually engages its users in helping to maintain and improve the product; they work for free because they believe in the cause: choice and control online.

STVP has created a "community of believers" throughout academia who also share its passion and support for STVP's philosophy. For many years, STVP led a series of annual conferences in Europe, Asia, Latin America, and the US to bring together entrepreneurship educators from across these regions to advance entrepreneurship education. STVP would share its approach and encourage others to do the same. Professors around the globe have tremendous respect for STVP's approaches and its role as a thought leader in this field. More importantly, there was incredible bonding that took place among the participants. There was a deep sense of camaraderie and mutual support. STVP provided these events as a service to its peers, but the events paid immeasurable dividends back to STVP in terms of what it learned, brand building, and other opportunities the events created for STVP.

A GO-TO DOESN'T SELL, IT SOLVES

In other words, a Go-To delivers killer results that have a profound impact on customers.

The Apollo Space Program didn't say, "We have a lot of really cool gadgets that can do amazing things." No. It kept the message focused on the outcome: "By landing a man on the Moon and bringing him home, we're going to win the space race as a symbol of the triumph of freedom over oppression."

Likewise, a Go-To brand already understands the business or consumer problem and walks in with a prescription for solving it. A Go-To doesn't answer the prospect's question of "What do you do?" with their own question of "What do you need?"

When pitching offerings, it's not enough to talk about the problem and what should be done about it. It's also not enough to share product functions and features or service capabilities. Instead, a Go-To brand delivers on its promises and provides value in the form of outcomes. By actively solving the problem for customers, it delivers astonishing impact.

- A Go-To provides not just a product or a service but also the *complete solution* required to give the customer a business or personal outcome.
- A Go-To leads the customer on a journey and *measures success in terms of results delivered.*
- A Go-To's sales activity is not transactional and "lead"-oriented—it is *long-term relationship- and account-oriented.*
- A Go-To seeks to be the customer's trusted business partner and *has the customer's long-term interests at the center of what it does.*
- A Go-To approaches the market with a set of targets it sees itself as best suited to serve and *cultivates a presence among those targets*—it builds a community of believers in its point of view and approach to solving the problem.

If you need a meal, Target will sell you the pieces—food, plates, utensils, etc.—and send you along. A fine restaurant will sell you a complete, satisfying dining experience, and for that complete solution you're willing to pay more. Taking that several steps further, the *Go-To* local restaurant will do this and be a gathering place for birds of a feather, know you by name, know your food sensitivities, make a custom dish at your request, and send you special offers.

A top-tier Go-To offers a very specific, and sometimes even quantified, value proposition. It talks in terms of specific business outcomes—for example, how much more quickly, less expensively, or more profitably you'll achieve your business goals and at what cost.

WHICH WOULD YOU PREFER?

A service that will monitor customer
dissatisfaction for your company
or
An offering that says, "We'll increase the
net promoter score of your unhappiest
customers by __% within six months"

A public relations (PR) firm that charges a monthly
retainer to manage your social media accounts
or
One that says, "We'll charge you $__ to achieve 100
percent aided awareness and 60 percent unaided awareness
among your top __ prospects within the next year"

A law firm that charges you an hourly fee
or
A firm that says, "We're so confident we can win
this case that you owe us nothing until we win a
judgment for you, and then you pay us a percentage"

Because it is so focused, a Go-To is able to do all of this through efficient, behind-the-curtain operational excellence. It has a low cost of delivery, relative to someone doing the same thing on a one-off basis, through tools, processes, and technology. A Go-To hires and trains people focused on its area of expertise who can jump in and immediately add value. And it has a "trusted partner offering superior results" value system and culture.

Unlike retailers in the mid-1990s that jumped onto the internet as a side business, Amazon made the online channel its only business, initially focusing just on books. Its operation was so efficient that, rather than create their own online channels, companies like Toys"R"Us, Target, and Sears Canada, among others, contracted with Amazon at the time to run their retail websites. Another major key to Amazon's success is its fulfillment operation, which reduces its shipping, inventory, and other operating costs. *Wired* magazine once called it "the world's most nimble infrastructure for the transfer of things..."

A GO-TO CONSTANTLY ADJUSTS AND ADAPTS

A Go-To brand keeps an eye on the horizon to stay ahead, because the world is continuously changing—market conditions, customer needs, and other factors that impact a company, like the economy, politics, regulatory policy, technology, and so on.

A Go-To maintains humility and a healthy paranoia. I've been in meetings with the senior leadership at Accenture during periods of record growth and profits, and you'd have thought from the conversation that the company was on the verge of going out of business. The executives in the room understood that Accenture's fortunes, like those of any company, could turn on a dime. The team had the same earnest attitude toward its strategic planning activity as a struggling startup. And rightly so.

A Go-To also realizes that regardless of how unique its current offerings are, it will face competition. The market will invariably begin to fill with copycats going for a slice of that pie, so the Go-To must watch its back and work to stay ahead of the pack. Airbnb dominates the online home-sharing sector now, but can it stay ahead, especially if the hotel industry decides to enter that business?

Technology companies, in particular, can't stand still for three seconds before a competitor pops up or market conditions change. Oracle started as the only relational database company, but of course competitors came along, followed by new technologies. Though Oracle still maintains solid leadership in the overall database space with over 40 percent market share, it is no longer the same company. It has built on its strengths and entered many other solution areas, such as digital marketing technology.

As of this writing, Apple, Google, and Microsoft are the world's three most valuable brands, according to *Forbes*, but you'd never know it from the intensity pulsing throughout the headquarters of all three. None look the same as they did in the early days, and they all know that their offerings could become obsolete at any moment. They are always working on their next innovations.

In recent years, some stalwarts like IBM have suffered for not embracing the trend toward cloud computing quickly enough. Toys"R"Us failed to properly adapt to market changes, including the rise of online shopping. Over the next decade, disruptors will include blockchain, the Internet of Things (think Nest thermostats but applied to nearly any kind of consumer or industrial device/product), changing consumer behavior, cleantech, widespread adoption of digital platforms for mature sectors (à la Alibaba, PayPal, etc.), the sharing economy (e.g., Uber), and the sheer speed of change in almost any industry.

A Go-To understands that companies that don't change or don't change fast enough often perish. According to an Innosight 2018 study summarized in the briefing, "Creative Destruction Is Accelerating," half of today's S&P 500 companies will be replaced over the next ten years; and whereas companies in 1958 stayed on the index an average of sixty-one years (per the 2012 version of this study), that average tenure is projected to shrink to just twelve years by 2027.

As Andy Grove put it in his book *Only the Paranoid Survive*:

> the person who is the star of previous era is often the last one to adapt to change, the last one to yield to logic of a strategic inflection point and tends to fall harder than most.

A GO-TO TAKES A LESS-IS-MORE APPROACH

The Apollo Space Program was funded by the government and had to use its resources wisely.

Likewise, because a Go-To brand is so focused, efficiency is built into its sales, marketing, and delivery activities. Every action revolves around a single theme. The company has to produce fewer marketing deliverables. By generating momentum in the marketplace, other people are promoting the company on its behalf. The company interacts with fewer unqualified prospects. Selling costs are lower—the field marketing activity has a higher conversion rate from prospects to customers. The solution-oriented nature of the offering results in long-term relationships and higher lifetime customer value. Every activity related to its product or service is highly focused. Every experience learned with one customer is applicable and can therefore be applied to the next customer. Nothing is wasted.

> *[Steve] Jobs would say it's more important to say "no," even to good projects, than it is to say "yes" too frequently, which is a mistake that most companies make.*
> —Adam Lashinsky, senior editor, *Fortune* magazine, and author of *Inside Apple*

My teams have been so resource constrained in both large and small companies that it forced us to be incredibly efficient. We focused proactive efforts only on core targets. Every deliverable served multiple purposes—for example, presentations' speaker notes were repurposed for blog posts, white papers, e-books, campaigns, and articles. Every piece of market intelligence went into an internal library available to the global team. Annual client conferences served as the nucleus of a powerful year-round client/lead nurturing and thought leadership program. Like a Rubik's Cube, everything was interconnected, interlocking.

RECAP AND ACTION ITEMS

ANYONE CAN DO IT

These qualities and actions are what can separate you as a Go-To from the me-toos as well. They are the crux of a market-dominance strategy. By establishing your company as the Go-To expert in its chosen markets, you are the first name that comes to mind when a prospect has a particular problem to solve. You become widely known and respected as the primary thought leader on a particular market issue, have unmatched expertise in a particular market, charge premium prices, and earn high margins. These huge profits then enable you to invest heavily in R&D, the development of your people and culture, brand building, your clients, other marketing activity, and a first-rate approach to everything you do. These profits enable you to keep your eye on the horizon and invest in adapting to market changes. And these are what enable you to *remain* exceptionally profitable, with sustainable margin and revenue growth far above the industry average over time.

ACTION ITEMS

You can access tools or download worksheets for each of these action items at apollomethod.com. Have some colleagues join you in doing these exercises. It's helpful to do these with a colleague who may have differing perspectives.

1. **Define:** We'll get into specifics later, but for now, what topics and/or market problems within your sector are you (or your company) obsessed with and capable of potentially "owning"?

2. **Analyze:** For one of the Go-To brands in your space that you identified at the end of chapter 2, rate on a scale of 1–5 how they're doing in each of the eight strategies in this chapter. Write down some ways in which they exemplify each of these areas.
   a. Focus
   b. Beachhead
   c. Obsession
   d. Ownership
   e. Conviction
   f. Results
   g. Change
   h. Less-Is-More

3. **Reflect:** On a scale of 1–5, rate your own company performance on each of these areas and write down some things you would change.

Want to become a Go-To? Here's how: first, let's get a sense of the big picture, and then we'll take it phase by phase, step by step, finishing with a one-page action plan to get you started.

PART III

HOW

(Image: NASA)

CHAPTER 4

THE APOLLO METHOD FOR MARKET DOMINANCE

Overview

Now that we know the components of what a Go-To brand does differently, how does a company implement all of that as efficiently as possible, especially when resources are limited? And let's face it, they usually are.

We can organize the various steps and tasks as a four-phase framework: **Launch, Ignite, Navigate, Accelerate.**

The essence of the approach is this: A company wishing to become a Go-To targets a specific market and identifies a common, critical, and urgent problem that no one else is adequately addressing; it develops a unique solution to this problem; and then it leads a movement in the marketplace around its approach, establishing itself as the top-of-mind Go-To brand. Meanwhile, it also sets out to deliver on its promises by building out the solution and helping clients successfully implement it. As the solution begins to penetrate the market and pick up speed, the company continually monitors market forces, adjusting its strategy and solution as needed to meet changing customer needs and stay ahead of the competition.

As we saw in chapter 3, focus is at the core of this approach. While other firms shine a broad spotlight on the market, a Go-To uses a laser beam. And it proactively focuses its energy on a small number of high-impact, interdependent initiatives powered by a clear, focused strategy to burn its brand right into the minds of the collective target market.

This chapter offers a very brief synopsis of each phase. **In chapters 5–8, we'll walk through the step-by-step implementation playbook for each phase, including an action plan of specific activities and the deliverables you'll need to produce, getting into the details and looking at some examples.**

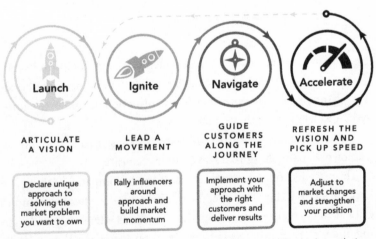

Apollo Method for Market Dominance—Overview Diagram. The high-resolution, printable image is available at apollomethod.com.

PHASE 1: LAUNCH

To get to space, you have to first literally get off the ground. You start with the launch, and it takes a certain amount of energy and thrust to achieve that. Similarly in business, you must develop and then aggressively propel your vision for the market and a unique approach to a common, critical problem into the marketplace. Develop a provocative, compelling, and seminal point of view on why companies should be concerned about this problem. Select a beachhead market on which to concentrate for initial traction, and stay focused on a limited scope of activity so as to not diffuse your limited resources, the way that NASA stayed focused on the Moon as a start.

Put your stake in the ground by publicly declaring your ownership for the market problem in a manner that sets you apart, the way Kennedy *launched* the Apollo Space Program with an audacious high-profile speech. For you, this may mean publishing a seminal article or making an announcement at a high-profile conference. "Ownership" here means a strong, abiding commitment to take the lead in helping the market address the issue on an ongoing basis, the way Apple took the lead in solving the problem of unlawful music file sharing. Or the way Salesforce took the lead in pushing companies to embrace the cloud. And you never deviate from that central theme. Everything you do and say revolves around it.

Launch

ARTICULATE A VISION

Declare unique approach to solving the market problem you want to own

- Identify a common, critical problem no one else is addressing
- Develop a point of view
- Define a unique approach

Chapter 5 will take you through the detailed steps and action plan of the **Launch** phase and case studies on how others have done it. For example, we'll examine how Tesla *launched* around "high-performance electric cars" with its Roadster sports car as a first step in a longer-term vision of having electric cars go mainstream and an even longer-term vision for self-driving vehicles. We'll also look at some of the early **Launch** activities of Airbnb, the iPhone, and Amazon, among others.

PHASE 2: IGNITE

In order to reach escape velocity, a space vehicle needs a multistage rocket. The first gets it off the ground, but additional rockets continuously *ignite* to achieve enough speed and thrust to escape the gravitational pull of the earth, enter space, and gain and sustain momentum. In business, you must do the same: Continuously *ignite* the marketplace around your theme—your point of view—and build momentum for your solution. Continuously evangelize the message and lead a movement in the marketplace. The Apollo Space Program faced huge skepticism in its early days and built a groundswell with aggressive PR, lobbying, and education programs to ignite the support of the American public and Congress.

LEAD A MOVEMENT

Rally influencers around approach and build market momentum

- Evangelize the message
- Build momentum

Ignite

Chapter 6 will lay out the **Ignite** phase and its steps in detail, though in essence, the goal is threefold:

1. Become a valuable and integral part of your market as a thought leader.
2. Establish your approach (solution) as the widely recognized, de facto standard.
3. Get visionary customers willing to be your guinea pigs to help you develop and improve your solution as you prepare to take it to market.

Over time, generate a level of demand in the marketplace that exceeds your supply, which allows you to increase prices and be selective in who you accept as a client.

Indeed, some Silicon Valley marketing firms have generated so much demand that prospects must convince the provider to take them on as clients, often offering up equity in addition to full-fee retainers.

During the early part of the **Ignite** phase, your goal is to convert the most influential people in your market into believers so that they will begin to evangelize on your behalf. These are often particular industry analysts, journalists, and pundits. There are usually also a few individual powerbrokers. They may be venture capitalists, financial analysts, a current or retired CEO. Sometimes they are people "off the grid" with all kinds of connections. If you know your market well, you probably know who they are. Through this core group of influencers, your message and story gains access to a vast network of other influencers and prospects. If your early efforts are the spark, these people are your kindling. Through them, your message and awareness of your solution will reach the "tipping point" and begin to spread like a wildfire.

You will also start to talk to visionary prospects, who will give you feedback and help you hone your message. (If the market is truly ready for what you're offering, they will also start to buy from you and help you refine your offering. More on that in chapters that follow.)

High-profile examples of people who have *ignited* markets around their points of view and solutions are Steve Jobs, Elon Musk, and Walt Disney, but there are many others we'll also learn about in chapter 6.

The more you're starting from ground zero, the more spark and kindling you'll need. Examples are startups or companies entering a new market space, as we did in the late '80s with Accenture's Communications Industry Group. When you are a complete unknown or lack credibility in the eyes of the market, the curve will be steeper and take longer; however, there will come a "tipping point," after which you'll start to gain momentum.

Coming back to Salesforce as an example, it serves as a superb role model for systematic, focused "market ignition." With Marc Benioff as a luminary and spokesperson in its early days, the company *ignited* a movement around "software-as-a-service." Marc was an unstoppable force, evangelizing the message everywhere he went with his "no more software" lapel pin. He and the rest of the company focused on a singular and simple point of view, exploited client testimonials, met with analysts, and did everything possible to draw attention to the message. Frequently, they didn't even discuss the Salesforce offering. They didn't need to. It was a natural answer to the question, "Well, if no software, then *what*?" What was once a tiny upstart competing with industry giants is now widely regarded as the Go-To for companies that need sophisticated customer relationship management (CRM) capabilities without a complex, expensive, and disruptive implementation and infrastructure to manage. Salesforce drew the software-as-a-service map and then put itself on it, front and center, starting with salesforce automation and expanding from there.

PHASE 3: NAVIGATE

Even while continuously igniting, a rocket simultaneously must *navigate* a course to reach its destination. Likewise, you need to help clients efficiently *navigate* the journey toward solving their problems. Market dominance is not a mere public relations exercise—you must deliver on your promises. You must go beyond a product or service and put a total solution in place—something that delivers a valuable *result* for customers. A solution may be composed of people with particular skillsets; hardware and other physical products, software, services, tools, methodologies, other intellectual property, training programs; alliance partners; and more. NASA conducted the **Navigate** phase with these elements, including a cadre of aerospace contractors, academic institutions, and systems integrators. Together, they executed a series of *Apollo* missions, each of which took the program closer to its ultimate goal and beyond.

**GUIDE CUSTOMERS
ALONG THE JOURNEY**

Navigate

Implement your approach with the
right customers and deliver results

- Deliver on promises
- Help customers navigate the journey
- Provide "whole product"
- Build "community of believers"

Oracle has done this very effectively. Its scope includes database products, professional services, training, partnerships with other vendors, and so forth. Many systems integrators today can't (or don't want to) provide the end-to-end solution themselves, so they certify and promote other hardware and software vendors, consulting firms, and other service providers with complementary capabilities.

Successful *navigation* also requires outstanding business development and client service skills—gaining and keeping a client's trust. This means doing the right work for the right clients with the right people. There are a host of other operational implications here, such as opportunity management, appropriate measurement and rewards, recruiting, excellent delivery, and project management capabilities. You want to reduce your costs, increase your speed to market, and be as efficient as possible to keep customers happy and raise barriers to competition the way Amazon did with free, expedited shipping.

In a solution-selling situation, you are going to be targeting accounts and taking a relationship-building approach to sales rather than a transactional (get in and get out) approach. You will use the **Ignite** phase to introduce yourself to target accounts, continuing that effort in the **Navigate** phase, where you'll approach them, learn what's happening in their organizations, and work together with them to solve their problems using your unique approach or solution. You'll also build a community of believers in your solution among customers, targets, and the industry.

We'll walk through the details step by step in chapter 7 and look at case examples from companies like Disney, Pixar, Harley-Davidson, Amazon, Vitamix, Apple, and others.

PHASE 4: ACCELERATE

After gaining market traction and momentum, pick up the pace and continually watch your back. NASA constantly monitored the Soviets' progress and adjusted its program accordingly. Once the Cold War dissipated, NASA changed its approach altogether to an international, collaborative effort and broadened to explore other planets and galaxies.

The market you have *ignited* as the Go-To brand will quickly fill up with me-too firms, so you must *accelerate* to stay ahead. And like a rocket aiming for the moon, you are aiming at a moving target. During the **Accelerate** phase, you'll *keep* a close eye on the horizon (e.g., market trends, technological developments), continually refresh your vision, and maintain that delicate balance between broader penetration and focus. You must adapt quickly to the changing environment by evolving or reinventing. If you provide human resources outsourcing services, you know that many are in the game now, and broad skills are a ticket to entry. How will you stay ahead of the pack and stand out? What makes you special?

REFRESH THE VISION AND PICK UP SPEED

Accelerate

Adjust to market changes and strengthen your position

- Build loyalty
- Constantly monitor the market
- Stay ahead

Since its rebirth, LEGO has been very careful to balance the traditions and focus that put it on the map with innovations and product extensions that will keep it there. It has to continuously find ways to entice customers to remain loyal and add to their collections of bricks rather than look to knockoffs or alternatives.

If you have successfully dominated your chosen markets and are the established Go-To, you can consider whether and how to broaden. LinkedIn started by targeting Silicon Valley technology executives before expanding to information technology executives in other cities and then executives in other industries. Typically, you will expand into contiguous market spaces, meaning they relate closely to the markets in which you're established. They may be similar in geography, demographics, psychographics, buyer needs and values, etc. Retailers select their expansion markets very carefully, often by geography and demographics. Or you may decide to broaden your offerings within your existing markets, since it's easier to sell to existing customers. We often see this in technology sectors. Oracle, Cisco, IBM, Salesforce, and many others like them have dramatically expanded their software and service offerings in the enterprise space, often through acquisitions.

We'll look at the specifics of how to maintain your competitive edge and broaden your base in chapter 8, along with the steps to take and examples of who's doing this well and who isn't. We'll analyze why once-dominant firms like Blockbuster, Siebel, and Tenneco are now complete unknowns to new generations of businesspeople, which would have been unthinkable during those companies' heydays. We'll also look at case examples at companies like Netflix, Harley-Davidson, Apple, Salesforce, and Amazon as they adapt to change and face market challenges.

MUST DO ALL FOUR FOR *SUSTAINABLE* DIFFERENTIATION AND GROWTH

Many companies may temporarily achieve Go-To status and enjoy healthy prices and associated margins by succeeding at one, two, or even three of these phases. However, their success will be short lived. *You want sustainable differentiation, high margins, and growth.* Therefore, you need *all four phases*, just like a chair needs four legs. This is because each serves a very important role in achieving a sustainable Go-To position.

- **Launch:** Without this, the company lacks a higher purpose and is just another product or service provider. You won't have a distinctive point of view as a foundation for market leadership or a clearly differentiated offering and positioning.

- **Ignite:** Without this, you'll be a well-kept secret unable to generate market attention, excitement, and support, so gaining market momentum will be a long, hard, expensive slog, if you succeed in gaining it at all.
- **Navigate:** Without this, you won't deliver customer impact or generate those healthy and growing revenues and margins.
- **Accelerate:** Without this, you may have short-term success but will soon succumb to competition or adverse market forces.

VRBO (Vacation Rentals by Owner) was in a category by itself for years and widely used as a resource for connecting travelers directly with vacation rental owners. It performed **Navigate** well and had business, but it never developed or conveyed a vision and point of view (**Launch**). It never demonstrated thought leadership or generated momentum in the marketplace (**Ignite**). And it didn't do much to adapt as online buying behaviors and travel trends changed (**Accelerate**). When Airbnb came along with a new approach, offered a provocative point of view about connecting travelers with local hosts, generated lots of market buzz, and created a sense of community among hosts, it scooped up mindshare. Many travelers didn't even know VRBO was a competitive alternative. Airbnb continues to *accelerate* with new offerings, while VRBO merged with Homeaway, which is now chasing Airbnb by adopting some of its practices.

PHASES ARE NOT NECESSARILY SEQUENTIAL

For the sake of explanation, I talk about these phases as though they occur sequentially. In reality, this is usually not the case. Very often, and ideally, activity is occurring concurrently across two, three, or even four of the phases. The Apollo Space Program worked on all phases concurrently.

When Apple decided to create the iPhone, it operated in total secrecy, even within the company, for as long as it could, wanting to have a complete, working product before announcing it to the world. It did some pieces of the **Launch** phase (analyzed the market; developed a point of view, approach, vision, an offering concept, and rough prototypes). It then focused on the offering development portion of the **Navigate** phase, which needed to include lining up manufacturers and partners like AT&T and having customer support capability in place. Early proponents of the project conducted very limited **Ignite** activity and only internally. They had to get key people on board, including convincing Steve Jobs that Apple should produce its own phone and getting him behind the vision for how it could be done. About two years after conception of the vision and once the product was well on its way into production, the marketing team produced **Launch** materials and the presentation that Steve Jobs would use for the big, splashy public announcement in January 2007. The product went on sale just six months later as another part of the **Navigate** phase. **Ignite** activities followed that to get the media and market influencers behind this revolutionary offering and to convince developers to create apps for the App Store that would roll out about a year later, an **Accelerate** initiative that would make the iPhone truly powerful and unique at the time.

The phases most likely to occur concurrently are **Ignite** and **Navigate**, because most companies simply can't afford to wait until the market is fully developed before rolling out an offering and generating revenue. In practice, one of the first things you'll be focused on is winning your first few clients and developing core components of the offering as quickly as possible. Those first paying clients are critical for what is commonly called, "proof of concept," meaning evidence that you're building something the market actually needs, wants, is ready for, and is willing to pay for.

Learn the method as presented, as though it's a sequential flow. Then when it's time to start executing, analyze your situation, look at where you are in the process within each phase, and develop your action plan accordingly. Determine the sequence in which you execute based on your circumstances, market, and resources.

DOES THIS APPLY TO THE ENTIRE COMPANY OR JUST A PIECE OF IT?

The iPhone was just one of many initiatives at Apple at the time, with activities that mapped to the Apollo Method which were specific just to that product (and actually conducted without the knowledge of most people at the company); yet, the product vision, positioning, overall aesthetic, and role of the product within its market as a disruptor were consistent with Apple's overall positioning and brand image. Conversely, at a startup, the company and its first product are one and the same, so everything happening at the company revolves around that first offering.

The best way to answer the question of how broadly you apply the method across the organization is going to depend on the company's maturity, the scope of the company's business activities, and the markets it serves. Suppose your company is large, complex, and diverse like Richard Branson's Virgin Group. Your company probably has an overall brand strategy designed to appeal across markets. But the company is organized into business units that have their own goals, target specific markets, and provide offerings tailored to that market. All business units must present a consistent Virgin brand to the market, but each needs to tailor that brand to what's appropriate for each market. In this case, you would want to apply the Apollo Method at the business unit level, guided by the context of the company's overall vision, strategy, brand, business goals, etc.

In a company like Procter & Gamble (P&G), where business units and brands are fairly autonomous and each have their own strong brand presence in the market (e.g., Tide detergent), your Apollo Method planning and execution activity would mirror that. If there is some connection and interdependence between units, such as when several units sell the same product set to different markets, it's ideal if there is some level of umbrella Apollo Method planning and execution that then trickles down and gets customized at the individual market level. For example, you wouldn't want completely disparate sets of visions, messaging, and positioning. You would want an overarching vision, message, and so on that is then customized as needed for each market.

If your company is small, you should be doing this at the overall company level. This helps you remain appropriately focused. As you successfully penetrate and develop a reputation in your market and decide to go deeper into specific market segments or broaden, you may decide to apply the Apollo Method to each market segment. We did this within the Communications Industry Group at Accenture. We had penetrated the billing arena and were ready to start penetrating other areas, such as wireless and operations support systems (OSS), which were the information systems that made the public-switched network run smoothly. The Communications Industry Group was a single business unit but had become big enough to warrant several subunits, each targeting a specific market segment. Each of those subunits effectively had its own Apollo Method plan (though it wasn't called that at the time) for dominating a particular aspect of that market segment.

UPCOMING CHAPTERS STEP THROUGH THE METHOD

A good strategic framework is easy to understand and difficult to execute well. That is what makes it valuable in providing competitive advantage. It's one thing to state a vision and quite another to achieve and sustain it. No sooner did Kennedy declare the Man on the Moon goal than the Soviet Union followed suit. The difference lay in Apollo's ability to plan and follow a methodical implementation program, lead a unified effort among multiple teams, and overcome obstacles.

In the next four chapters, we'll talk about each of these phases in more detail and go through a step-by-step approach for executing them. For each phase, I'll start with an overview that lists all of the steps, the key projects/programs involved, and the related deliverables. I'll then walk through each step in detail, along with examples, hitting the highlights of what's involved in executing it. We'll end each chapter with a worksheet you will fill out to get started on your own plan.

Though I could write an entire book on each phase of the method, you'll see that many of the steps involved are fairly intuitive and that you already do much of what's required. This simply organizes and integrates them so that all of your strategic, marketing, and delivery activities are working together to move you toward a dominant position in your chosen market(s). There are some unique twists, and I've put most of my emphasis on those. The real magic in the Apollo Method for Market Dominance lies in having the right strategic intent each step of the way and in the details of how you are executing these activities.

RECAP AND ACTION ITEMS

The Apollo Method for Market Dominance consists of four major phases that may happen sequentially or concurrently in the journey toward becoming the Go-To brand in your space. Sequence and timing will depend on your particular situation.

1. **Launch:** The first phase, **Launch,** is all about deciding on and publicly declaring what you want to stand for in the

marketplace. You *launch* yourself into the market. This includes a unique and prescriptive point of view on a common, critical, and urgent market problem, and a unique, results-oriented solution.

2. **Ignite:** The second phase, **Ignite**, is about building momentum. You build support among powerbrokers and continuously *ignite* a movement in the marketplace around your point of view and solution. This is where you also start to convert visionary early customers, who help you refine your offering and prove your concept.

3. **Navigate:** The third phase, **Navigate**, is where you walk your talk and guide customers along the journey. You deliver on your promises to the marketplace. During this phase, you develop and take your solution to market and thrill customers with powerful results they are willing to pay you well for. You also put the infrastructure and processes in place that will lower your operating costs and give you speed to market and other efficiencies.

4. **Accelerate:** The fourth phase, **Accelerate**, is all about picking up speed to further cement your status as the Go-To and stay far ahead of the pack, since me-too copycats will inevitably emerge. During this phase, you will watch your back, monitor changing conditions ahead, and continuously innovate and adapt.

This approach goes beyond having a great product or service. It positions you as a true market leader in reputation *and* in execution, who sets the industry agenda and leads the charge in eradicating a common, critical, and urgent problem plaguing your market. **The key is to do not one, not two, not three, but *all four of the phases* in order to achieve sustainable differentiation and position yourself for sustainable, profitable growth even in crowded markets.**

ACTION ITEMS

You can access tools or download worksheets for each of these action items at apollomethod.com. Do these with one or more colleagues. When you get into the real work in the following chapters, you'll find that a team approach is essential.

1. **Visualize:** Without having any specifics just yet, think for a moment or write out what it would be like to declare your own moonshot to the marketplace, generate all kinds of excitement and support in the market for your solution, and have customers clamoring to buy it. Envision and write out what it would do for the market and for your company to become the Go-To for a crucial market problem you're uniquely able to solve.

2. **Analyze:** For the Go-To in your industry that you looked at in the chapter 3 action items, write a short blurb on how they've gone about each of these four phases based on what you know or can quickly research.

Now it's time to roll up our sleeves and get our hands dirty. In the remaining chapters, we're going to dig into each of the phases in detail, walk through the process step by step, and hear stories of how others have done it. This will be fun. You'll also create your strategy as you go so that by the time we're done, you'll have a one-page flight plan you can start implementing ASAP.

CHAPTER 5

LAUNCH PHASE

Take Ownership of a Market Problem and Solve It

True story. The global managing partner of a prestigious management consulting firm had finally landed a face-to-face introductory meeting with the CEO of Exxon. This would be the partner's big opportunity to generate an enormous flow of business for his company for years to come. Despite being a top energy industry expert, he prepared like crazy. Ultimately, he walked in with an eighty-slide presentation covering anything and everything related to the energy industry and his firm's credentials. He was ready to pull out and discuss in blinding detail whatever the CEO might be interested in. The CEO greeted him cordially and said he wasn't interested in seeing any slides. He had only one, very simple question. Sadly, it completely stumped the partner, rendering him speechless.

The question was, "In a sentence or two, what does your firm want to mean to the energy industry?"

Being able to answer this question is what the **Launch** phase is all about.

To position you for the key success factors spelled out in chapter 3, the fundamental strategy of the **Launch** phase is to figure out and then declare a market vision and point of view around a problem you will take ownership for eradicating and to propel your unique proposed approach into the market, potentially even before you've developed it. This is because you are not just announcing a product or service. You are announcing your intent to be the market's ongoing thought leader and driver around that issue. People get excited about Tesla not because it's another electric car manufacturer. People get excited because Elon Musk has articulated a higher purpose of making electric cars ubiquitous for the sake of the planet and has offered a long-term vision and roadmap for getting there.

In 1935, outdoorswoman Mary Anderson and her husband were deeply frustrated with how difficult and expensive it was to buy high-quality ice axes and other outdoor equipment, so they decided to find "a better way to purchase gear." Driven by their vision for a cooperative with strong buying power that would serve people who are serious about outdoor living, they led the formation of Recreational Equipment, Inc. (REI).

Remember, we saw in chapter 3 that to stand out and accomplish Go-To status, it is imperative to focus on a very specific segment of the marketplace and decide *what you want to be known for*. Not only will the right customers gravitate toward you, but others in the industry will also help spread the word on your behalf. They can only do this, however, if they can relate to what you're about and remember it top of mind. For that to happen, you must keep it simple and convey your moonshot in only a couple of words. Google started with "paid search." Facebook wanted to "connect *everyone*."

Starbucks wanted to be "the third place," one's bridge between work and home.

Be not afraid. "Focused" does not mean small; it means specific. You want to pick a large, dynamic, high-growth market that suits your strengths.

But what if there is already a Go-To brand in your chosen field? Subdivide and carve out your own territory. The industry analyst arena is a good example. Gartner owns the overall IT space, so Forrester Research has positioned itself as the authority in areas like consumer internet, online retail, marketing technology, and social media.

OVERVIEW

As the saying goes, "If you don't know where you're going, any road will get you there." In business, resources are usually too tight to stumble around indefinitely until we meander our way to the destination. Many a company would have been saved with a better up-front understanding of the market and how it wanted to uniquely fit into that market. This is what you're trying to accomplish during the **Launch** phase.

ARTICULATE A VISION

Declare unique approach to solving the market problem you want to own

Launch

- Identify a common, critical problem no one else is addressing
- Develop a point of view
- Define a unique approach

Yours is likely a huge industry and no one company can dominate the entire sector. Your market is also likely very crowded, with every major player targeting some aspect of it. This first phase is essentially classic strategic and business planning but with an emphasis on carving out your own territory. Think of your industry as a boardroom with its leaders sitting around the table, each representing a company. Your job is to find the unoccupied seat and claim it.

Kennedy chose the Moon. What will you pick?

During this phase, the goal is to very clearly answer these major questions:

1. What is our vision for the market and what market problem are we solving?
2. What's our point of view and unique solution to the problem?
3. What do we want to uniquely mean in the marketplace?
4. What value will we provide to customers?
5. How will that spell success for our company?
6. How will we roll this out to the marketplace?
7. What minimal infrastructure do we need to support the business?

After going through the process that follows, you will gain clarity and be able to articulate these answers in a compelling manner for yourself and your stakeholders—employees, customers, partners, investors, and market influencers. The **Launch** phase lays the foundation for everything else that you'll be doing and literally launches you into the market.

I'll go through this process in a logical sequence, but be aware that you may need to reorder the steps based on your situation. Or your process may be iterative, depending on how well developed your market and organization are. If so, develop a rough version of a particular deliverable, work on some other activities that help you gain more clarity, and then come back to refine what you've done.

LAUNCH Yourself Into the Market

ARTICULATE A VISION

Pick a Problem

- Focused, unoccupied market space
- Market vision
- Common, critical problem to "own"

Develop POV and Seminal Approach

- Unique point of view—manifesto
- Unique, results-oriented approach

Define Your Meaning and Value

- Unique meaning in the market
- Value you provide customers
- What spells success for your company

Declare Ownership

- Seminal thought piece

Establish Infrastructure

- Minimal

This is something you can do at the company level, business unit level, or business solution level, depending on your scope of responsibility and the size of your organization. For the sake of discussion, we'll assume you are responsible for a business unit (profit center) that serves a particular vertical industry such as healthcare.

There are five major steps, with a series of activities in each. Here is a quick-reference list, and then we'll go into detail on each, along with examples of how some companies have done them:

1. Define the common, critical, and urgent market problem you are going to "own."
   - Conduct an in-depth market analysis.
   - Segment the market.
   - Conduct a thorough internal assessment.
   - Place your bets—target a focused, unoccupied market space to dominate.
   - Clearly profile your target companies and buyers.
   - Develop a vision for where the market needs to go and decide on the market problem you will seek to own.
2. Develop your unique point of view on the problem and fresh approach for solving it.
   - Develop a unique point of view on the problem.
   - Define your approach to solving/addressing the problem.
   - Validate market need, target segment, and point of view with potential targets and industry thought leaders.
3. Define what you want to uniquely mean in the marketplace, what value you will provide to customers, and how that will spell success for your company.
   - Define your positioning.
   - Define your business vision.
   - Draft business strategy and other plans—how you will deliver on the promise.
   - Develop your unique core message platform.

- Define your proprietary offering for implementing your approach (your solution).

4. Tell your story and establish ownership of the approach (publish it).
   - Develop an anchor diagram, schematic, or infographic that captures your solution.
   - Develop a "stump speech" (executive presentation), e-book/white paper, and brief article that convey your point of view and approach.
   - Publish the point of view to put a stake of clear ownership in the ground.

5. Establish the infrastructure you will need to support the business.

In more familiar terms, here are the programs and projects involved in doing the above and which you're probably accustomed to executing. With the Apollo Method, however, there is a particular focus and continuity among these.

- Situation Assessment
- Vision Development
- Market Selection
- Positioning Strategy
- Point of View Development
- Service Offering Definition
- Business Strategy
- Operations Planning
- Market Launch
- Operating Infrastructure Development

Here are examples of the deliverables you produce during this Phase:

- Vision and Strategic Plan
- Business/Operating Plan
- Strategic Marketing Plan
- Investor Presentation (if a startup or asking for internal funding)
- Supporting documentation and working papers
- Anchor Diagram
- Executive Presentation ("stump speech")
- Seminal article, white paper, and/or book
- Website
- Service/Product Offering Conceptual Design

As you can see, this can be a lot of work. If you are a greenfield startup, all of this may be done by one or a few people. If you are a larger organization, you will likely need and want to involve people from various functional areas, including strategy, sales, marketing, and product management. Regardless, you should use professional program/project management practices, starting with a work plan, schedule, and name of person responsible for leading each task. Get agreement on all of this up front so that there aren't turf wars along the way. You want to avoid the common conflicts between sales, marketing, and product management, for example, to ensure a unified effort everyone will stand behind when it's time to execute.

STEP 1

Define the Common, Critical, and Urgent Market Problem You Are Going to "Own"

A college student typically has two years to dabble in a variety of subjects, and then he or she has to pick a major. Junior and senior years are the time to go deeper into a subject in order to tackle more sophisticated material. Students are still allowed to be opportunistic by taking a few electives. But for the most part, they have to focus.

Likewise, it's time to pick your major. Remember, your aim is to commit to a market, have a vision for where it needs to go, and develop such a superior ability to meet its needs and evolve with it that prospects actively seek you out and are willing to pay you a premium. Your aim is to become a part of the fabric of the market you serve, the way Harley-Davidson is within the premium heavyweight motorcycle market. To be such an integral member and a supreme expert, you must focus and then identify the unique market position you want to occupy. You must select your market.

This is possibly the toughest part of this entire process—picking the right market and right problem to focus on—but it's also the most powerful. If you do this well, you'll be set. The rest just falls into place from there.

So where do you begin? Look for the competitive white space. Find a common, critical, and urgent market problem that no one is adequately addressing and solve it. Become associated with it. Own it.

Anne Wojcicki, co-founder of consumer genetic testing company 23andMe, wanted to "give people direct access to their medical data."

Airbnb saw an empty seat in the hospitality industry and plopped down into it, devoting itself to helping travelers "live like a local."

IN-DEPTH MARKET ANALYSIS

When the Soviets thrilled the world by sending the first human into space, Kennedy gave his vice president a task in a memo dated April 20, 1961, saying:

> I would like for you as Chairman of the Space Council to be in charge of making an overall survey of where we stand in

space...Is there any...space program which promises dramatic results in which we could win?

Johnson turned to the experts, soliciting input from NASA, the military, Congress, and industry before and even after recommending that we aim for putting a human on the Moon.

Start with a very in-depth market analysis of your general domain. If you aren't already a deep expert in the field, seek help and then set about to become one yourself. Involve subject matter experts in your own company, industry analysts and other luminaries, and trend watchers. Get out of the office and go talk to customers, prospects, and others who live the business challenges day after day to find out where the sector is going, what challenges they are struggling with, and what no one seems to be addressing. Study the market as it is and develop a vision for where the market is going.

Because Steve Jobs was initially opposed to the idea of being in the phone handset business, Apple worked with Motorola to create an "iTunes phone" called the Rokr. Even after realizing the product was going to be an embarrassment, Jobs used the project to gain market intelligence from the many interactions with Motorola and Cingular (now AT&T). According to Richard Williamson, an original leader of the iPhone project at Apple, "Steve was gathering information during those meetings." He wanted to figure out what would be involved in controlling the handset design after all. Many external and internal meetings and debates later, Jobs came around and went all-in on making the iPhone.

Be sure to distinguish between fads (short-lived) and trends (lasting changes that will occur over time). You don't want to chase fads. They come and go away quickly to leave you hanging. Falling or rising commodities prices are a fad, for example. A statewide drought in California turned out to be a short-term issue, but the challenge of long-term water management in that state is a broad trend that will endure.

You can certainly generate a good, short-term income stream from a fad, but it won't sustain you long term. Many companies are reaping huge profits building applications on other companies' platforms such as Facebook or Apple's iPhone. But what is going to happen if those platform providers change their policies or some other platform eclipses them in popularity?

Be sure to distinguish between fads (short-lived) and trends (lasting changes that will occur over time). You don't want to chase fads. They come and go away quickly to leave you hanging.

In the technology and medical device sectors, for example, there is a big difference between being a service provider that latches on to the hot vendor of the day (fad) versus specializing in the overarching market problem (trend). Installing a third-party system is commodity work, unless you make it part of a solution for which you are a thought leader and the best-in-class provider. Maybe you capitalize on that vendor's popularity while it lasts, but be ready to quickly switch horses, so to speak.

Many companies made lots of money capitalizing on the Year 2000 or "Y2K" scare in the late '90s, when it was feared that computer programs coded with two-digit years would not be able to handle the transition to the new millennium and would crash. It turned out to be much ado about nothing, but there was sufficient concern to induce *$100 billion in spending in just four years*. Once the year 2000 arrived, especially when the anticipated problems didn't materialize, the market evaporated almost overnight and put many companies out of business.

The exception to this is fads that you're in a position to quickly capitalize on without betting the farm and then just as easily abandon, which is what the more successful companies did with the Y2K fad—they capitalized on the spending surge but weren't depending on it for long-term market positioning or growth.

Obsess over trends and anticipate where they are taking the industry. For example, the rise of cloud computing is a trend. The move toward clean, sustainable energy is a trend. The growth of mobile applications is a trend. The use of artificial intelligence is a trend. The Internet of Things (IoT) and blockchain are trends. Population growth is a trend. Aging of the baby boomers is a trend. Very often, you can extrapolate out, project fairly accurately what the implications will be, and identify where the market opportunities are.

Obsess over trends and anticipate where they are taking the industry.

Jeff Bezos was working for a hedge fund in the early 1990s. As part of his research, he encountered a report saying the nascent internet was growing at 2,300 percent per year. He later said, "That's huge—nothing usually grows that fast outside a petri dish." Through additional research, he created a list of twenty products that were ripe for online sales and settled on books as the top choice. When he couldn't convince his employer to jump in, he quit and started what is now Amazon. He did what Tina Seelig likes to teach entrepreneurship students at the Stanford Technology Ventures Program: "Find a tsunami and stand in front of it."

As a starting point, read everything you can get your hands on. You'll find source information, much of it free, all over the internet. Search for white papers, articles, top-tier trade publications in your industry and content marketing hubs focused on your domain. Look at the agendas for major conferences in your sector to spot patterns for emerging trends. Investment banks and research firms such as Gartner publish market trend and forecast reports with useful data. Analyze your own customer and operations data, along with third-party growth projections, research on budgeting trends (how consumers and businesses expect to allocate their spending in the future), and data on venture capital investments—follow the money. Be mindful of ensuring that sources are credible and unbiased. The rule of thumb is to dig and research until you're not hearing anything new. Stop only when most of the information from disparate sources is repeating what you've seen elsewhere.

Market timing is always tricky, so your aim is to concentrate on market challenges and opportunities that are going to catch on in whatever time frame you need. The bigger opportunities are also often the ones that will have longer lead times in terms of how long it takes the market to come around to it. Eventually, all cars could be self-driving, but that may take years or even decades.

The trends more likely to bear fruit in the near term are also sometimes the ones that other people are also eyeing, like predictive data analytics. Ones that are perhaps already saturated or are so easy to solve that they will soon become saturated may not make sense for you at all. Or if you still feel they're attractive, you should dissect them to find the unmet, more challenging, and specialized market problems. The key factors to consider are:

- What broad market do you currently serve?
- Where is the market going?
- What are the unmet needs today?
- What are the competitive threats?
- What common, critical problems will the market face tomorrow?

If you want help structuring, such an analysis, Michael Porter's Five Forces Model is an oldie-but-goodie example of a useful analytical framework. You can find more examples at apollomethod.com.

Importantly, stand in the shoes of target clients. Get firsthand perspective and input from them by contacting executives in your target market and asking them a few questions:

- What are the three biggest problems your business faces today?
- What would it be worth to your business to solve these problems?
- What do you anticipate will be the three biggest problems your business faces over the next five years?
- What will it be worth to your business to solve these future problems?
- What is impossible to do in your business, but if it could be done, would fundamentally change it?
- What would that be worth?

Dig deep with them. Use these questions as a starting point for probing conversations about what's happening in their world, where they see things going and what they'll be spending money on in the foreseeable future. Be sure to talk not just to prospective customers but also to industry influencers and pundits. Customers operating in the heat of battle every day don't always have the capacity to poke their nose out and look at the horizon. They are too busy dealing with the here and now. Plus, most people are not particularly adept at anticipating where the trends are headed. Financial analysts, market analysts, trade journalists, industry strategists, data providers, and other market watchers can be invaluable here.

When Leland Stanford and his wife were debating how best to serve the children of California after losing their only son to typhoid fever in 1884, they solicited input from leaders at Cornell, Yale, MIT, and others. It was Harvard president Charles Eliot who suggested they start their own university. Stanford asked him what investment it would take, to which he replied, "Five million dollars."

MARKET SEGMENTATION

Segment the marketplace according to common characteristics, as opposed to traditional breakdowns, such as industry or business function (or age, income, etc., for consumers). Look for common problems and patterns, such as culture, behavior, competitive pressures, how readily they adopt new technologies, the role that emerging trends will play in their businesses and industries, and so forth. Develop profiles of particularly attractive segments. This is exactly what Jeff Bezos did in coming up with his list of twenty potential markets.

INTERNAL ASSESSMENT

When Johnson received Kennedy's memo asking for a recommended space program goal, the first thing he did was conduct an internal assessment, as summarized in his reply memo to Kennedy. The US led in "communications, navigation, weather and mapping" but lagged in "large rocket engines…[and] technological accomplishments in space," he wrote. "The US has greater resources than the USSR for attaining space leadership but has failed to make the necessary hard decisions and to marshal those resources to achieve such leadership."

In an environment of constant, rapid change, how do you select and commit to a direction? Like Johnson, look at your strengths, weaknesses, opportunities, and threats (commonly called a SWOT analysis). Your company can't be all things to all people, so later you are going to look for the intersection of external unmet needs and your own strengths and requirements.

Conduct a thorough assessment. List the *distinctive* competencies, strengths, and qualities that truly set your company apart. This includes

Begin With Your Strengths

Your Distinctive Competencies, Strengths, Qualities, and Potential

clarity on your organization's values, culture, and characteristics, because you want to include a good cultural fit between your chosen market and your organization. If your company culture is extremely fast moving, likes to show fast results, and thrives on the adrenaline rush of constant change, the utilities or government sectors may not be for you.

When starting Entre Nous Aesthetics, the Go-To medical spa in Menlo Park, California, serving Silicon Valley's movers and shakers, the founders, Dr. Jane Weston and physician assistant Sandra Ewers, were very clear as to their values. They aim for very natural-looking, flattering results. This is one of several core values that inform their decisions about who they seek to serve and what those clients want to achieve.

TARGET SEGMENT

In order to narrow down and select a target segment, you may have to eliminate before you can dominate, just as Bezos did in narrowing his list of twenty down to just one. In an industry overflowing with opportunity, market selection is a process of elimination. Now that you have conducted an assessment, look for the overlaps between the unmet market needs and your organization's strengths and qualities.

Now identify which segments you will not serve. Consider eliminating market segments that:

- Are of no value to your future (not profitable, strategic, rewarding, helpful toward skill development, etc.)

Start to Narrow Your Options

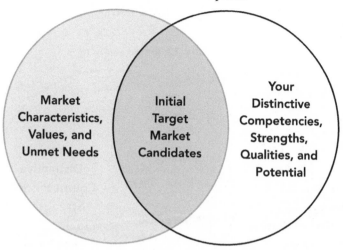

- Are already dominated or saturated and can't be subdivided in a way that makes sense for you
- Are slow-growth markets
- Lack competitive pressure of their own or the need/motivation to change
- Are completely price sensitive, with buyers not willing to pay for value
- Are not a good cultural fit for what you are or want to become
- Are slow to embrace change, innovation, or new methods
- Don't particularly suit your strengths
- Are outliers (don't have much in common with the other markets you serve—have buyer values that are radically different from your other markets; require a very different skillset; etc.)
- Will require intellectual property and skills that cannot be cost-effectively transferred from customer to customer
- Have no clear gathering spots—are hard to reach as a group

Now eliminate markets that other companies can just as easily serve or where you're at a competitive disadvantage.

Your Initial Target Market Candidates

It is invaluable to make very conscious decisions at this point about which markets you will not serve and to document them. This is very handy down the road when the temptation to proactively pursue that market segment starts to rear its ugly head. You can remind yourself as to why it's not a good market for you.

Now it's time to decide what market you intend to own as the Go-To. Refine your criteria, with a strong weighting toward readiness for what you're offering. The good news is that if done well, your market analysis will almost scream it at you the way Bezos's analysis screamed, "Books!" to him. If you are tempted to broaden somewhat or aim for multiple segments, you should prioritize them into a Target Market Dartboard. Put the core target in the bullseye, and work your way out from there. It should make very logical sense as to what the markets are, how they relate to each other, and how they relate to your company's expertise. For Amazon, it was buyers of books, then CDs and videos, then gifts, and so on.

It's ideal if penetration of your core target market will help you win over the second market, which will help you win over the third market, and so on. You want markets that influence each other.

The key here is to ensure that the core market is narrow and specific enough to be able to gain a foothold

Prioritize Your Target Markets

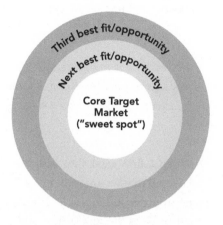

If you are targeting multiple segments, prioritize them into a Target Market Dartboard, with the highest-priority market in the bullseye, followed by the others in order of priority. This will help keep you focused.

without being so small or restricted that you will have trouble expanding later. GoPro started as a way for surfers, skiers, mountain bikers, and other such athletes to document themselves in action, and it expanded from there. The core market needs to be large and lucrative enough to support your initial growth objectives. *It's also extremely important that this be a market you can reach efficiently—that there be a network among the targets and central mechanisms for reaching them* (e.g., a central trade organization, efficient distribution channels). You also want to double-check your market analysis and look out on the horizon. How prone is this sector to market cycles? What cycle is it currently in, when is the next downturn going to happen, and will you be able to balance it out with other business? Are there any disruptive trends on the way that are going to dramatically impact your market? For example, payroll processing for the newspaper publishing industry is not a growth market, because newspapers are in decline. Employment numbers are shrinking, not growing.

The key here is to ensure that the market is narrow and specific enough to be able to gain a foothold without being so small or restricted that you will have trouble expanding later.

When I first went into business, I did my market elimination and overall market analysis, knowing I needed a very specific target niche in order to be visible. I initially decided to focus on professional services, because it was still a relatively small market at the time in terms of spending on strategy and marketing services; it was an untapped market; and it was one I understood well. Back then, marketing was a very young and immature discipline in this industry. There was a huge opportunity to declare ownership. However, upon further analysis, I realized some things.

First, there were many subsegments in what seemed to be an already very narrow, specific niche: law, medicine, advertising, public relations, management consulting, private equity, accounting, environmental consulting, market research, information technology, and the list went on. Second, market forces, cultures, business practices, terminology, business models, and so on varied widely among these sectors. Third, there were easy ways to reach people within these sectors but not across them. Under a microscope, they were distinctly different markets. Some were also more sophisticated than others from a marketing standpoint. Also, I lacked expertise in some and had no interest in working with others.

Another thing I realized is that it would not be long before a lot of people decided to do just what I did—leave their positions at professional services firms and start leveraging their expertise as consultants. The needs of these companies are so specialized that the supply would start to grow to meet the demand for marketing help. And sure enough, that is exactly what has happened. Whereas years ago, there were few marketing consultants of any kind who specialized in professional services, today there are thousands.

I decided to play to my strengths and make IT services my bull-seye target, which was a huge market unto itself. Within that, I narrowed the market even further based on geography, industries they served, types of services they offered to their customers, company culture, level of marketing sophistication, etc. I developed a very specific profile of who I wanted to target and ended up with a Target Market Dartboard, ranging from core targets to outer targets (which meant they were nice to have but not worth proactive investment). This told me exactly who I was talking to with my thought leadership material, articles, website content, and so on.

For small companies without the money to aim at an entire market or for some offerings, it may be that your core target market is a finite list of specific companies. What matters is that they share buyer values, have the same relevant business problems, listen to the same set of influencers, and share other characteristics that will allow you to appeal to and serve them in an efficient manner.

MARKET VISION AND PROBLEM TO OWN

In chapter 3, we talked about obsession and some examples of Go-To companies like Salesforce, Cisco, Facebook, Kaiser, Amazon, and others that are each obsessed with the market problem it wants to own.

In chicken-and-egg fashion, you can either start with the market vision and let that point you to the current gaps and obstacles that pose market problems, or you can identify the problems and develop a vision for what an end state could look like. For example, believers in cryptocurrency have a clear market vision that the rest of us don't yet understand. They see what a cryptocurrency economy will look like and the current obstacles to mainstream use. That gap between the vision and the reality highlights many potential problems to tackle. Steve Jobs had a vision for digital devices that would stream music, and he needed the music companies as partners. However, the gap was that music companies were being burned by free streaming and sharing and didn't trust it. The problem to solve, then, was "How do we enable *paid* streaming and get both music companies and consumers on board?"

In contrast, Elon Musk famously starts with big, societal problems and then develops an end-state vision. How do we get people to "embrace electric cars" (Tesla)? How do we enable people to "live on other planets" (in case that's ever necessary) (SpaceX)? How do we "solve the problem of soul-destroying traffic" (The Boring Company)?

Now it's time for you to develop your market vision and decide which market problem *you* intend to own. What problem would you like to take chief responsibility for eliminating? Be sure to select a market problem that is common, critical, and urgent. You want a common problem most companies or consumers in the sector face. According to the former head of Apple's Human Interface Group, Greg Christie, "Apple is best when it's fixing the things that people hate."

Be sure to select a market problem that is common, critical, and urgent.

Unless you have Musk's deep pockets, you want the problem to be critical in that it's a very high priority to your targets. And you want it to be urgent so that they will be motivated to take action now and pay a premium for it, valuing speed-to-results over cost. *The lower on Maslow's Hierarchy of Needs it is (the more tightly it's linked to survival), the more quickly buyers will respond and the less price sensitive they will be.*

Pick something you and the organization will be passionate about. It needs to be a problem the organization is feverishly devoted to solving. Elon Musk views electric cars as so vital to our future that he wouldn't begrudge anyone else for being more successful at it. Asked about competition from GM during a CBS *60 Minutes* interview with Leslie Stahl, Musk said, "If somebody comes and makes a better electric car than Tesla, and it's so much better...that...we go bankrupt, I still think that's a good thing for the world."

It's impossible to do justice to such a complex topic in just one portion of a chapter, but the most important thing to remember is that market selection is an analytical process. As you work on this, constantly test and validate your choices in the marketplace with objective outsiders and prospects. If your hypothetical area of focus feels risky or uncomfortable, you have more work to do.

CHECKING YOUR WORK

Now that you've selected a market and business problem, here are some criteria to help you verify you've got the right one.

- **Does anyone else currently own it?** It's best to pick competitive white space, as many call it. Be sure there isn't already a Go-To for the market issue you specialize in. If there is, either go back to your analysis or see whether you can subdivide, the way Forrester Research subdivided the technology industry analyst space owned by Gartner.

- **Does it play to your distinctive strengths?** Do you have a credible track record? Do your people already have expertise in this area? In a high-touch, consultative sales situation,

people will only sell what they know. I was once with a
business-to-business (B2B) cloud infrastructure company
that had only ever worked on front-end consumer support
and online retail systems. The board hired a new president
whose main expertise was in supply chain management. This
company didn't have a single credential in that area, yet he
built a strategy around it and declared it as the business we
would be in. Needless to say, we got nowhere, because the
rest of the salesforce had no expertise, no contacts, no ability
to credibly discuss it, and no passion for it.

- **Will the market grow fast enough to support your revenue
  growth goals?** You want to be sure the market for this
  problem is not only big enough now but will also grow with
  you and at a pace that will sustain your business.

- **Will people pay a premium to solve this quickly?** Is there
  currently enough urgency around this problem to drive
  people to take action? The more urgent a problem is, the
  more people are willing to get moving and to pay to solve it.
  Will they value speed, expertise, and results and be willing
  to pay well for those? And do prospective buyers have the
  budget?

- **Are there clear gathering spots for this market and
  business problem?** Be sure that you can efficiently reach
  large chunks of your target audience. We'll do this in depth
  in **Ignite**, but for now, here is an acid test: if it's not easy to
  identify the top dozen or so events, publications/websites,
  and influencers you need to target to reach this market,
  your market may be too broad or poorly defined. I've made
  the mistake in the past of not giving enough credence

to this filter and then having a hard time cost-effectively reaching targets.

In summary, you ultimately want to answer three questions:

1. Who specifically are we targeting? (market segment you specialize in, a profile of your ideal customer and buyer set)
2. What is our market vision and the unique market problem or challenge we will solve? (in a sentence and then boiled down to one to three words)
3. What will companies gain by being able to solve this problem? (the strong central benefit and what it is worth)

AN EXAMPLE

Here are two extremes on how to do this market analysis, and then of course there is everything in between. The first extreme is very quick and dirty, but it can be a very valid approach: relying on the top experts in the field to basically tell you where things are headed, what the big problems are going to be, and therefore where the big opportunities are going to be.

An example of this was Accenture's foray into a new market in the late '80s. Then still a unit of an accounting firm, the company had just been through a global strategic planning process and saw a growth opportunity in the telecommunications industry. It appointed senior partner Al Burgess to head what was then a nonexistent practice. Divestiture had taken place in the US market only a few years prior in which the AT&T monopoly had been broken into seven "Baby Bell" local telephone companies (telcos), the "long-distance" company, and Bellcore (now part of Ericsson), which managed and maintained the complex software and systems used by all of the telcos. In most other countries, the telcos were still government run. Mobile technology was still in its infancy. And only a handful of large equipment manufacturers were considered qualified to provide any kind of hardware or software to a highly specialized industry with very complex, proprietary technology needs. Burgess's job was to break into it. And he had only a few weeks to figure out what the beachhead would be.

He was given a revenue target and "seed funding" of a couple hundred thousand dollars, with the understanding that he could ask for more once he had a compelling plan and business case.

The first thing he did was hire a boutique strategic consulting firm that was purely focused on the telecommunications industry, with a special emphasis on the US market. This was a small firm of only a few people, but they were deep, deep experts with vision. At the time, almost no one knew as much as they did about what was wrong with these companies and where things were headed. The company's services were very expensive and very worth it. Burgess asked them where the problems were, and they had one word: billing. The phone company's billing systems were completely antiquated and inflexible, yet the boutique consulting firm could see that value-added services, competition, and higher customer expectations were on the way. Its vision was that billing was going to become a competitive weapon, because it doesn't do much good to offer new services if you can't bill and get paid for them—the phone companies were going to live or die on billing over the next ten years. But there was an even bigger problem. If the market moved at bullet-train speed, telcos moved like old, lumbering freight trains climbing a mountain. They were going to need help, and no one out there was ready to give it to them. Now, if there is one thing that the consulting unit of an accounting firm knows how to do, it is building flexible billing systems. Burgess had his market.

Now fast-forward several years, when he took the other extreme. The practice had established itself as the Go-To for billing and had grown organically to a few hundred million dollars in revenues, and it was time to refresh the vision. The business unit assembled an international team of market research experts and strategists with industry expertise; conducted an in-depth market growth projection using numerous secondary sources; conducted primary research, consulted with various external experts, and prepared a detailed trends report predicting upheaval in the industry. It also developed a vision for what the market would look like in ten years and the problems companies would face during that time frame. The team then validated the report with outside experts, published it, and distributed it worldwide. There were six people working full-time-plus for about four months, plus legions of others coming in and out. This effort drove the development of a new vision and strategy to top $2 billion in revenues within a short period, again through organic growth, which the organization achieved.

STEP 2

Develop Your Unique Point of View On and Solution to the Problem

As expressed in his January 1961, State of the Union address, newly installed president Kennedy had a strong point of view that "we must prevent the arms race from spreading to new nations, to new nuclear powers and to the reaches of outer space." The speech included a direct overture to the Soviet Union to set the Cold War aside and join the US in a cooperative approach to space exploration, which they declined. Shortly thereafter, the Soviets reached a milestone when cosmonaut Yuri Gagarin became the first human in space. At that point, Kennedy became very clear on the imperative: the US must demonstrate dominance in space to ensure it doesn't become a literal battleground. In his "Moon Shot" speech that May, he expressed his point of view on and solution to the problem:

> If we are to win the battle that is going on around the world between freedom and tyranny…the dramatic achievements in space which occurred in recent weeks [a Soviet sent into space] should have made clear to us all…the impact of this adventure on the minds of men everywhere who are attempting to make a determination of which road they should take [democracy vs. communism]…We go into space because whatever mankind must undertake, free men must fully share.

He then announced the Moon landing goal as the solution, adding:

> No single space project in this period will be more impressive to mankind, or more important for the long-range exploration of space…

When I was chief marketing officer for a startup some years ago, our law firm invited me to a presentation about branding. I thought that was odd, because I don't usually associate law firms with dishing out branding advice any more than I think of marketing firms giving out patent law advice. I was intrigued and attended. The presentation turned out to be so powerful and valuable that not only do I still remember some of the information they shared, but I also continue to regard that firm as experts in this area.

The reason is that they had a clear, compelling, and provocative point of view on branding challenges I could expect to encounter and offered advice on what to do.

- It was clear—I understood it.
- It was compelling—it got my attention.

- It was provocative—it engaged me and made me think, question, debate, and ultimately buy into it.

Their presentation happened to be very engaging and entertaining, but it could have been as dry as dirt and I would have still found it incredibly valuable. What was the result? It completely transformed my view of the firm and how I might be able to benefit from their services. It made them credible. It gave me the sense that they could immediately walk in and solve my problem without a learning curve. It made me want to ask, "Can you come help me?"

It gives you a platform for getting in the door, and the more provocative and audacious it is, the faster and wider that door will open.

Having a strong point of view on a market issue is absolutely essential to differentiation, especially in crowded markets. Done well, this will make people sit up and pay attention. A point of view is a strong opinion about what's wrong and what needs to be done about it. The Apollo Method for Market Dominance has four "ABCD" criteria for a strong point of view:

- **Actionable:** It must be prescriptive in nature so that the audience can actually act on it.
- **Bold:** It should be game changing or mind bending in some way and be a large leap beyond traditional thinking and approaches.
- **Controversial:** It should be provocative and counterintuitive and stir debate.
- **Distinctive:** It must be completely unique and distinctive, memorable, and clearly set you apart.

Kennedy's point of view certainly met all of these criteria.

You've probably come to realize by now that people don't usually want to hear about your product or service unless they're already very predisposed to buying it or there is some big news about it that they need to hear.

This is especially true of the media, industry influencers, and qualified prospects just entering the sales funnel. What they are interested in is new information that might help them in some way. They don't want to hear about you. They want to hear about them or something related to them. Most of all, people love free advice. A point of view provides it.

Actionable

Bold

Controversial

Distinctive

We're not just talking about any ol' free advice. It needs to be a unique perspective focused on the common, critical, urgent market problem you've selected and, generically speaking, what it will take to fix it regardless of whether you're involved. It gives you a platform for getting in the door, and the more provocative and audacious it is, the faster and wider that door will open. That's because people are inherently curious. If you say something that blows their preconceived notions out of the water, they won't be able to resist hearing you out.

If you say something that blows their preconceived notions out of the water, they won't be able to resist hearing you out.

Tesla "believes the faster the world stops relying on fossil fuels and moves towards a zero-emission future, the better." Many previous electric car efforts had stalled, because they had a limited market, only appealing to the "tree huggers," as a car manufacturer had put it. According to co-founder Martin Eberhardt, Tesla decided that the solution was "an electric car that would appeal to people who love cars." What the world needed was an electric sports car that broke the usual "compromise between performance and efficiency" and would get people excited about electric cars. Having no idea at the time as to how they would actually accomplish this, the founders set out to try.

The Verde Group, a North American market research firm, tells companies they can actually *"profit* from customer dissatisfaction." Now, you can bet that draws some attention. Verde's research and experience shows that if you convert a dissatisfied customer into a satisfied customer, they actually become more loyal than a customer who was satisfied all along. Actionable? Check. Bold? Check. Controversial? Check. Distinctive? Check. And it's directly relevant: the Verde Group specializes in helping companies do just that— identify dissatisfied customers, understand why they're unhappy, and develop strategies for how to make them happy.

The Verde Group, a North American market research firm, tells companies they can actually "profit from customer dissatisfaction."

In pursuing market dominance, you are going to become a thought leader in your industry. Your point of view is going to be your foundation for all future thought leadership, marketing, selling, and delivery activity. It is your basis for leading the rest of the market and setting the market agenda. It will be the underpinning for everything to come.

What you want to do is develop a point of view on the market problem that is separate from you and does not discuss your solution. It should, however, be a natural lead-in for your solution, should the listener ask.

A simple framework for a point of view is:

1. Here's *why* (insert trend/issue) is creating a problem/challenge for you.
2. Here's *what* you need to do to solve the problem (this should imply your solution and its benefits without specifically mentioning it just yet).

At the highest level, it's just a couple of sentences, which can then be elaborated upon in as much detail as one wishes. For example:

- **Why:** For ships at sea, the prevalent use of radios to manually communicate with each other and plan their routes is prone to user error, which causes collisions and consumes excess fuel.
- **What:** Instead, all ships should be electronically tracked as part of a monitoring network that optimizes routes and speed, which would reduce fuel consumption and increase safety.

At this point, even if you don't already know what your solution will be, you now know the key trend, market problem, and sector you're focused on. There is great value in articulating your point of view, because the analytical process may direct you to a unique solution.

Later, once you've defined your solution, we'll build on this structure to create a complete, succinct message platform.

YOUR SOLUTION TO THE PROBLEM

Once Tesla decided that the market needed a car that would get people excited and actually *crave* electric cars, it strategically decided with much forethought that its solution would be to start with a sexy, high-end sports car that many wanted but few could afford. "What better way to show that electric cars can perform?" it thought.

Your goal is to define a solution that delivers such a powerful result for the customer that they are willing to pay a premium.

Now it's time to define *your* solution. It's okay if you're not prepared to develop anything just yet. Keep it high level and conceptual. It could take any or all of several forms: a tangible product, a service, a framework or method, and/or training offerings. Your goal is to define a solution that delivers such a powerful result for the customer that they are willing to pay a premium. You want value-based pricing, not cost-plus pricing. There are some ideal criteria—the more of these it meets, the more powerful it will be.

- ☑ Truly solves the problem
- ☑ Is easy for targets to get their heads around during the evaluation process
- ☑ Delivers a killer result that has a profound impact on customers—ideally one that is tangible and quantifiable
- ☑ Has a very clear and, ideally, quantifiable value proposition (a no-brainer cost-benefit ratio)
- ☑ Is unique and very obviously superior to past and present alternatives
- ☑ Delivers results more quickly and easily than competitive alternatives
- ☑ Offers value that eclipses implementation disruption or pain
- ☑ Is a radical departure from standard industry practices in a way that is substantially more effective

- ☑ Makes the customer want to enthusiastically tell others about it
- ☑ Encourages ongoing loyalty and a long-term customer relationship

Take the idea to a few people for some initial feedback and refine your concept again. When ready, develop a sketch or diagram and then a prototype (nothing elaborate—use rapid prototyping techniques and come up with the fastest, easiest way to try it out).

Marc Benioff first conceived the idea for Salesforce while still working at Oracle and sought out a colleague with expertise in the market, Magdalena Yesil, to get her reaction. As she describes it:

> And one day Marc called me and said, "Listen, I need to have lunch with you because I have an idea I need to bounce off of you." And the idea was taking a Siebel Solutions [the leading salesforce automation provider at the time, which cost millions to implement], boiling it down to the 20 percent or 10 percent of the functionality that most people used, leave the other 90 percent behind, and turn that product into a, you know, software-as-a-service model. We didn't use the word "software-as-a-service" at the time. We didn't have the word "cloud." It was a very basic idea. We did have a [market] space for those of you who remember that, so it wasn't a completely out of the box idea. But it was out of the box in the sense that we really had a multi-tenant environment that we were going to basically be hosting the software in. So when Marc and I had lunch that day, I already believed that the end of enterprise software was coming as we knew it. It was too expensive for midsize and small companies that couldn't really afford it at all.

An interesting example in the consumer space is Proactiv Solution, the wildly successful acne treatment system made famous through infomercials. Prior to Proactiv, acne treatments were either strong prescription medications or weak over-the-counter options that consumers had to cobble together on their own. Dermatologists Katie Rodan and Kathy Fields created a total solution by pulling together various, mostly common ingredients into a three-step system, which now generates over $1 billion annually. The perceived value is so high that customers willingly pay more for the kit than they would by putting the pieces together themselves.

Now update your point of view with your solution so that it tells a complete story. (Step 3 will explain how to formalize this into a message platform.) Check to be sure it meets these criteria:

- ☑ Unique and differentiating
- ☑ Prescriptive—declares your opinion/philosophy and approach
- ☑ Establishes ownership for fresh perspective and solution
- ☑ Addresses common, critical, urgent industry problem
- ☑ Says, "We understand your problem and have a uniquely effective approach for solving it"

At this point, you have a part of the market you plan to focus on, a particular market problem you want to own, a groundbreaking point of view on what companies should do about the problem, and a proposed, unique solution. It's time to test it in the marketplace.

VALIDATION

The April 28, 1961, Johnson memo to Kennedy recommending a Moon landing as the US solution to winning the space race began with, "…The examination will continue…" This would be one of the two largest, nonmilitary undertakings in the nation's history (the other being the Panama Canal), and no one wanted to see the US president make a declaration to the world that the public would not get behind or that would be impossible to afford or execute. Conversations about going to the Moon had been occurring within NASA and among other stakeholders in its ecosystem for a couple of years. By the time Kennedy got his own mind around it, key people within NASA were already won over and some of the early thinking about how to make it happen had already occurred. Still, significant due diligence occurred within the White House, NASA, and other entities to determine what it would cost, where the talent would come from, what partnerships and facilities would be needed, and whether it was, indeed, doable. Kennedy himself agonized over such a monumental commitment, soliciting opinions from scientists, engineers, and other experts and making his final decision only after weighing the costs, risks, alternatives, and effort required.

Likewise, you must take draft material regarding your target market, business problem, and solution around to experts inside your company, market influencers, potential customers, and anyone else you can get your hands on who knows more than you. Ask them to poke holes in what you have. Ask whether they agree on the market need and opportunity. Determine whether the market urgency is there and whether people will pay a premium to solve this. Get a sense of what you'll be able to charge—what it is worth to the customer to be able to solve this problem. Ask them whether you are sufficiently focused. Find out what they think about the market issue. Learn about competitive alternatives. Actively seek out the flaws in your work. These conversations will also help you fill in details and flesh out the concept even more. There are product development methodologies out there that provide even more detail on how to do this. See apollomethod.com for a few examples and links.

Beyond bouncing the idea off colleagues over lunch, Benioff immediately built a rough, web-based salesforce automation tool in one month and then had people try it out. As he recalls it:

> I invited friends and colleagues to visit the apartment [the team worked out of], which I called the Laboratory, and asked them to test the prototype and offer feedback. Michelle Pohndorf Forbes, a family friend who was in sales, was one of the first people we invited to cycle through the prototype. She constantly reminded us to make the site easy to navigate with as few clicks as possible. My friends who worked at Cisco shared everything they hated about using traditional enterprise software products, and they walked us through what wasn't working for them. We listened and then responded by designing salesforce.com to be all the things that traditional software wasn't.
>
> Unlike the way software had traditionally been developed—in secret—everyone was welcome at the Laboratory. When a group of Japanese businessmen were in town, they came to see what we were creating. We eventually became a stop on a tour for visiting Korean businesspeople who were interested in seeing an American startup. Being inclusive of potential users from large and small companies across the world helped us gain valuable insight.

Another valuable role this activity plays is that it kicks off your selling effort and helps you build early pipeline. In prior steps, you've already talked to people about their problems and what they're looking for (meaning, you've prequalified for a need). Now you're coming back with a potential solution. You get feedback and learn more about what they're after. They get to help shape and mold the solution to their specific needs. It's also an opportunity to ask them who else you should talk to. Invariably, they will recommend conversations with other stakeholders and influencers at their company who will eventually need to buy into the solution, and they will often also refer you to peers at other companies. It's a win-win and a great way to get your first customers.

Another valuable role this activity plays is that it kicks off your selling effort and helps you build early pipeline.

I must confess that I have made grave mistakes on this task in the past, falling into the same trap as all of the others who inspired Steve Blank to create his Customer Development methodology, which emphasizes involving customers in the product development process. At a few prior companies I worked with, we would take our draft material to information technology industry analysts and ask them what they thought. Some call these "How much do you love us?" meetings. We would listen very carefully only for positive reinforcement. I remember sitting in a meeting once with some Gartner analysts who were telling us that our offering was too comprehensive for a company our size. They also had some positive things to say. We walked out fixated on the positive and conveniently ignoring the negative. We had worked so hard and were already so invested in our idea that we just couldn't bear to hear that it was off base. Even though it's human nature to want to be right, I should have known better. Time proved them right, and we adjusted, though at a cost.

Instead, these meetings need to be "Tell us everything that's wrong with this" conversations. The earlier you go to the experts with your draft material, the less invested you'll be and the more willing you'll be to hear constructive criticism. Be open to it. Seek it out. It will save you time, money, and risk in the long run and give you a better solution that the market will actually help you craft.

STEP 3

Define What You Want to Uniquely Mean in the Marketplace, What Value You Will Provide to Customers, and How That Will Spell Success for Your Company

"Positioning is the act of designing the company's offering and image so that they occupy a meaningful and distinct competitive position in the target customers' minds."
—Philip Kotler, *Marketing Management*

"The goal of positioning...is to create a space inside of the target customer's head called 'best buy for this type of situation' and to attain sole, undisputed occupancy of that space."
—Geoffrey Moore, *Crossing the Chasm*

POSITIONING STATEMENT

Clearly, Kennedy's goal was to position the US as the Go-To for space exploration. The work you did above in defining your target market, business problem you'll own, and solution possibly resulted in lots of words, and now your task is to boil it all down into a positioning statement that captures what you want to be uniquely known for. This is a one- or two-sentence summary of what business you are in, who you serve, and what differentiates you. It serves as a compass for guiding the company's vision, strategy, and operating activity—it is the company's theme. It should also inspire the listener to want to know more. It states what you do and implies what you don't do. A positioning statement is not supposed to say everything you do or always stand alone, though it can if it needs to. It may not even be used externally as is. It's meant to be a strategic guidepost. The positioning statement may also be aspirational. It may state what you intend to become, even if you're not there yet.

My favorite format for a positioning statement is an adaptation of one widely used in Silicon Valley. You would mostly use this for internal purposes and then tweak later for external use. The format is this, and obviously you can wordsmith as appropriate for the situation, as shown in the examples:

> For _____(target market), we are the Go-To for _____ (customer problem/result) in order to achieve _____ (benefit). Unlike _____ (competitive alternatives), we use _____ (unique method/solution) to achieve _____ (tangible, quantifiable outcomes).

For example, Salesforce's first positioning statement would have sounded something like this. At the time, most salespeople in these companies used their own phones and contact systems to maintain prospecting data, and companies relied on spreadsheets for forecasts:

> For small and midsize B2B companies who do direct selling, we are the Go-To for salesforce automation in order to sell more, predict revenue more accurately, and keep treasured prospecting data in-house when salespeople leave the company. Unlike installed software, such as Siebel, which costs months and millions to implement and maintain, we use software-as-a-service in the Cloud to have customers up and running in just hours for a mere $75 per month per user.

Using this format, the positioning statement for Recreational Equipment, Inc. (REI) would sound something like this:

For upscale outdoor enthusiasts across the US, we are the Go-To for a well-lived life outdoors in order to fully experience the transformational power of nature. Unlike for-profit outdoor gear and clothing retailers, we are a member-owned cooperative that also provides complete support—expert advice, rental gear, education, inspirational stories, travel experiences, and environmental stewardship—to help customers achieve the unbridled joy of safely being outdoors while also supporting a healthy planet.

Once you have your positioning statement, test it for differentiation and dominance potential:

- ☑ Can anyone else make the same claim? Can you own it? Does it clearly set you apart, make you unique in the market? Is anyone else out there already saying the same thing?
- ☑ Does it speak to a common and urgent, critical need/problem/challenge for a specific group of targets? Does it apply to a definable market segment? Does it provide a springboard for a unique point of view?
- ☑ Is it hard to achieve (and therefore duplicate/imitate)? Is it defensible?
- ☑ Does it require/imply what marketing professor Phillip Kotler calls a "strategic architecture"—rely on multiple dimensions of marketing strategy, thereby making it more difficult to imitate?
- ☑ Does it speak to the types of industry/company/buyer/situation you want?

☑ Is it highly valuable to your target? Is the market ready? Will results be more important to them than price (justify high margins)? Will you be able to make performance-based deals in some cases?

☑ Can you sum up the positioning in one or two words? Can you sum up the target in one or two words?

☑ Will your organization be capable of delivering on the promise?

☑ Will your people relate to it? Be willing to live it?

☑ Will it make the buyers who hire you look good and be successful in their companies and their markets?

☑ Can organizations further down the hierarchy in your company apply a more specific version of the positioning in their own markets?

☑ Is it obvious, simple, and clear? Is it credible in the marketplace?

BUSINESS VISION

Marc Benioff has described his vision back in 1999 as being bigger than salesforce automation, saying, "I saw an opportunity to deliver business software applications in a new way. My vision was to make software easier to purchase, simpler to use, and more democratic without the complexities of installation, maintenance, and constant upgrades." This was a radical idea that would take time for companies to embrace.

When Google bought four-year-old Nest in 2014 for $3.2 billion, it wasn't just for Nest's smart thermostat product. It was for the bigger vision: "To reinvent unloved but important devices in the home…"

The Alzheimer's Association states that its vision is "a world without Alzheimer's disease." It's an ambitious outcome with no clear end date at this time, but that hasn't stopped the organization from declaring it and publishing a ten-year vision on its website that aims for major strides toward the ultimate goal. Its stated mission is "to eliminate Alzheimer's disease through the advancement of research; to provide and enhance care and support for all affected; and to reduce the risk of dementia through the promotion of brain health."

Jeff Bezos's vision from the start was to provide "an everything store" and that books would be just the first step.

Stanford University has published its vision for being "a purposeful university" focused on "knowledge, learning and innovation for a rapidly changing world" at ourvision.stanford.edu following a year-long effort involving multiple, campus-wide design teams.

Your positioning statement is now a nice capsule of what you want to mean in the marketplace. Put some meat on those bones now by developing your business vision. This is a document (often done in presentation format) that literally states what the company is going to look like in five or ten years—what your end game is. It should talk about the target market, the business problem and solution, and what you mean to the industry by the end of this period. It should specify the business model, high-level revenue and margin goals, and the organizational model. You should have a section titled, "We'll know we're successful when…," which lists some goals such as external recognition of your leadership position and market share goals. It's also powerful to include a list of fantasy headlines, which often help a company's employees visualize what you're shooting for.

It's surprising as to how many organizations pass on creating a written vision like this. Some use an "investor pitch deck" or annual plan as a proxy, which are usually more akin to business plans than a vision. The value of having a vision document like this is to get your entire team on board and able to literally envision the destination you're all aiming for.

It's imperative that you write it down, agree on it, and get everyone on board. It's one of the most powerful tools you can have for moving your team forward. You'll find a template at apollomethod.com.

BUSINESS STRATEGY AND OTHER PLANS

Next, draft your business strategy and other plans. (You can use this book as a framework for those.) The vision is what you're going to accomplish, and the strategy specifies how you're going to accomplish it. This should include information about your targets; your approach to business development and selling; market and image development plans; how you will develop and deliver your solution; how you will hire, develop, and retain people; investment requirements; etc. You'll also want to specify how you'll execute all of this by developing annual operating plans, marketing plans, sales plans, etc. You can use the other components of the Apollo Method discussed in the next three chapters as a framework for any or all of these.

Both the Alzheimer's Association and Stanford have published high-level versions of these on their websites with much underlying detail developed behind the scenes. You can find links to these in the chapter end notes, plus templates and links to additional examples at apollomethod.com.

MESSAGE PLATFORM

In order to communicate internally or externally, you need a core message platform. This boils your story down to just a few sentences in order to brief someone. The more unfamiliar someone is with you, the less capacity they will have to retain information about you. That's why it is crucial that you be able to succinctly communicate what you are all about.

It's well documented that the ideal number of items that people can retain and focus on is three. You always want your messages to come in sets of three. Have three core, high-level messages. If/when a listener is interested in diving into more detail, have three messages under each of those, then three, and so on. It's like peeling an onion. If someone only wants the highlights, you have your story in three sentences. If they want more, you can work through the layers to their content.

A problem with the way many companies do their messaging is that they either start with the solution (to which the audience often asks themselves, "Why would I need that?"); or they start with the problem and then immediately dive into their solution without properly priming the audience for why that particular approach is superior to other options. It's like jumping right to the punchline for a joke that requires a build-up.

Of the various story frameworks out there, I find the Why/What/ How Storyline to be the most effective way to simplify a complex company or product message and reel an audience in.

A way to get around this is to talk about the problem and then merely offer a point of view for what should be done about it (the Point of View from Step 2 earlier in this chapter). This primes them for your solution without the mental barriers that naturally arise when you start to pitch or sell something. By the time you discuss your unique approach to eliminating the problem, they have heard and likely bought into the rationale behind it.

This story flow is called the Why/What/How Storyline. I initially developed it for my own use and then found it valuable for clients as well. Of the various story frameworks out there, I find it to be the most effective way to simplify complex company and product storylines and reel an audience in. It tells even a complex story in just three sentences:

- Core Message 1 answers *Why* customers in the market have a problem.

- Core Message 2 answers *What* they should do about it.
- Core Message 3 answers *How* you've solved the problem and the result you deliver.

Kennedy basically pitched the "Moon Shot" goal in this fashion. Paraphrasing the portion of his famous speech quoted earlier in the chapter, he said:

- **Why:** Outer space should be a place of peace and freedom that benefits all mankind, and yet recent accomplishments of the communist Soviets, who wish to stifle freedom around the world, have positioned them to "own" outer space.
- **What:** As a world power, the United States needs to step up and do what it takes to win the space race in order to protect freedom and humanity from tyranny in space as well as on Earth.
- **How:** To that end, we are going to safely take a man to the Moon and bring him home, which will clearly establish US dominance in space on behalf of the free world.

When first introduced, smart thermostats were a classic example of people asking, "Why would I need that?" The Why/What/How structure answers the question right up front in the sequence in which objections enter the audience's minds. Using this framework, the pitch for Nest's smart thermostat, for example, sounds something like this:

- **Why:** Even with programmable thermostats, each household wastes hundreds of dollars per year and adversely affects the environment by overheating or overcooling rooms, particularly when occupants aren't home.
- **What:** What people need is a thermostat that will "learn" their behavior, optimize room temperature accordingly,

and let them manage the home remotely when they are
gone (e.g., tell it to warm the house up for their return or be
alerted if the furnace is acting up).

- **How:** We've created Nest, a smart thermostat that reduces
  energy bills by 10–15 percent, programs itself based on
  how you live, and allows you to manage your home from
  anywhere using a phone-based app.

Once you have your basic three-sentence storyline, you can add
color commentary as appropriate for the situation. For example, in
a sales situation, you may want to preempt objections during the
What. Nest may say:

Now, you might be thinking, "My thermostat automatically
lowers the temperature when I'm at work." Yes, but what if
there was a way to know the most cost-effective time to warm
the house up before you get home based on the weather that
day and have it happen automatically?

Conversely, you may need to boil your three sentences down to just
one. In the case of Apollo, Kennedy may have said, "[why] To keep
the communist Soviets from 'owning' space, [what] the US needs
to dominate on behalf of the free world [how] by putting a man on
the Moon."

There will be many instances in which it is more appropriate to
speak to audiences in a thought leadership capacity, meaning they
don't want to hear about what you are selling. Or you may be in a situation when they think they don't want to hear what you're selling.
The beauty of this framework is that you can deliver just Message
1 (why they have a problem), which will lead them to want to hear
Message 2 (what they should do about it). In some cases, you'll stop
there. But in many cases, they become naturally curious and ask you

for Message 3 (how you've solved the problem). If you articulate these properly, the discussion very often naturally leads into peeling the onion, and you get your opportunity to elaborate.

In complex organizations or hierarchies (e.g., multiple product lines within a business unit), there would be a top-line story per the above, and then each sub-entity would have its own flavor of the story adapted to their situation but still in line with the top-line story.

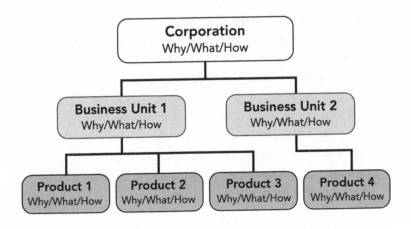

You can find more detail on the rationale for this message framework, how to apply it, and additional examples at apollomethod.com.

BRAND STYLE

When we talk about "brand style," many may think of the elements that make up a brand's identity, such as a logo, color palette, and general look and feel, but it goes beyond that. You need to define your brand's overall, distinctive personality and desired image—how your company will package itself. It's the flair (or lack thereof) that you bring to what you do. There is usually a heavy emphasis on the visual aspects, but there are many nonvisual aspects as well, like the voice, tone, values, and behaviors that define your brand.

Even the Apollo Space Program had a very purposeful brand style. Realizing that it would have to win and keep the public's hearts and minds over an extended period, NASA created a visual identity that included an official Apollo insignia (logo), along with a unique official patch (logo) for each Apollo mission. It decided the overall brand style, particularly its tone, would be open, honest, nonpartisan, and fact based, as opposed to the propaganda-oriented spin used during World War II or the stealth approach used by the Soviets.

Left: Apollo Space Program official insignia *(Image: NASA) Right:* A sampling of Apollo Space Program mission patches *(Images: NASA)*

Apple technology offerings are all about simple elegance, and therefore so is the brand style. This extends not just to the minimalist visual elements of its brand and products but also to the verbal and written elements. A brand style must be completely authentic and must complement the unique value you are seeking to deliver to customers. You aren't going to fool anyone. It won't work to package your company as hip and edgy if, in reality, it's fairly conservative. The market will see right through that and dismiss you as a fraud. Define a style that fits the company and culture. Or build a company and culture that fits the brand you've defined. Either way, make sure they are in sync.

FedEx is the Go-To for overnight delivery. Its brand style conveys the kind of "energized efficiency" that sets the company apart. Its ingenious, colorful logo (Can you spot the hidden arrow?) and uniforms support this, along with the strategic use of white space on its trucks, envelopes, and so forth. Unnecessary bells and whistles would be inconsistent with its desired image.

Can you spot the symbolic arrow hiding in plain site within the FedEx logo? *(FedEx service mark used by permission.)*

REI's brand style, including store design, supports its Go-To status as a total solution for a lifetime of outdoor living. Customers walk through tall timber structures that seem to symbolize trees in a forest and enter an interior that its architecture firm, MG2, says, "...speaks to a comfortable relationship between its customers and nature..."

Tree-like timber structures and other elements of REI store designs are part of a brand style that supports its Go-To positioning around outdoor living.

As part of its overall playful, rule-breaking image, Google has a colorful logo designed to work on screens of all sizes and sometimes replaces it online with homepage doodles that celebrate special occasions.

Google's colorful logo supports its playful, rule-breaking brand image.

Some companies have a strong brand with little or no distinctive style, but they are missing an opportunity. A distinctive style will really make your Go-To brand sing and differentiates it that much more. Apple has both substance and style, and look at what a difference it makes in terms of brand equity and emotional connection to its avid fans.

OFFERING DEFINITION

Before jumping to action on making Kennedy's dream a reality, NASA had to figure out what the broad approach would be and what it would take. As with any "design" initiative, they began with a simple diagram and some general strategies.

This is the lunar orbit rendezvous concept for getting humans to the Moon and back, as presented by NASA's John C. Houbolt. It is an example of how even the most complex undertakings can begin with a simple conceptual diagram. *(Image: NASA)*

It's time to define your offering. Beyond possibly a prototype, you are usually not developing anything yet. This is a conceptual design with a bit more detail on what the offering consists of and, in broad strokes, what it will take to make it a reality. By thinking it through first, you are likely to find some of the fundamental structural flaws in your thinking before spending money on development. For example, you may realize that you don't have to build as much of it yourself as you originally thought. It's useful to think of some typical customer scenarios and what's involved in realizing the full benefits.

- **Broad concept:** One phrase or sentence that captures the offering
- **Primary initial use cases:** The initial, common customer scenarios for using this offering

- **Unique selling proposition (USP):** Game-changing factors that will set this apart and aspects that make it a complete solution that provides, ideally, a killer outcome
- **Value-pricing business case:** How the value will be framed for customers so that customers focus their cost-benefit analysis on results rather than your effort/cost to produce
- **Revenue/pricing model:** How the pricing will work (not what that actual price will be at this point but the general approach, such as a subscription model, one-time purchase, etc.)
- **Existing alternatives to eclipse:** What's currently in the market that you are going to leapfrog—keeps you focused on quantum rather than incremental improvement
- **Initial customer partners:** Handful of customers who will play a role in shaping the offering as it is developed (sometimes they also help fund the development)
- **Conceptual diagram:** A simple drawing or infographic illustrating the offering and how it will work
- **Offering execution matrix:** A list of the major components of the offering (e.g., software, physical components, services, etc.) and for each:
  - Whether to buy or build
  - Whether to create in-house or partner
  - Whether the component will have to be customized to an individual customer
  - Whether the component will become proprietary intellectual property
- **Infrastructure:** What will need to be in place in order to develop and support the offering (e.g., facilities, technology, skills, recruiting, legal, accounting, etc.)

- **High-level investment required:** A rough idea (grounded in an analysis) as to how much money it will take
- **Partners:** Outside entities that will play a role (e.g., manufacturer, data center, customer support outsourcer)
- **Channels:** How you will distribute the offering

The architects of the Apollo program did all of this, only adapted for a noncommercial environment, of course. The program had to consistently eclipse the Soviet efforts that were still underway; it had to demonstrate superior value to justify its enormous "price"— benefits like economic growth and improved weather forecasting, medical equipment (e.g., CAT scanners, kidney dialysis), consumer products (e.g., modern athletic shoes, freeze-dried food), electric power grid control systems, advances in computing, military competence, and more. The architects had to figure out which pieces of the effort had to be built versus bought from industry. They evaluated what the overall investment would be for the life of the program. They identified university partnerships across the US in a coordinated effort to encourage academic projects and the growth of research centers that would produce skilled engineers and PhDs. In terms of infrastructure, they also articulated a vision for developing technology capabilities and facilities in the US southwest, which eventually led to Houston as a base.

In **Navigate**, you'll go into quite a bit of detail as you prepare to make the offering a reality. However, at this stage, once you've worked out all of the above, it's useful to boil everything down to a one-page blueprint that captures the concept and what's going to be involved in pulling it together and delivering it to customers. Taking inspiration from Alex Osterwalder's Business Model Canvas, here is the Apollo Method format you can consider. Remember that you're building off the Why/What/How Storyline you developed earlier.

For additional guidance, there are Customer Development, Lean Startup, and other methodologies that provide more detail on how to create your offering concept efficiently, without overengineering it and with input from the market. You will find links to these on apollomethod.com.

APOLLO METHOD OFFERING BLUEPRINT					
OFFERING CONCEPT	**PRIMARY INITIAL USE CASES**	**UNIQUE SELLING PROPOSITION** (including game changers and what makes this a complete solution)	**VALUE-PRICING BUSINESS CASE** (to customers)	**REVENUE/ PRICING MODEL**	
EXISTING ALTERNATIVE(S) TO ECLIPSE					
INITIAL CUSTOMER PARTNERS					
CONCEPTUAL DIAGRAM	**OFFERING EXECUTION MATRIX** List of major components on left, with checks in columns for: • Buy vs. Build • Create in-house vs. partner • Repeatable vs. customized • Whether it results in proprietary IP				
	Components	Buy	Build	In-Hse	Ptr	Custom	IP
INFRASTRUCTURE	**HI-LEVEL INVESTMENT REQUIRED**	**PARTNERS**		**CHANNELS**	

It's very useful to lay out your offering concept in blueprint fashion so you can evaluate its market appeal and what it will take to bring it to market. This also allows you to quickly test it with other people. You can use the Apollo Method Offering Blueprint as a framework or a format of your choice.

The following example imagines what such a blueprint for Airbnb could have looked like in 2008. (A more legible image to fully digest and use as a model is available at apollomethod.com.)

APOLLO METHOD OFFERING BLUEPRINT

Hypothetical Case Example: Airbnb

OFFERING CONCEPT	PRIMARY INITIAL USE CASES	USP	VALUE-PRICING BUSINESS CASE	REVENUE/ PRICING MODEL
Web-based service matching travelers & local hosts/owners	• Traveler wants a local experience or feel "at home"	• Traveler: More than a bed – live like local, feel like houseguest	Instead of just "rental by owner," get a complete, unique, local experience from hosts we curate	Take a % of rental fee from both guest and host
ALTERNATIVE(S) TO ECLIPSE VRBO & Homeaway, Hotels	• Host wants extra income	• Host: Best practices, insurance, privacy		
INITIAL CUSTOMER PARTNERS Founders and friends of founders				

CONCEPTUAL DIAGRAM	OFFERING EXECUTION MATRIX						

Components	Buy	Build	In-Hse	Ptr	Custom	IP
Website		✓	✓			✓
Online property platform and mapping		✓	✓	Vendor		✓
Content management system	✓		✓	Product		
Registration, payments, account database	✓		✓	Product		
Host training and resources, e.g., checklists		✓	✓		Some at first	✓
(and so on)						

INFRASTRUCTURE	HI-LEVEL INVESTMENT REQUIRED	PARTNERS	CHANNELS
• Development team and technology • Host recruiters and trainers • Host insurance • Professional photography for host listings	$XX,000 seed funding for proof of concept	• Web development vendor • Third-party products for site • Insurance provider • Photographer network	• Craigslist integration • Huge conventions with hotel shortages • Meetups and events

Here is a hypothetical offering blueprint for Airbnb as a startup in 2008. The details are unimportant in this example and are for illustration purposes only. You can find a larger, more legible image at apollomethod.com.

STEP 4

Launch This Into the Market

CORE, STARTER-TOOLKIT MARKETING ASSETS

Kennedy's speech to announce the "Moon Shot" goal was a carefully orchestrated publicity effort by the president and media-savvy NASA. Knowing the event would stoke a frenzy of curiosity and follow-up questions by everyone ranging from the public to Congress to other national leaders, NASA public affairs had to have information in place and be ready with press kits, briefing papers, spokespeople, and so on.

Even if your public launch won't make quite a splash, you need to develop a few communications tools in advance. All messaging follows the Why/What/How Storyline above. These are, at minimum:

1. **Brand style:** Brand Definition, Identity, and Standards
2. **Infographic:** Anchor diagram that serves as a visual overview of your solution
3. **"Stump speech":** An overview presentation that can be shortened or lengthened depending on the situation and audience; for startups, this may double as the front end of the pitch deck; design two version of the slides:
   a. A presentation version: Highly visual with few words, suitable for live audience
   b. A stand-alone version: Enough information for someone to get the gist from flipping through it
4. **White paper or visually interesting e-book:** A manifesto that provides more color commentary; cites research and case examples when applicable; and lends credibility (usually five to ten pages)
5. **A brief article:** Suitable for a blog, trade publication, and social media; a 700- to 1,500-word capsule of the stump speech and manifesto
6. **Website:** The home page (or landing page if in a larger organization) should clearly and immediately convey the why/what/how; the site should feature the offering concept, its infographic, and links to the manifesto and article, in addition to typical website content; many sites use video overviews to great effect

All six assets say the same thing in different formats and at different levels of detail for different forums. All should follow the structure of your core message platform and elaborate as appropriate. You want audiences to regard them as groundbreaking. And importantly, they should be provocative and controversial. You want them to stir people up.

Use and test these deliverables internally and with friendly outside stakeholders.

If you do a high-profile event that will attract significant attention, you may also want a press release, media training, a spokesperson with prepared talking points, and so forth. Think ahead to what your audience will crave under the circumstances and be ready.

Use and test these deliverables internally and with friendly outside stakeholders. In addition to getting important feedback on how well they are communicating the message, this process becomes a way to gain internal buy-in and get everyone in the organization singing from the same songbook. This will also help you refine what you've got so far.

Once slightly refined, test these materials with friendly influencers, customers, and prospects externally who can give you feedback and help you tweak them.

If you are part of a larger or existing organization, you may need a few other tools, such as a cheat sheet that specifies the top-line messages, elevator statement, etc. that make it easy for nonexperts to deliver the message; training sessions to educate others on the vision, point of view, solution concept and strategy; and so on.

STAKE IN THE GROUND

Now you're ready for prime time. Put a stake in the ground by announcing your point of view. This, of course, is what Kennedy accomplished with his speech. Regard this as your big debut—your opportunity to publicly declare ownership of the market problem and introduce your solution. Depending on the circumstances, you can either do this as a big splash or as a "soft launch."

You don't necessarily need product at this point—right now, you are claiming ownership of the point of view and approach.

If the market is fairly well developed and you believe your offering is stable, meaning that you are confident you have it figured out and that the fundamental nature of it won't change much over the near term, you may want to make a big, public splash. This might include a news release and significant proactive media and blogger outreach, email campaigns, a high-profile announcement at an industry tradeshow or customer event, etc. The goal in this case is to garner as much attention as possible in the shortest amount of time possible with continued payoff.

Salesforce did this to beautiful effect when it launched the company and its "end of software" campaign in February 2000. It started with an announcement at a major event called DEMO, a leading technology conference for debuting new offerings. A couple of weeks later, it staged a playful mock protest at the main user conference of the industry goliath at the time, Siebel Systems. Two dozen "protesters" it had hired marched with anti-software signs and chanted anti-software slogans like, "Red rover, red rover, software is over." Attracting plenty of attention, they handed out invitations to a party that evening—a coming-out ball for Salesforce with an "End of Software" theme, military style, to represent its "battle against the established software industry." Benioff wore army fatigues. To gain admittance, one had to bring old software to put on a trash heap. There were "Software-Free" zones, a "Prisoners of Software" section, and games like, "Throw the Disk in the Toilet." The provocative message and creative execution of the theme attracted nearly thirty media outlets such as *The Wall Street Journal*, USA *Today*, *Vanity Fair*, and *Fortune*, an impressive turnout for a completely unknown company made possible by a clear theme and differentiating thought leadership delivered in a fun and fresh way. Needless to say, the company generated enormous buzz, garnering over one hundred media mentions and a "Top Company to Watch" award at the DEMO event. With a working offering at that point, it signed on more than 1,000 customers within two weeks.

Now, before you go out and throw an expensive, high-profile party, be mindful of your audience and the times. Lavish shindigs became so commonplace during that era that they lost their usefulness. After a time, freeloaders in attendance couldn't tell you whose party they were at. It worked well for Salesforce, because in Marc Benioff's words, "Although we wanted our guests to enjoy the party...the event also carried a much larger mission. Unlike other dot-com parties, which functioned to introduce a company and its products, we needed to introduce an entirely new market (on-demand, or SaaS, or cloud computing) and promote a new way of doing business."

When planning your own launch, carefully consider existing market noise, your target audience, your objectives, and of course, your budget. There are many ways to accomplish the goal, and the launch is just the first mile of a marathon that gets continued during the **Ignite** phase.

If you are in a still-evolving, emerging market or if time is of the essence, even when you don't have all the kinks worked out, you may want to do a soft launch. This allows you to evolve your message and content once you're out there and as feedback continues to come in. Entre Nous Aesthetics, the medical spa based in Silicon Valley, was still completing the build-out of its new facility and refinement of its point of view and unique approach when it opened its doors. The business was a spin-off from plastic surgeon Dr. Jane Weston's medical practice, and so it was fortunate enough to have clients from day one. Those clients were very loyal and enjoyed being in on the new venture even as Entre Nous put the finishing touches on its office space. Entre Nous focused its initial **Launch** activities on current clients, making them aware of the point of view and new offerings. In this way, it was able to gauge the reactions of established clients and get invaluable feedback. With this input and experience under its belt, the company then conducted a public launch with new targets.

Soft launches like this are very common in emerging technology fields, when the market as a whole is still trying to figure out what label to put on a collection of companies, regardless of how different they are from one another. In Silicon Valley, it's very common for a company to "pivot" by redefining its category, positioning, business model, and even its product or service long after it has launched. This can create some confusion, but in emerging markets, the "fail fast, learn fast, adapt" mantra has high value in terms of funding, partnerships, and so on. PayPal's original concept was cryptography for handheld devices. It went through several more iterations before becoming a person-to-person money transfer system.

Regardless of which approach you take, your aim is to put a stake in the ground so that down the line, when me-toos come along and try to claim they are the first in this area, you will be able to point back to a specific point in time. This is especially important if you have intellectual property such as copyrighted material and trade names that you want to protect. Beyond that, this action mainly gives you bragging rights of being the first when the market starts to fill up and you are working to defend your Go-To status and reputation as a thought leader and innovator.

At the same time, you should launch your website, of course, which also highlights your point of view and solution.

STEP 5

Establish the Minimal Infrastructure You Will Need to Support the Business

Immediately after Kennedy's decision to go to the Moon, NASA had to get ready for the thousands of people it would be hiring. Facilities and the political decision of where to locate them was one of the many first priorities. NASA administrator James Webb also made the decision to avoid bureaucratic slowdowns by using 80–90 percent of the budget on third parties, with NASA oversight and management, a policy put in place early on and continued even today. Within just a few months of Kennedy's announcement, he also established the ambitious and innovative Sustaining University Program (SUP) to increase the national "output" and diversity of outstanding science and engineering talent, since NASA was going to have an insatiable appetite for new recruits. This included beefing up science and technology programs at more than just the handful of elite schools at the time and funding substantial research grants and facilities expansion.

You have announced yourself to the market and are just getting warmed up. Now is the time to get business basics in place. For a startup, this means establishing administrative processes, workspace, business functions like HR and finance, etc. But keep it to a minimum until you have a stable revenue stream.

Marc Benioff began by recruiting and hiring three people with technology and customer relationship management (CRM) software backgrounds to develop the prototype. He rented a one-bedroom apartment in San Francisco next door to his home and furnished it with card tables and folding chairs, a bean bag, lamps, and computers. Using his summer-job experience at Apple as inspiration, he put an immediate focus on culture by hanging a picture of the Dalai Lama over the fireplace and a picture of Albert Einstein on the wall as symbols of the company's guiding principles.

For an established organization, this may mean infrastructure related to developing and selling your offering, such as a team (whether on payroll, retainer, or contract), product development and manufacturing capabilities, etc. When Paradigm Consulting (a pseudonym) decided to start an Internet of Things business unit, it initially assigned a mere handful of people—a leader, a couple of business development executives, and a business analyst. They put a few tools in place for managing research and market development activity and otherwise leveraged the rest of the organization for other infrastructure and support.

We'll cover sales, marketing, and delivery in the **Ignite** and **Navigate** phases, but some of that hiring may need to occur here. You'll know the proper timing once you lay out your implementation plan across all four phases. (This is covered later as well.)

Now is the time to put your infrastructure fundamentals in place so that you are ready and supported when you rev up sales efforts and business starts coming in. You want people up the learning curve and the kinks worked out of your processes by game time. Just be sure not to overinvest. You want to layer in infrastructure on a just-in-time basis as you build a stable revenue stream with healthy margins that support ongoing investment.

RECAP AND ACTION ITEM

The primary objective of the **Launch** phase is to figure out and declare what you want to be the Go-To for—the one "thing" you want to mean and in what marketplace, captured in just a few words. You must determine the problem you intend to own in a particular market, formulate a unique solution to that problem, and then publicly declare intellectual and execution ownership for that problem. You also need to develop a concise point of view on that problem that you can boil down to just three sentences as a start:

- *Why* there's a problem
- *What* needs to be done about it
- *How* you've uniquely solved the problem

Once you've identified your Go-To positioning, identify the baseline items you'll need in order to declare ownership and get your operation started. Then put your stake in the ground and get ready to go *ignite* the market around your point of view and approach!

ACTION ITEM

You can access an online tool or download the worksheet for this exercise at apollomethod.com. You and your team will get optimal results by first completing the steps outlined in the chapter. However, even based on where you are today, you can take a first stab at completing this summary worksheet. Once done, you'll know what you want to mean and how you'll *launch* yourself into the market. Next, we'll find out what it takes to ignite a movement.

Launch

ARTICULATE A VISION

Planning Worksheet

What is the profile of your overall target market?

_____

Fill in your Target Market Dartboard.

Core target market:

Next best fit/opportunity:

Third best fit/opportunity:

What is your market vision and the common, critical, urgent problem you'll own? _____

_____

What is your point of view about this problem?

_____

_____

What is your unique solution to this problem? What evidence will prove it works? _____

_____

What must you do to validate your solution in the market?

_____

_____

What is your unique positioning statement?
"For _____, we are the Go-To for
_____ in order to achieve
_____ (benefit). Unlike
_____, we use _____
to achieve _____ (quantifiable outcomes)."

What is your business vision? _____
_____

What is your message platform? (three sentences)

1. **Why** they have a problem

_____

_____

2. **What** they must do about it

_____

_____

3. **How** you've solved the problem

_____

_____

Define your brand style _____

Sketch the anchor diagram for your solution.

When and how will you put your stake in the ground to declare your intent to "own" this problem?

_____

_____

What baseline tangibles will you need in order to declare ownership? (e.g., Website, seminal article, etc.)

_____   _____

_____   _____

What minimal infrastructure will you need?

_____   _____

_____   _____

CHAPTER 6

IGNITE PHASE

Lead a Movement in the Market Around the Problem and Solution

I once had the pleasure of seeing Al Gore give his climate change presentation live. Like most of the general public at that time, I knew little about the topic but was curious about what he had to say.

As most people know by now, it was a stunningly effective presentation. By the time he was finished, I was in tears. He did more than just share impressive statistics. He was passionate, and I could feel the emotion coming off him from a couple of hundred feet away. There were about 20,000 people in the audience, and he converted just about each one of us into a believer. Judging from some of my conversations afterward, quite a few people were on their way to becoming evangelists to help spread the message on his behalf.

Al Gore had come a long way since his defeat in the controversial presidential election in 2000, after which he had gone back to

Nashville to recuperate and ponder his future. His wife, Tipper, convinced him to pick up the cause he cared most about and had devoted much of his political career to: climate change. He went down to his basement and pulled out an old stack of slides that had been gathering dust for years. It was a presentation he had been giving since he was a junior congressman in the late '70s. You're probably aware of where the story went from there...an Oscar-winning movie and a Nobel Peace Prize. But just to give you a sense of his humble beginnings as a climate change evangelist, the first time he used the slides, he literally put them into a physical slide carousel, some upside down and backward! (That might have continued for a while had Tipper not insisted he graduate to a computer.)

From there, Al Gore gave that presentation over 2,000 times. Starting out, he would give it to anyone who would listen. He focused his proactive efforts on small, handpicked audiences in order to get some momentum going. But if there were ten people gathered in someone's living room who wanted to hear it, he would show up. There was ridicule at first. How could the former vice president of the United States and the guy who won the popular vote for the presidency have sunk so low as to have become a door-to-door salesman for global warming? Even worse, how could he be peddling what some then considered to be a ridiculous message? This wasn't on people's radar at the time. What was the big deal? These were 9/11 times. Weren't there more important things to be talking about for a guy of his stature? But he persisted.

Slowly but surely, word began to spread. The audiences became larger. And after about 1,000 deliveries, he hit the tipping point. Laurie David, then-wife of *Seinfeld* co-creator Larry David, was sitting in one of those audiences and was so moved that she wanted to create a platform for reaching not thousands of Americans but multiple millions of people worldwide. She wanted to make the movie. And she did. *An Inconvenient Truth* became a blockbuster. Everything from there is history.

Al Gore put this topic on the map and transformed the world's perspective on it. He did it by focusing on what he believed to be a common, critical, urgent problem that could be summed up in two words: "climate change." He created a controversial, provocative point of view that got people's attention. He had a simple, top-line message that could be expanded upon infinitely and was backed by as much detail as anyone wanted to hear. And he tirelessly promoted the message, starting with influential people who could evangelize on his behalf once they became believers.

This is what the **Ignite** phase is all about. The fundamental strategy in this phase is to lead a movement in the marketplace around your point of view and approach, beginning with highly influential powerbrokers who can help evangelize on your behalf. Over time, you build momentum, which amplifies the sales and marketing activities of the **Navigate** and **Accelerate** phases.

GOING VIRAL

If focusing on a particular market problem and identifying the unique solution you'll offer are the most important strategic elements of the Apollo Method, the **Ignite** phase is possibly the most important execution element. It's also the one that is most commonly attempted by companies. And the one that is most poorly implemented.

Before we examine why that is, let's look at what you're trying to accomplish here.

Think about it. You've defined what you want to mean in the marketplace, and that meaning is built around a problem that really matters to companies or consumers in your market. You've developed a vision and provocative point of view on a common, critical, and urgent market problem. You've defined a solution. Now it's time to provide market leadership. Your goal during the **Ignite** phase is to establish yourself as the preeminent thought leader on your topic, convert others to your point of view, and inspire them to want to take action. You want to start an epidemic. You want to lead a movement. You want to get everyone on board. Most of all, you want to get other people evangelizing on your behalf. You want to literally *ignite* the market around your point of view.

Over time, a shift will occur—you will be the key influencer and powerbroker, and you will be the one others are clamoring to meet.

In the beginning, you want to *lead* this conversation and be at the center of it. Eventually, it will take on a life of its own. If all has gone well, the "masses" in your market will be talking about it with or without you; however, your name will come up often, and conversations among the key powerbrokers will involve or be about you. In the beginning, you may well have to work hard to meet key influencers. Over time, a shift will occur—*you* will be the key influencer and powerbroker, and *you* will be the one others are clamoring to meet. You will be sought out.

When Marc Benioff first started talking about software-as-a-service (SaaS) for companies, it wasn't a brand-new concept. In the 1960s, it was called time sharing (sharing large, expensive computing power located off-site). In the 1970s through the 1990s, terms like "service bureau," "outsourcing provider," and "application service provider" included companies that managed another company's data and software off-site. But the suggestion to kill on-site, installed software altogether was radical at a time when companies like Oracle, Siebel, Microsoft, IBM, SAP, and Accenture were making a fortune selling and/or installing complex systems for clients' in-house use; so venture capital (VC) companies wouldn't invest in Salesforce at first. Early investor Magdalena Yesil was helping Benioff raise money and not only got turned down by partners at her own VC firm but at all other firms she approached. They told her, "The idea of having [companies] give you their customer data, their sales data, outside their firewall…that's crazy. Change your model." But Salesforce held steadfast to its "religion." Benioff began as the lone pied piper, touting the end of traditional, installed software and what a boon that would be for companies. That was 1999. He persisted, and soon other voices joined in. Initially, SaaS was closely associated with Salesforce, and Benioff in particular. However, over time, it caught on as a movement and became standard operating procedure.

With limited resources and lots of market noise, you are going to want to do this in a highly strategic way. And here is where many companies go wrong.

FIXING THE CONTENT MARKETING MISTAKE

Though not a new technique, many companies now have "content marketing" programs in which they produce useful information, such as "Five Tips for…" articles and so forth, to share with the market via blogs, social media, and so on. The problem with how these programs are executed is that the content and messaging are all over the map instead of centered on a central point of view. Yes, all of the content usually relates to what the company offers. After all, the purpose of content marketing is to create awareness and then move prospects through the buying cycle and/or to further engage customers through informative or entertaining content. But marketers produce a veritable smorgasbord of material—articles, e-books, white papers, social media posts, case studies, infographics, and all kinds of piecemeal chatter. It's as if companies are throwing toilet paper at the market to see what will stick.

Like so many others, one B2B company I won't name produces thousands of these items per year; but if you were to lay them all next to each other, you would understand the general category the company fits into but not what their overarching point of view and approach are. You would not come away with that "one thing." You would come away with about ninety "things." The company has a different meaning to different customers, depending on what part of the company they get exposed to. As a result, this company has very low market awareness, despite significant marketing investments and exceptional products and services.

Blogger David D. Parker articulates this beautifully in terms of his personal social media presence, but the same happens to companies:

> I was reflecting on the story about The Blind Men and the Elephant. As the story goes, each man touches one part of the elephant and describes what he thinks an elephant looks like...Each assumes the entire elephant resembles the one part he was exposed to. The same can happen to our audiences, if we aren't careful to present a cohesive picture.
>
> I started using social media as part of my job search strategy...I jumped into Tweeting and Linking-In and Facebooking with gusto; but since, I've begun to ask myself, "Am I showing people the whole me or just one side of the elephant?" Someone who follows me on Twitter sees the side of me that is interested in corporate social responsibility. Or social enterprise. They also see me tweeting about OpenAgile, which is a way of applying agility to environments beyond software development. And I tweet about the persecution of members of the Baha'i Faith in Iran, which is an injustice that I am very concerned about. Does my social media presence paint an

accurate picture of me? Or do the individual parts create confusion in the market? Most of all, do they build on each other to establish a cohesive personal brand with a central underlying theme? Probably not."

Most companies approach their content marketing efforts the way David has been approaching his social media efforts to the same effect.

By contrast, the Stanford Technology Ventures Program (STVP), for example, takes a very cohesive approach to all of the content it produces. All messaging and material revolve around "entrepreneurial leadership" in the technology arena. It produces a podcast, videos, academic research papers, emails sent to subscribers, talks, and so forth. Regardless of which form a given piece of content may take, it connects back to the central point of view.

WHERE LESS IS MORE

What you'll find in the **Ignite** phase and carry into the **Navigate** and **Accelerate** phases is use of precisely the same tactical activities any company would use but centered on a coherent theme with a very strategic, systematic approach that allows the tactics to build on each other. The most difficult execution challenge is not *what* to do but *what not* to do. There are simply too many options in the marketplace—hundreds, if not thousands, of potential campaigns and initiatives, sponsorships, media outlets, social media tactics, events, and the list goes on. There is no shortage of ideas, just a shortage of budget and execution capacity. A central tenet of the **Ignite** phase is narrowing down your options to what's most important and what will have the most impact.

Your game plan is to focus on the "vital few" people and activities that will yield maximum results and be executed in such an integrated fashion that they all build on each other to gain the most market momentum with the least overall effort/cost. Over time, the market will do the work for you. The end result is a cohesive brand image for market consumption with the added benefit of getting outsiders on board to trumpet your message and bring prospects into the relationship life cycle for you.

Your game plan is to focus on the "vital few" people and activities that will yield maximum results and be executed in such an integrated fashion that they all build on each other to gain the most market momentum with the least overall effort/cost. Over time, the market will do the work for you.

During Apollo, the NASA public affairs organization consisted of just 146 employees in fifteen locations nationally. Relative to the size of the overall program, this was miniscule. Their strategy was to sit at the top of an information dissemination pyramid that then leveraged external resources—primarily news reporters and PR and marketing departments of the corporations involved in Apollo—to get the word out. Knowing that the emotional power of Apollo would be the visuals, the Vital Few would be the three major TV networks at the time and a magazine whose primary emphasis was stunning photojournalism.

Targeting the right people who have influence over a lot of people is the key. I'll discuss sample tactics and tools later in the chapter, but these will come and go with time, as technology evolves and the influence of various channels changes. It used to be that traditional media (e.g., newspapers, magazines, trade publications, radio, TV, etc.) were a key channel for the **Ignite** strategy, but the rise of social media, and digital marketing in general, means these channels now rival traditional media for the **Ignite** phase in many markets. What isn't going to change is the fundamental principal of efficiently leveraging a relatively small number of highly influential channels and individuals in order to establish awareness and credibility with a very large number of prospects.

Done well, this is a very powerful strategy that gives you maximum bang for your buck. You will never have the kind of sales and marketing budgets you'd ideally like. You'll never have capacity to take advantage of all of the brand building and lead generation opportunities that present themselves. How do you decide where to put your limited resources? How do you get your point of view out there? How do you build awareness of and support for your solution? How do you identify, prequalify, and start to build relationships with those "Innovator" and "Early Adopter" prospects? How do you get them to self-select and start seeking you out?

Answer: You're going to start an epidemic.

GUNNING FOR THE TIPPING POINT

Love him or hate him, there is no denying that Donald Trump's campaign did a masterful job of dominating media coverage and the national conversation while running for US president in 2016. He beat a crowded field of seasoned Republicans with establishment support by having a crystal-clear point of view on the state of the country as captured in the "Make America Great Again" slogan (central theme) emblazoned on red hats and stoking fears and a sense of urgency around immigration, the economy, and Hillary Clinton (three of several subthemes). Not afraid to stand out and be derided as a misfit, he relentlessly pounded on his point of view, supported by many surrogates with influence in key markets. This generated tremendous momentum, over $2 billion in free publicity and fervent zeal among supporters, who showed up to rallies by the tens of thousands.

Think of the **Ignite** phase, in part, as a political campaign. You are going to evangelize the heck out of your point of view and get the market fired up about it. You are going to create a sense of urgency. And you're going to enlist the help of key influencers to get visibility for your issue and help you spread the word. In traditional marketing terms, **Ignite** is essentially a combination of market development and image/awareness building but with a very focused method to the madness.

We'll cover the details of how to do this throughout the chapter and assume a worst-case scenario: You are coming in cold. No one knows who you are, what you do, or why they should care. If you have a jump start with market awareness in your domain, all the better.

The best explanation for how and why the **Ignite** phase works can be found in the terrific book *The Tipping Point* by Malcolm Gladwell. If you haven't read it yet, I strongly recommend that you do.

In a nutshell, tipping points are "the levels at which the momentum for change becomes unstoppable." In the book, Gladwell takes a sociological view, defining a tipping point as "the moment of critical mass, the threshold, the boiling point." He explains how viral epidemics like AIDS and SARS start with some kindling and then catch on at some point to spread like wildfire. The point at which the wildfire starts can often be traced to a few key people responsible for a disproportionate volume of infections in other people. His research, backed by numerous examples and case studies, demonstrates that the same happens in the spread of ideas, products, messages, and behaviors.

I had an interesting tipping point experience shortly after arriving in the San Francisco Bay Area (before social media was a thing). I was seeking a regular meetup after work on Fridays, so I decided to start one. I didn't know anyone but had six friends who knew *lots* of people. They agreed to cohost and invited their friends, which led to attendance of about fifty within a few weeks. When a guy named Alf, who held his own ad hoc happy hours, got wind of it and scheduled one of his events to coincide with ours, attendance bumped to around ninety.

Then we hit the tipping point. Someone on the email list sent it to someone named Victor, who made his living as virtual CEO for early-stage startups in Silicon Valley. He was also a "social connector." He had a website list and daily email of social events (a precursor to sites like Meetup and Eventbrite) that went to a massive opt-in list. He promoted it, and on week six of our happy hour, about 250 people showed up.

One of them was Maria, another social connector who spread the word to her huge email list. From there, we made it onto a few more similar lists.

At that point, we went viral, and weekly attendance swelled to over 500. Before long, the event took on a life of its own and became the Go-To gathering spot for the technology and finance communities, which was in full swing by then.

Now take these same principles and apply them in your market: an offering that fills a need; identification of a small set of highly influential people with large networks in your target market who really believe in what you're all about; and initial outreach efforts tightly focused on these people who will help you reach a broader audience.

These dynamics are what make social media so powerful and are a marketer's dream come true, provided you work this channel properly. Contrary to the way most people approach it, the game is a matter of quality at this point, not quantity. You want to get to the key people—the people at the top of the influence pyramid in your target market. If you win them over, you will win hundreds, possibly thousands, of others.

HOW TO START AN EPIDEMIC

Ever get envious of companies that seem so successful in getting everyone to talk about them while you languish in anonymity?

Let's first understand the underlying principles of moving toward and reaching a tipping point. Malcolm Gladwell listed "three rules of epidemics." You are going to leverage these as you seek to lead a movement and rally people to your point of view.

THE LAW OF THE FEW

There are a relatively small number of people who can make a large difference. "The success of any kind of social epidemic is heavily dependent on the involvement of people with a particular and rare set of social gifts," says Gladwell. There are three types of people, and they can sit anywhere in almost any organization. One of the many reasons Tesla was so successful during the **Ignite** phase of its journey toward Go-To status is that Elon Musk embodies all three of these archetypes. As you read the following three profiles, think of two to three people you know who fit the part.

- **Connectors** know a lot of people. They are social glue who know everyone. They move among many different subcultures and niches, collecting contacts along the way. Their networking tentacles seem to reach everywhere. Every community, every industry has them. (I call these "tree trunks with vast root systems," because their networking reach and influence extends far beyond the obvious. I'll come back to this later.) In business, they are absolute gold mines—you win just one of these people over, and they will connect you with many, many other key people with barely any effort on your part. But it is sometimes hard to know who they are just on the surface. You have to get to know them or learn of their reputation. This is not a job title; it's a personal characteristic. Sometimes these people naturally fall into certain roles—consultants, lawyers, trade association leaders, talent agents, lobbyists, executive recruiters, publicists, or executives who have been around for a long time. But often not. Chances are, if you give it some thought or ask around, you'll figure out who they are in your sector.

- **Mavens** are information collectors. They have a combination of knowledge and social skills that give them tremendous credibility and therefore tremendous power to start a word-of-mouth epidemic. They are deeply passionate about their area(s) of interest and are motivated to share this information. In business, these are often journalists, bloggers, industry analysts, financial analysts, other researchers, pundits, and consultants. They are experts in a particular area, like the tech support person you always call upon when your computer goes berserk. They are the ones who always seem to have the answers.

- **Salesmen** are people who persuade. They are usually charming, charismatic, upbeat, likable, and extremely good at building rapport with other people. Obviously, they are often in business development, marketing, or sales. They may be lawyers, politicians, activists, lobbyists, or celebrity spokespeople. They may even be customers. But you often find them elsewhere as well. Frequently, they are respected industry thought leaders with wide reach or name recognition.

THE STICKINESS FACTOR

This is how memorable something is and how much impact it has. A man on the Moon. "Software is dead." A rebel on a big, loud Harley-Davidson motorcycle. "Sticky" means that people can readily recall it top of mind and instinctively feel inclined to pass it along. It moves people to act. During **Ignite**, you will find out whether your point of view, positioning, and messages are sufficiently sticky. If not, you'll want to refine them. (For an excellent, fun elaboration on what makes something sticky, read the book *Made to Stick: Why Some Ideas Survive and Others Die* by Chip Heath and Dan Heath.)

The Apollo Space Program decided to employ two primary strategies to make its "Moon" message stick throughout the decade: one founded on hope, the other, fear.

Just age forty-three when he won the presidential election, Kennedy had beaten Richard Nixon on a platform of youth and vitality packaged as the "New Frontier." The space program, with its foundation of science and technology, formed the nucleus of that vision. This "quest" theme tied into the heroic storyline of exploration, pioneers in the "wild, wild west," and the urgency of being first.

The other strategy was to stoke a fear of losing. One can't overstate the Cold War hysteria during the 1950s and '60s, when schoolteachers would spontaneously scream "Drop!" to give young children "duck and cover" practice in case of nuclear attack. Kennedy positioned the "Moon Shot" goal as being central to achieving world leadership. It would determine whether other countries aligned themselves with the US, rather than the USSR.

The press ate it up. They had all the elements of a compelling saga: hero (the US, as represented by the astronauts), villain (Soviets), and a roller-coaster hero's journey in the form of a drama that would unfold over eight years. Each of the missions would be a cliffhanger in itself ("Will they succeed?"), building to the *Apollo 11* climax of that first step onto the Moon's surface—*if* it was to happen at all.

Even then, no one would breathe a final sigh of relief until the *Apollo 11* astronauts had splashed down and emerged from the spacecraft alive and well.

THE POWER OF CONTEXT

As Gladwell puts it, "Epidemics are sensitive to the conditions and circumstances of the times and places in which they occur." You need the right context in order to reach a market tipping point, and small things can make a big difference. You can't necessarily create context, but you need to be aware of context and can capitalize on it. For example, but for two defining moments, the Apollo Space Program might have never happened. In March 1961, Kennedy had been resisting his space advisors' urgings to accelerate the US space program, concerned about cost and how it would be received politically. But on April 12, 1961, the Soviets put Yuri Gagarin in space, a humiliating defeat for the Americans. Just a few days later, the calamitous Bay of Pigs invasion took place: 1,400 US-backed Cuban exiles launched an attempt to overthrow the Soviet-backed, communist Cuban dictator, Fidel Castro. They failed miserably. Over 1,100 were captured and another 114 killed. Left to choose whether to send the US military to intervene, Kennedy backed down, fearing he could spark World War III with the Soviets. At that point, he needed to restore national dignity and reconsidered ramping up efforts in space, sensing the public would embrace this. By the end of May, he had given his speech announcing the "Moon Shot," and the wheels were in motion. According to space historian Roger D. Launius, this was "the unique confluence of foreign policy crisis, political necessity, personal commitment and activism, scientific and technological ability, economic prosperity, and public mood." To Gladwell's point, timing matters.

"Context" is why you did so much analysis and preparation during the **Launch** phase to gauge what's happening around you. You don't want to be too early, or the market won't catch on quickly enough for you. Amana offered the first countertop microwave oven in 1967, but it took another twenty years for microwaves to reach 25 percent market penetration among US households. Adoption was tepid throughout the 1970s, and then three aspects of context worked together to accelerate adoption during the early 1980s: there was a surge in married women working outside the home and seeking time-saving conveniences; food company Swanson started offering microwave-specific foods; and foreign manufacturers drove prices down. People saw the microwave oven's utility, and market adoption started to take off.

Unlike Amana, you want the wind at your back, as was the case for Marc Benioff when starting Salesforce. After resisting for years, companies had finally started to embrace salesforce automation and had begun to embrace the internet. The dot-com boom was in full swing, so there were oodles of small companies in need. And when the recession hit in the early 2000s, even large companies didn't have the capital budgets to make massive software purchases or make long-term financial commitments. A pay-as-you-go option like Salesforce suddenly became very attractive.

Tesla had the wind at its back in 2006 when it announced its revolutionary luxury electric sports car with a range of over 200 miles. The first practical electric cars hit the market in the late 1800s and were quite popular by the early 1900s until the mass-produced Model T overshadowed them. Electric car interest then waxed and waned until the early 1990s when new regulations motivated automakers to act. GM released the EV1 in 1996, which amassed a cult following. Toyota released the hybrid Prius in 1997, and rapid adoption by celebrities made it a global hit. Meanwhile, Al Gore was steadily increasing public awareness of global warming. By the time Tesla came forward, the market was primed.

The personality types and conditions that drive epidemics as discussed above are the enablers of successful political campaigns and what have helped social movements like suffrage, civil rights, gay rights, and others to gain momentum to reach a tipping point. These are how drunk driving went from being a joking matter in the 1970s to a highly illegal and prison-worthy matter a decade or two later. These are why only 14 percent of US adults smoked cigarettes as of 2014, compared to 42 percent in 1965, despite the highly addictive nature of cigarettes and a ubiquitous presence in TV shows and movies (a known influence in getting people to start smoking when young).

Those "overnight sensations" in the entertainment industry—actors, singers, musicians, stand-up comics, etc.—are often anything but. Instead of "tipping point," it's called a "breakthrough" moment or "breakout role." Lady Gaga was regarded as an overnight sensation at age twenty-two when her megahit "Just Dance" dropped in 2008, but she had been performing for over eight years by then. To reach that point, she had applied these same principles.

Musicians and comedians might start by singing in small venues that powerbrokers are known to frequent, like the Bluebird Café in Nashville or the Comedy Store in Los Angeles. Eventually, they open for larger acts or work their way into larger venues. They build a following through social media. All along the way, they are using these low-risk venues to hone their craft, improve, get more comfortable in front of audiences, make and learn from mistakes. Lady Gaga experimented with and developed her public persona during a burlesque show dubbed, "Lady Gaga and the Starlight Revue," which she and a partner performed at Manhattan clubs. By the time artists hit the big leagues, they are seasoned and know what their audiences want. By the time they are selling songs, they have enough of a following to turn it into a hit. Most importantly, they've built a loyal base of superfans who will devour everything they produce, which keeps them from being one-hit wonders.

You are going to do the same.

OVERVIEW

Again, your goal during the **Ignite** phase is to build a groundswell of support for your point of view and approach that will provide a solid, enduring foundation for your market presence. In politics, they call the point of view a "platform" and call these early-stage activities "building your base."

These activities commonly fall under the "market development" banner, because you are essentially creating a market and demand centered on the problem you have identified and are solving.

LEAD A MOVEMENT

Rally influencers around approach and build market momentum

Ignite

• Evangelize the message
• Build momentum

Here is what you want to accomplish during the Ignite phase:

- Draw industry attention to the problem—become a player and lead the market conversation on this topic
- Aggressively and continuously evangelize the message internally and externally
- Convert key industry executives and other influencers
- Establish your unique message as a common topic of discussion
- Establish a clear, top-of-mind association between you and the message in the minds of your targets
- Gain momentum
- Begin to sell to innovative customers

IGNITE the Market Around Your Point of View

LEAD A MOVEMENT

Become an Industry Player

- Get "inside" the industry
- Draw attention to the problem

Convert Influencers

- Target key powerbrokers and connectors
- Evangelize POV internally and externally

Gain Momentum

- Establish POV as common topic of discussion
- Become associated with it

Convert "Innovators"

- Convert vocal customers who are "innovators"
- Refine offering with them

The underlying strategy centers on efficiency and sustainability. In biology, nature doesn't ask each plant to directly deliver its pollen to a million other plants one at a time. Instead, it gets pollen onto the bee, which the bee then propagates across plants just in the course of its normal activities. Who will your bees be?

Understand that this is not where sales promotion happens (that comes during the **Navigate** phase). The **Ignite** phase is all about your point of view and building philosophical support for your approach to solving the problem.

Perhaps one of the greatest case examples of the Ignite phase in action is the well-orchestrated marketing and public relations effort underlying the Apollo Space Program. When Kennedy announced the "Moon Shot" goal, NASA understood it would be just the beginning of a long and sustained public affairs undertaking. NASA documents state that:

> While Congress enthusiastically appropriated funding for Apollo immediately after the president's announcement, NASA Administrator James E. Webb was rightly concerned that the momentary sense of crisis would subside and that the political consensus present for Apollo in 1961 would abate.

Apollo would consume, at times, 3–4 percent of the federal annual budget during the 1960s, even as the Vietnam War competed for funding. NASA would have to continuously sell the Moon—to Congress for annual funding, to the public for support, and even to employees and contractors who would be making sacrifices and working, at times, around the clock to deliver on the promise. But how?

Several key strategic decisions proved pivotal.

The first is that NASA Public Affairs decided its bees—its key influencers—would be the three national television network news outlets at the time, city newspapers, and *Life* magazine (more on this later). It would focus on educating the media, who would then evangelize the message on NASA's behalf on nightly television news and in daily newspapers. It would also heavily leverage the public relations and marketing departments of the many corporations involved in Apollo as contractors. This would allow NASA's scant resources to go a long way. By nurturing and feeding these various communications channels and partners, NASA fueled inbound interest. More media outlets joined in, like local radio and television stations. Over time, it was indirectly able to reach nearly every US citizen and millions around the world with robust information that was almost a science education unto itself. Through this, NASA built and sustained a rabid fan base for the program.

The second strategy was critical for gaining and keeping credibility and the trust of these channels, especially the reporters: *transparency*. Openness was a congressional mandate for NASA upon creation, but Apollo public affairs strategist and leader Julian Scheer took this to a whole new level, saying, "We're going to get information out, and we are going to tell the truth." He had been a reporter himself and knew the frustrations of trying to wrest reliable information from the government. In the past, the military had influenced space program communications policy and made it difficult for the media to obtain information. The Apollo policy was the opposite—proactively provide very detailed, straight, and factually correct information without spin.

This included the jaw-dropping, historic live television broadcast of the Moon landing, which almost didn't happen. When the notion of live television was first floated, both the astronauts and the engineers objected, because it seemed superfluous to the primary mission and would add weight, one of the most sensitive factors in planning the Moon landing. But Scheer and a few others went to bat. It took years, but they finally prevailed. About his discussions with the engineers, Scheer said:

> Weight was a critical issue, no question about it. But I insisted, "You're going to have to take something else off. That camera is going to be on that spacecraft..."

Astronaut Tom Stafford agreed, saying:

> What better way to take viewers along to the Moon than by using color television?

This extreme openness and authenticity, even given the risk of cameras capturing human foibles in real time (e.g., accidental cursing by astronauts while is space) and failure (e.g., an aborted lunar landing by *Apollo 13* due to an onboard explosion that almost prevented the astronauts from returning to Earth), engendered tremendous trust and a symbiotic relationship between NASA Public Affairs and its main conduit for *igniting* the market: reporters. NASA added an unprecedented human element to real-life space exploration by putting astronauts front and center and granting media access to engineers and scientists working behind the scenes, and almost no questions were off limits unless the information could potentially put the mission or astronauts at risk. For the same reasons the transparency of today's social media builds strong bonds between brands and their constituents, this strategy proved enormously powerful for keeping the public engaged in the multiyear Apollo endeavor. At the time, this felt like a national security risk to some but like an important and distinguishing feature of "the American way" to others.

A third important strategy that worked for NASA was its journalistic approach to content—what some today call brand journalism. For starters, it hired mostly ex-journalists who understood what reporters wanted and how to prepare ready-made information for them without any spin. Then the Apollo program consistently disseminated meaty, prepackaged information ready to turn into news stories. This made the reporters' jobs easier and helped educate them on such a technical and scientific topic so they could accurately translate for their audiences.

For the same reasons the transparency of today's social media builds strong bonds between brands and their constituents, this strategy proved enormously powerful for keeping the public engaged in the multiyear Apollo endeavor.

This information campaign centered on the theme of "a new frontier." Over the course of the program, NASA and its corporate partners created thousands of media-ready documents that included bylined articles, press releases, background materials, television news segments, and radio broadcasts that incorporated interviews and sound effects. It even provided scale models of the spacecraft that television anchors like Walter Cronkite used as props during their evening broadcasts. For schools and civic organizations, NASA produced documentaries and sent frontline people to give talks, including the astronauts themselves.

The *Apollo Spacecraft News Reference* is just one example of how elaborate this content campaign was. Like almost all materials produced during the campaign, it was a collaboration between NASA and its contractors such as Grumman Aircraft Engineering Corporation and North American Rockwell. Each of these press packages contained over one hundred pages of details about the space vehicles and onboard systems, complete with elaborate diagrams, illustrations, photographs, and charts, all organized into tabbed three-ring binders. As Walter Cronkite put it, "I took NASA's manuals and books, and I did my homework. I studied like fury."

The production of all of this content—creating it, ensuring the technical accuracy of every word, diagram, and caption, and then producing it in the predigital era of typewriters, hand-laid graphics and printing presses—was an enormous task that wasn't central to the primary mission of getting a human to the Moon. But it was indeed central to *igniting* the market for sustained financial, political, and public support.

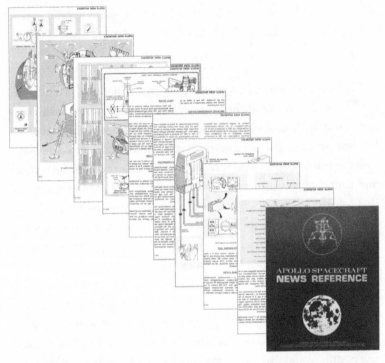

This edition of the *Apollo Spacecraft News Reference* was created by NASA and Grumman Aircraft Engineering and consisted of 267 pages of detailed information and diagrams about the lunar module, command module, crew personal equipment, and so on. It's one example of NASA's journalistic approach to content, designed to ignite influencers' support for the program and, by extension, public support. *(Cover image—David Meerman Scott and www.apollopresskits. com; inside pages—NASA)*

To dig even deeper into the juicy details, read the marvelously researched book *Marketing the Moon: The Selling of the Apollo Lunar Program*, written by two marketers, David Meerman Scott and Richard Jurek, which tells many behind-the-scenes stories.

Yes, it was a different time. There was no such thing as a public internet, cable television, social media, personal computers, or any of that. In some ways it was much harder; in some ways it was easier. Yet the fundamental challenge was and still is: How do you, with limited resources, rally a market around your point of view and approach to a problem or challenge? How do you get the market behind you?

Throughout this chapter, as I share the steps you'll need to take in *igniting* your own market by driving toward a tipping point for your offering, you'll see specific examples of classic strategic marketing and brand-building activities that NASA expertly used to gain and maintain support of the program, weather a few storms, and *ignite* the public's imagination. Through these efforts, it gradually built excitement, culminating in a televised landing on the Moon eight years later that was enthusiastically watched by 600 million people around the world.

As a testament to how critical these outreach efforts were, Wernher von Braun, chief architect of the *Saturn V* superbooster that propelled men to the Moon, stood up at NASA's Manned Spacecraft Center as *Apollo 11* astronauts were headed back to Earth and acknowledged the reporters gathered in front of him:

> I would like to thank all of you for the fine support you have always given the program. Because without public relations and good presentations of these programs to the public, we would have been unable to do it.

Here are the steps you'll take to **Ignite** your market:

1. Prepare a game plan and materials.
2. Prepare luminary as spokesperson—hone messages, train, rehearse, coach.

3. Meet with vocal key influencers to share point of view, obtain input and feedback, and convert into proactive supporters evangelizing on your behalf.

4. Evangelize the messages and point of view to carefully selected gatherings of target audiences (media, events, social media, etc.).

5. Publish thought leadership and draw attention to it.

6. Assume a leadership role in key organizations to set the industry agenda, promote the point of view, influence others, and set the agenda.

7. Build awareness among "Innovator" and "Early Adopter" targets/prospects who will be vocal and whose lead others will follow.

8. Monitor, measure, and refine.

Bear in mind that the underpinnings and how-to of the **Ignite** phase could be a book in itself, though I am boiling it down here to just one chapter. Also, the specific detailed tactics within each of these steps are going to vary widely depending on your market, offering, industry, budget, timing pressures, and situation. Don't get tangled up in any of the specifics that follow if they don't directly apply to your situation. Look for parallels and extract whatever guidance you can. Ultimately, what matters is that you use the market expertise you gained during the **Launch** phase to inform your decisions during this phase.

I'll offer information on some specific tactical channels below, but realize that these will ebb and flow in influence over time as technology, tools, and market dynamics change. Or they may not apply to you at all. The principles, however, are timeless. So stay focused on the strategy behind **Ignite**, and you will achieve your desired outcome of *igniting* the market around your point of view and solution to help establish brand recognition, prestige, and a strong base.

STEP 1

Prepare a Game Plan and Materials

One month after Kennedy's "Moon Shot" speech, the US Senate took up a funding bill the House had passed before the speech and amended it to include the full $1.8 billion NASA had requested for the year ($18.5 billion in today's dollars), which passed effortlessly in both chambers. This unheard-of congressional expediency occurred only because Vice President Lyndon Johnson had been highly strategic in paving the way in advance for bipartisan support with key congressional leaders during the previous two months.

When you are just coming out of the gate, it's simply not feasible to reach out to anyone and everyone in your target market. You have to be very thoughtful about how you spend your precious, limited time and resources. This means you want to start with the people who have the most reach and influence in your market. If you can convert them and get them preaching your message on your behalf, you gain tremendous leverage. Therefore, you must first figure out who these Vital Few are.

The key is to really analyze the powerbrokers (people, media, channels, etc.) in your market and focus on the smallest number that will yield the most results. Apply the 80/20 rule here, only perhaps make it 99/1—which 1 percent of the countless business development and promotional vehicles available to you will yield 99 percent of what you need in order to reach that tipping point?

When I ran Entrepreneurship Week for Stanford University and was promoting it to the local community, I would always reach out to one of our alumni, Guy Kawasaki, who is a renowned author and has a huge blog following that overlapped closely with who we were targeting. I could tell just from the immediate bump in our website traffic when Guy's post promoting our event went online. One post by him on our behalf was worth a hundred promotional activities anywhere else.

When prioritizing, map the audiences you'll reach through a particular tactic to the buyer profile you're after by using a bell curve and buyer breakdown popularized by Everett Rogers of Ohio State University in his seminal 1962 book, *Diffusion of Innovations.*

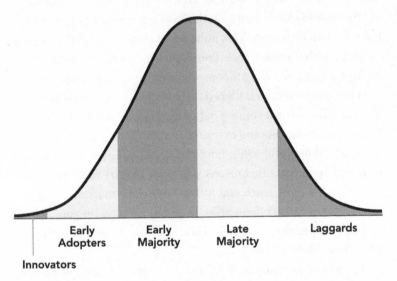

The Innovation Adoption Curve illustrates how and when buyer groups gravitate toward innovations. It emerged through research over the course of decades and was popularized by Everett Rogers. *(Image:* Diffusion of Innovations, *Rogers.)*

This is an important model for understanding profiles and characteristics of buyer groups based on when they'll gravitate toward innovations relative to other members of the same social or economic system. A topic addressed by thousands of studies and publications since at least the late nineteenth century, it came to the forefront in the 1950s through various academic publications by

Rogers and others on "how farm people accept new ideas." However, it has broad applicability and is a useful model for figuring out who to target with new offerings and how and when to do so. (There are various names for this curve in academic and business literature. I'll refer to it as the Innovation Adoption Curve.)

This is an important model for understanding profiles and characteristics of buyer groups based on when they'll gravitate toward innovations relative to other members of the same social or economic system.

- **Innovators** (2.5 percent of the market) are early customers with "extremely high" risk profiles who jump in blindly to willingly adopt groundbreaking offerings without the need for evidence that it works. In fact, if it doesn't work quite right, they'll help improve it. They immediately see the vision and are happy to be guinea pigs and part of the experimentation process in exchange for having first access. These are people who waited in line overnight for the very first iPhone before they even quite knew what it was. They are the people who will participate in medical clinical trials when they have non-life-threatening conditions. They are the ones who provide seed-round and Series A financing to startups.

  Elon Musk offers a great story of how forgiving Innovators can be. Tesla was breaking new technology ground in developing its first model, the Roadster, which he looks back on as a "basket case" experience. In a 2016 shareholders' meeting, he described taking Google co-founders Sergei Brin and Larry Page for a spin, and the sports car wouldn't go above ten miles per hour. "I was like, 'I swear, guys, it goes way faster than this,'" he said. But Brin and Page "were kind enough to put a little money in the company despite the world's worst demo."

Musk had another disastrous yet profitable demo while unveiling the futuristic Tesla Cybertruck at a high-profile event in November 2019. In a demonstration meant to show off the truck's "armor" windows, the glass shattered. That didn't stop the Innovators. At least 50,000 orders poured in immediately following the event.

- **Early Adopters** (13.5 percent of the market) have a "high" risk profile. They jump in once the big kinks have been worked out, but they are still willing to take risks and accept mild imperfections in exchange for early access. These are the people who will try a new medical device or medication as soon as it obtains Food and Drug Administration (FDA) approval. They bought the Prius when it was first introduced, finding comfort in Toyota's quality reputation but willing to take a chance on a new hybrid. They provide Series B financing to startups that have paying customers, have proven themselves, and are ready to grow.

- The **Early Majority** (34 percent of the market) has a "moderate" risk profile. It embraces innovation but wants to know other people are buying it and experiencing success, and it wants to hear strong evidence of that success. It also wants the kinks worked out first. This group waited at least a couple of years to get a smartphone. It wants to hear plenty of patient testimonials and understand the side effects before trying a new medication. Enterprises in this group want case studies and milestone objectives. Investors in this group are Series-C types who jump in once a startup is quite successful and just needs funding to scale. Note that there is often a pause in market adoption timing between saturation of the Early Adopter market and uptake by the Early Majority, as the Early Majority takes a wait-and-see approach; so you must be prepared to hang in there during that "chasm" (as author Geoffrey Moore calls it) or "trough of disillusionment" (as research firm Gartner calls it).

- The **Late Majority** (also 34 percent of the market) has a "low" risk profile. It is more cautious. It wants all of the kinks worked out and adopts the innovation only out of necessity and on the basis of lots of long-standing evidence. This group got smartphones a good five years after they hit the market. It only tries "new" medications that have been around for years. It consists of enterprises that have elaborate contracting procedures that eliminate most of their risk. Investors in this group invest in startups *after* they've become unicorns (meaning companies worth at least $1 billion).

- **Laggards** (16 percent of the market), also called Late Adopters, take no risks at all and are the very last to adopt, often ultimately waiting until the innovation isn't any longer an innovation. These are people who *still* don't have a smartphone or only bought it because nothing else was available. If they use social media, it's just because it's the only way to keep in touch with relatives. Enterprises in this group only change technologies when the old product is no longer supported. Investors in this group only invest in Blue Chip companies and bonds.

We're going to come back to the Innovation Adoption Curve throughout the book, especially as you identify your target customers, but **the thing to understand now is the importance of pursuing powerbrokers and influencers who will help you reach Innovators and Early Adopters without getting too far afield with the Early Majority or Late Majority.** If you are out in front of them too soon, this audience may reject you out of hand and put up walls that become tough to break down.

An Apollo example of someone who tried to "jump the curve" and got burned for it was aeronautic research scientist George Low, head of NASA's Office of Manned Space Flight (OMSF) for Apollo precursor Project Mercury in 1958. Attesting to his talent and brilliance, a former colleague recalled that "George was good at everything. He was worth about ten men." Openly advocating as early as 1959 to aim for a lunar landing when that concept was still unpopular with politicians, he led a planning session in 1960 to discuss the feasibility of doing so. He described his vision for landing a human on the Moon in detail to 1,200 attendees from government, the aerospace sector, and academia. The press ran with it. At the time, President Eisenhower still viewed Project Mercury as a one-off initiative to counter the *Sputnik 1* accomplishment and had no plans to fund a new and audacious, ongoing enterprise to the Moon. The presumptuousness of Low's announcement and plan so enraged him that he instantly erased astronaut flight funding from NASA's 1961 budget. Though others later persuaded him to restore the budget, a lunar landing was out. Eisenhower was a big believer in the importance of large rocket boosters but was not an Innovator or Early Adopter when it came to manned space flight. Low had hit him too early.

If you're after "Innovators," don't go after coverage in just any blog or publication in that market—go after the super-nerdy, trend-spotting blog or publication that every serious aficionado in that domain fervently devours. Where do the industry's newest, most mind-bending ideas always appear first? What do the truly innovative thought leaders read? Where do they get published first? (We'll get to the details of this in step 4.)

You also want to look at the materials and concepts you developed during the **Launch** phase and determine whether they are "sticky," or whether they need to be repackaged or repositioned in any way to ensure they'll grab your audience.

The challenge of figuring out how to make a concept sticky is that there are many ways to approach any given theme or message. Here's an example of the same concept packaged in two ways. In 1992, Georgetown University professor and linguist Dr. Deborah Tannen published *You Just Don't Understand: Women and Men in Conversation*, a book on differences in communication style and how they can inadvertently cause relationship breakdowns. It did very well, spending four years on the *New York Times* best seller list, eight months at number one. Two years later, however, relationship counselor John Gray came out with a book covering the same topic, only it more narrowly focused on romantic relationships and was packaged more provocatively: *Men Are from Mars, Women Are from Venus*. This book has sold over 15 million copies and turned into a cultural phenomenon spawning a pop-culture catchphrase, seminars, a Broadway show, a television sitcom, and more.

The only major difference was framing. John Gray's approach was much stickier. As related in a USA *Today* story:

> One night, Gray told women in the audience their husbands were like E.T., from a different planet, with different needs, speaking a different language. The women laughed, and one called out, "Where's my husband from?"
>
> "Mars," Gray replied. He knew he had a hook. "I had goosebumps, the hair rose on my arms," he recalls.

This Aha! moment and John Gray's ability to leverage it into a marketing juggernaut made him a household name and generated a fortune in the crowded field of relationship counseling through seminars, paid speeches, products, and other offerings.

Find your hook. Figure out how to make your message stick. This could be a process—you may have to refine it as you continue to talk to people in the market.

Your plan will also specify to whom you are going to convey your message and who/what you will use to gain leverage in the market. It will also specify the tools you'll need so that you can prepare them. If you are not familiar with common techniques like defining buyer personas, there are numerous how-to articles online that can help, or see apollomethod.com for links. Your plan should contain answers to the following, which the rest of this chapter will help you develop:

- What is the profile of your target market as a whole and by segment? (characteristics, locations, buyer values, structure and culture, etc.)
- Who are your audience group targets and target executives? What buyer personas are you after? Be very specific, and map them to the Innovation Adoption Curve.
- Who do they listen to? Who most influences them?
- How/where do they "gather"?
- What are the steps in the "customer journey" that they'll take? (How-to information on mapping the customer journey is available at apollomethod.com.)
- What evidence do you need in order to prove you are the best at what you do? What makes you truly different from the competition and substitutes?
- Who are the top twenty Connectors, Mavens, and Salesmen you must convert to your point of view—who are the key industry execs and other influencers the rest of the market

listens to and follows? Prioritize them. If you are severely resource constrained, pick just ten, or even five.

- What are the most influential publications you must target?
- Which events must you be part of?
- Which trade organizations are most important in this market?
- What else do you need to do to be considered a player in this market? For example, are there key partnerships/alliances? Particular customers you need to win in order for others to follow?
- Prioritize all of these in sets of three.
- Who will your leading luminary (face of the organization) be? Once you are building momentum, who else will you put out there?
- What tangible deliverables do you need in order to communicate with the above and **ignite** the market?

Assemble and summarize all of this into an action plan. If you are having trouble answering some of these questions, look to other market leaders in your space—where are they established? What path did they take to become well known?

In addition to your written plan, prepare the deliverables you'll need. Here are some examples:

- Stump speech (refinement of what you put together in **Launch**)
- Versions of stump speech tailored for particular audiences
- Sales presentation (one or more versions of your stump speech with more specifics on your offering, tailored to specific Innovator and Early Adopter buyer personas)
- Company overview presentation and credentials (as a supplement to your stump speech)
- Case studies and testimonials (if available)

- Social media editorial calendar
- Press kit (if applicable)

Also line up the people you'll need to help you get the **Ignite** phase done, such as social media and public relations experts, other communications people, your marketing team, and so forth.

STEP 2

Prepare Luminary as Spokesperson— Hone Messages, Train, Rehearse, Coach

The fear of nuclear annihilation during the Cold War was so palpable that a common joke at the time was, "What do you want to be *if* you grow up?" By the end of the 1950s, 60 percent of American children reported having nightmares about it. Meanwhile, machines were starting to automate workers out of their factory jobs, which made a severe economic recession in the US even worse. Exacerbating anxiety and distrust of the encroachment of technology into people's lives, despite its benefits, was Hollywood. During the 1950s, the science fiction genre went to the dark side. What had been low-volume, tame *Flash Gordon*-style serials now became a proliferation of terrifying tales about radioactive fallout, mind control, outer space, and alien or robot invasion, all of which served as metaphors for the nuclear holocaust and possible dominion over the US by communists—or worse, machines.

Meanwhile, space flight was machine driven, and some within NASA argued that it should stay that way for practical reasons. Others knew the public would not want space travel left to machines that could one day take on minds of their own, so they put "pilots" on board during Apollo-predecessor Project Mercury, even though they were effectively "Spam in a can," as characterized by renowned flying ace Chuck Yeager. After a few flights, ever the marketer, NASA even decided to change its vehicle vernacular from the passive "capsule" to the more human-controlled "craft."

Thus, it was clear to NASA that for Apollo, the astronauts themselves would need to become the face of the story. And people couldn't get enough. According to Captain Eugene A. Cernan of *Apollo 17* and the eleventh person to walk on the Moon:

> Because of the public's desire, we were called upon to share with the nation why we felt what we were doing had value; in fact, people began to demand no less. As a consequence, NASA would send us traveling throughout the country, one at a time, on what was called our "week in the barrel," public affairs duty...In addition, we went on goodwill tours after each of our missions, not only to major cities in the United States, but to world capitals as well...A personal association with someone who "had been there" is what everyone wanted.

Human stories sell. This is why you want to put a face on your message. Pick one person, to start, who will be the face of the company on an ongoing basis. It doesn't necessarily have to be the spokesperson from your launch. Kennedy made the big splash, and the astronauts carried on from there, with him stepping in for major interventions, like with Congress. Apollo's unique circumstances made it possible for several people to interchangeably play the public role of astronaut at any given time, but in your case, more than one will likely make it too hard for the audience to latch on. Even with Apollo, the luminary was "Astronaut," and not a collection of other people in other roles. Give them just one person, one voice, to remember. The exception may be when you are using experts with different skillsets or personalities to reach different market segments.

Thus, it was clear to NASA that for Apollo, the astronauts themselves would need to become the face of the story.

This is a crucial role, so choose carefully. Your spokesperson needs to be someone who is an expert in the field with a deep understanding of the industry problem and solution you are offering, but s/he doesn't necessarily need to be the *most* expert person; s/he needs to be the *most presentable and most relatable*—someone the audience will emotionally connect with, like they did with Steve Jobs, whose enthusiasm for Apple products was infectious. This person should be a charismatic ambassador with a strong presence, great speaking and presentation skills, and industry expertise. Richard Branson of Virgin Group is an example of a luminary who personifies the company brand. This person needs to be able to project confidence, speak to the issues, and fire people up the way Marc Benioff does on behalf of Salesforce. S/he needs to be naturally persuasive and genuinely passionate about the issues. It's ideal if this person is the lead executive for the part of the business targeting this market. If you are a smaller company, it's probably the CEO or president. If you are a business unit or product team, it's the executive in charge, product manager, etc. It could also be the CMO or head of sales. If the people in those positions don't fit the above criteria, choose someone else. You want someone credible who can also sell it.

Cernan offers a perfect encapsulation of the importance of the **Ignite** phase, the luminary role, and how to make it work:

Looking back, I must admit that I learned something from those weeks "in the barrel." If your desire is to bring others into your camp, they must know that you, yourself, believe in what they are hearing; your sincerity and passion must be evident. You must share your ideas with them—not talk at them—if you want to achieve your ultimate goal. To me, *that* is marketing, and it was a key part of the US space program that garnered the support of the American people.

Get your spokesperson ready. Help him or her hone the messages. Regardless of how media savvy or experienced the person is, provide formal media training focused on presenting your new story. Train, rehearse, coach. Role-play with listeners who push back or are disinterested. Let this person practice on insiders and then outsiders.

The presentation of the messages and story needs to be clear, crisp, and memorable. Most of all, it needs to have emotional impact. It needs to punch your intended audiences in the gut.

From here, for the sake of discussion, I'll assume you're going to be the spokesperson.

STEP 3

Meet with Key Influencers to Share Point of View, Obtain Feedback, and Turn Them into Evangelists of Your Message

Undaunted by his slap on the wrist from Eisenhower, George Low doubled down, and taking a cue from the **Launch** phase, he decided to document his point of view. He said, "I felt it would be important to have something in the files. We needed to be prepared to move out with a bigger program, should there be a sudden change of heart within the government and with the administration." Learning his lesson, this time he assembled just a small working group and quietly produced a detailed report on methods, schedules, and budgets for landing on the Moon in a decade. Engaging with key influencers inside NASA, he circulated the memo, keeping it all low key. By now, Kennedy was the newly installed president, but sending a human to the Moon was still a politically toxic notion rejected by some of his advisors. Some were even discussing the possibility of merging NASA with the military. However, that "sudden change of heart" to go to the Moon occurred in rapid succession (in just three months) when Jim Webb became NASA administrator and Lyndon Johnson was tasked with recommending an audacious goal: Webb shared Low's report, Johnson bought in, and Johnson sold Kennedy. That report provided a framework for Kennedy's "Moon Shot" and served as a technical and management springboard for Apollo. Ah, the stunning power of a strong point of view, even in the face of headwinds, and the magic that occurs when you convert the right influencers.

When thinking about **Ignite**, you want again to be highly strategic. It's essential that you identify the right people and determine how best to reach and persuade them.

Some call the people you'll be targeting "Opinion Leaders" or "Centers of Influence." Bryan Clagett, a longtime financial services marketer, explains it well:

> Centers of influence are those people (or organizations) that can boost your market access and credibility through referrals, testimonials, and simple, under-valued word-of-mouth. These are people who are generally very well established, are good networkers and who can introduce you to the kind of markets (or members) you need and are looking for. Ideally, you should be in the network of several Centers of Influence. So why is this important? The Roper Organization has conducted many studies on influential people for decades. They have found that the influential segment of the population is "remarkable for its consistency and typically deeply involved in their communities, both socially and politically."

Here, you're leveraging a phenomenon also seen in astrophysics and astronomy. In those contexts, this is called a sphere of influence and is a celestial body that exerts a dominant gravitational pull on a nearby body, such as a moon, despite the existence of a much larger object, such as the Sun.

You can see it in international relations as well, where a "sphere of influence" occurs when one country is able to exert power or influence over another country or area, even though it has no formal authority.

Many people talk about "Centers of Influence" in sales referral terms. This is limiting. You're after *market* influence for much broader reach and impact.

Dr. Tom Kosnik, a former adjunct marketing professor in the Department of Management Science and Engineering at Stanford, researches and espouses the concept of "Circles of Influence," citing environments like Silicon Valley and Singapore as examples. He describes this concept in the context of startups as follows, though it is also applicable to mature companies:

> Circles of Influence are informal networks that help early-stage ventures rapidly acquire customers, capital and talent in their target markets, which simultaneously increases the speed and reduces the risk of scaling a business.

To put a finer point on it, your first priority is to target the *most influential powerbrokers* in your space. These are the people with vast networks and whom everyone else listens to. I guarantee there are a handful of people in your industry who pull most of the strings. Earlier, I referred to these people as "tree trunks with vast root systems," because on the surface, they're just like anyone else.

But underground, out of sight, that one person or company can get you a meeting with almost anyone you want. They can make your name with a one-line endorsement. In San Francisco, Willie Brown is one of these people. Now well into his eighties, you'd think the former California assemblyman and former San Francisco mayor would be irrelevant, with his influence and contacts just relics of his glorious past. Not so. Willie Brown can still get almost anything done in San Francisco and possibly in the state of California with one phone call.

On the surface, a powerbroker just appears to be a single entity, like any other.

Research your sector and revisit lists you made earlier. Ask around. The "tree trunks" in your space may be attorneys, industry analysts, talent agents, executive recruiters, lobbyists, private equity investors, investment bankers, accountants, bloggers, reporters, activists, socialites, association or community group presidents, and the list goes on. Get them on your side, and you're made.

Marc Benioff was fortunate to count his boss and mentor, billionaire Larry Ellison, as both a friend and early supporter of Salesforce. Benioff was a young star at Ellison's company, Oracle, when he decided to start Salesforce with Ellison's blessing to work on the new venture during the mornings and head to Oracle for afternoons. He soon offered Benioff a sabbatical to work on it full time, invested $2 million in the young company, and joined its board. Benioff also once worked for Steve Jobs, who then became a friend and mentor, giving him the advice to create an application marketplace, advice

Jobs later followed himself with the Apple App Store. You can imagine the extra oomph it gave Benioff to have both of these powerbrokers and their vast networks available to him as he sought to build his business.

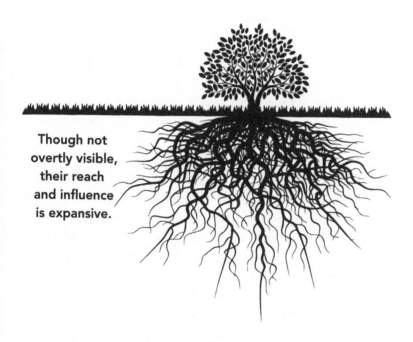

Though not overtly visible, their reach and influence is expansive.

Even though some of the influencers you target may have a social media following, this discussion is not referring to social media influencers who promote other people's products for compensation. In select cases, they come in during sales and promotional efforts in the **Navigate** phase, but they aren't useful at this point unless they are genuine thought leaders themselves who are going to give you instant, *enduring* credibility and proactively advocate *your point of view* in addition to your offering. Otherwise, they simply give you a momentary bump in awareness. No, we're talking about leaders who can sway other leaders.

This "tree trunk" dynamic occurs inside every company and throughout every industry, and you're going to leverage it. Refine your list of targets, make sure they are prioritized, and then set up your meetings.

FIRST, AN INSIDE JOB

"I had to do about as much public relations work inside as I did outside NASA."

—Jack King, NASA chief of public information during the Mercury, Gemini, and Apollo programs

Start inside your organization, if you haven't already gained full awareness and buy-in during the **Launch** phase. If you are a business unit that is going to need funding, support, and resources from "corporate," meet with internal powerbrokers who hold the purse strings or influence those who do. Educate them about the market need, opportunity, your vision of the role the company can play, and the economic opportunity for the company. Tirelessly meet with everyone you can and build support internally. If you are a smaller company, meet with each investor and board member individually if you didn't do this during the **Launch** phase. Keep at it until they are converted. They will also help you clarify and improve your story and get the next influencer/powerbroker on board. They do this for themselves, because there is safety in numbers; and it works to your great advantage.

Once that's done, turn your attention to others inside the organization. This is incredibly important, especially in matrix organizations where authority and influence is not hierarchical. Start with leadership executives, meeting with them individually. Work your way down the organization chart to include all employees. Have everyone in the company on board and make sure they understand the story. They should be able to tell the high-level story, but they should know to call you in to do the real storytelling for customers and others outside the company. Also share the story with other pseudo-internal stakeholders, such as partners and vendors.

NASA wanted to be sure the entire organization delivered the same consistent and convincing message, so it began providing a set of written quotes by NASA officials to its public affairs officers in hopes that the document would arm NASA employees with answers to questions they "might meet either in public speaking appearances or in other contacts with the general public."

Joe Young, a NASA mathematician who provided the computer programming for the research engineer who studied the physics of landing the lunar module on the Moon, described the early days of Apollo as an elevation in morale due to the thrill of the challenge. Recalling the energy in the air, he said:

> The goals were clear, and the people were excited about doing something of such monumental and unifying importance.

Marc Benioff recalls discovering he had not properly done this even while Salesforce was still young and how he fixed it:

> One day, early in our occupancy at the Rincon Center, our marketing director, a developer, a quality assurance person, and an engineer were in the elevator when another tenant in the building asked, "What exactly does salesforce.com do?" To my surprise, everybody gave a different answer.
>
> To ensure that everyone was on the same page (literally), our PR firm, OutCast Communications, produced a two-sided laminated card. It was a marketing cheat sheet that stated in one sentence what we did. It also provided information about the benefits of our service, our newest customers and partners,

and our most recent awards. With this card, we leveraged everyone—from developers to engineers to quality assurance people—as integral parts of our marketing organization.

The card would have been of little use if we had simply distributed it. Instead, we offered training to make sure that everyone was crystal clear on the message that we wanted delivered to the world. In the early days, we met with the whole company for brown-bag lunch sessions to go over the latest marketing pitch for the company. Even though we were small, it was essential to ensure that our marketing was focused and first class.

In an existing organization, be mindful that you are introducing a change, so you must handle it as any other. Start with one-on-one meetings and very small audiences in order to build a groundswell of support. The more people in the room, the more likely the naysayers are to infect the rest of the group, and you'll be met with resistance. Therefore, *always* walk into a group meeting having presold everyone or almost everyone in the room, especially the influential ones. It's much better to encounter this resistance one-on-one in advance so you can understand where it's coming from and address it. Also, the reasons may be very valid and require you to modify your work.

We did a great job of this internal selling with the Accenture Communications Industry Group and a terrible job at a cloud infrastructure provider I was once with. At Accenture, our luminary spokesperson was the business unit head, Al Burgess. He was dogged. We were trying to get internal resources and funding for our new initiative, so we created a stump speech about the market opportunity and what it would do for Accenture. He would jet off and meet with various influential partners in the firm (now called managing directors). With each meeting, he'd make more headway in building support for the vision and learn what was and was not resonating in the way he presented it. He'd come back to Atlanta, we would rework the presentation, and he'd jet off again for more meetings.

Once all of the people we directly or indirectly reported to had bought in, we gathered an extended team of people we'd be relying on to help make all of this a reality—sales and business development people, service delivery people, marketers, and anyone internally who was interested in the communications industry. We put together a three-day "seminar" in which we trained people on the industry trends and issues, presented the vision, established a sense of team and identity among this far-flung group of people, and fired them up. Because there was a central theme and message, they were able to quickly get their heads around what we stood for and come away with that "one thing" they would start to convey to their clients. In just three days, we had a team of people marching into the marketplace in lockstep.

This is exactly how politicians polish their rough edges and message to gather internal support before branching out—they start with one-on-one meetings with party members and then expand to small gatherings of friendly donors. They test their message, get feedback, obtain commitments of support, and refine their delivery. They then branch out into ever widening circles, the way still water ripples outwardly from where a thrown stone enters it.

In contrast, we made a big mistake in not gathering enough internal support at the cloud infrastructure provider I mentioned. It was a startup created by merging a collection of small independent companies. We had a lot of entrepreneurial people in the company whose trust was earned, not granted. Under a lot of pressure from investors to make a difference externally and move quickly, we put all of our focus on the outside market without first building enough internal awareness and buy-in for the vision and message. We underestimated the importance of doing this, even at a small company. The results were disastrous. No one was singing from the same songbook, there was a great deal of frustration and confusion within the organization, and doubts about the company's direction affected sales and client service. I can't overstate the importance of getting total stakeholder buy-in internally before you proceed externally, regardless of the organization's size.

NOW LOOK OUT

When ready to go outside, set up meetings with your list of target thought leaders, key industry executives that others seem to listen to, and other influencers. Sit down with each one. Share your point of view and invite discussion. Get them fired up. The outcome you want is for them to feel a sense of urgency about the problem and agreement on what needs to be done about it. For startups, these may be investor pitches.

This is exactly what Steve Jobs did when preparing to upend the music industry with the iTunes Store in 2003. At the time, the record industry was in a state of chaos, playing legal whack-a-mole with free file-sharing services and pirated music. Both consumers and artists themselves were beginning to revolt. Yet the industry seemed incapable of creating a solution that would catch on despite trying. Enter Steve Jobs. By 2002, he had developed a vision for creating an online music store. His point of view was that customers would be willing to pay for downloaded music if the service was really easy to use, had a great selection, worked well, and allowed them to download music à la carte instead of having to shell out $15 for an entire album just to get the hit they were after. It was a radical new model. He would have to get the record labels to buy in.

He started by meeting with dozens of influential artists like Bono, hoping for their help getting the labels on board. Wynton Marsalis said Jobs presented to him for two solid hours. "He was a man possessed," says Marsalis. "After a while, I started looking at him and not the computer, because I was so fascinated with his passion." Jobs also met with powerbrokers like Eagles manager Irving Azoff, who shared with the *Wall Street Journal*, "I've said 'no' to all of [the other online services],…[but] I liked [Apple's] product."

Jobs then called the president of AOL Time Warner, the behemoth at the time. As relayed by *Rolling Stone* in 2011 based on interviews:

> The president quickly patched in Paul Vidich, an executive at Warner Music Group, the storied label that acts including Madonna, R.E.M. and Neil Young called home. Vidich listened as Jobs snarled that the labels' digital-music services—clunky, pricey, unpopular options like MusicNet and Pressplay—had gotten it all wrong. Jobs had something better in mind, a new product that would actually get consumers to pay for online music in huge numbers. As he shared the beginnings of an idea that would eventually become the iTunes Music Store, Vidich listened in awe. "That's exactly what we need," Vidich told him.

Universal was next. Then came BMG, EMI, and Sony. Jobs soon had a demo to show them, which sealed the deal, but only after "long and painful negotiations" and a couple of concessions to his original vision: he had to copy-protect songs and limit them to Mac devices. The iTunes Store opened in April 2003, and sold over a million songs in the first week. Within six months, he was able to persuade the labels to offer iTunes to Windows users as well.

What made him effective was his genuine passion for the topic. "Steve was a magnetic personality and a fierce intellectual debater of all things music, ranging from piracy to specific discussions about lyrics," describes Lucian Grainge, chairman and chief executive of Universal Music Group.

These meetings can be challenging to obtain if you don't have any market presence, contacts, or influence going in. A compelling story and message is critical. Whomever you're targeting is insanely busy, but they will make time if someone they know and trust asks them to on your behalf; or they think you have refreshing insights that will be timely and valuable. Your outreach in setting up these meetings must convince them of this. Use a great hook and succinct why/what/how message that answers, "What's in it for me?" Then you must deliver.

If your story is well baked, start at the top of your target power pyramid like Jobs did. They will then convince the people below them. If you know it needs work, start at the bottom with more "forgiving" contacts and refine as you go.

Whatever the audience, these discussions should not turn into "hard sell" presentations, unless the person invites that discussion along the way. (If you are doing a good job, these meetings often lead to selling discussions, so do be prepared.) Jobs went in with a reputation and leverage you probably don't have in your target market, so he was able to come on strong. You, on the other hand, may get better results by handling these as thought leadership and relationship-building conversations with back and forth. (Actually, even Jobs did that with the labels.) Allowing the other person to contribute ideas starts to give them a sense of ownership in the point of view you're advocating. One of your goals is to learn about their needs, interests, and point of view so that you can eventually become even more useful to them as they may be to you. You also want to get guidance on the offering's perceived value and pricing. Most often, these are introductory meetings, and your primary goal is to intrigue them and get the next meeting. If it's a one-way presentation to an audience, keep it to thought leadership and encourage discussion and follow-up afterward.

When targeting enterprises, there is a temptation at this point to jump right into sales mode and get business development people to deliver these presentations. Do not succumb. They aren't going to be deep experts in the broader market context and trends, the point of view, and the philosophy driving the proposed approach/offering. They won't yet be in a position to give a deep-dive, educational presentation or have the passionate conviction that's needed. It won't come from the heart the way it will with your primary luminary. The sales or relationship management person's job should be to set up the meeting, attend, and let the luminary do the talking and persuading. The luminary has been immersed in the material. The luminary has the lessons learned as to how to tell the story and what resonates. The luminary is the person who will be able to sell it.

Sit down with each one. Share your point of view and invite discussion. Get them fired up. The outcome you want is for them to feel a sense of urgency about the problem and agreement on what needs to be done about it...This is exactly what Steve Jobs did when preparing to upend the music industry with the iTunes Store in 2003.

Many people feel the need to have a "reference customer" or success story at this point, which presents a Catch-22 if you don't have a fully developed product or haven't implemented anything yet. Fortunately, you don't necessarily need that. If you're truly presenting an educational, provocative point of view on a key trend or market issue to the right audience (Innovators and Early Adopters) who will learn something new, they will be all ears. And they'll get it. If you go into selling mode and become self-serving, you're in trouble. The exception is when you're offering something so desperately needed that the listener can't wait to get their hands on it.

In the technology world, the enthusiastic conversion of just *one* industry or financial analyst or pundit can be all it takes to put you on the map. Getting a mention in one of their reports can be a game changer. In consumer markets, it may be a celebrity or journalist. Regardless of your market, if you've done your homework and have focused properly, you probably know who that person or entity is and therefore whom to target.

STEP 4

Evangelize the Messages and Point of View in Carefully Targeted Media and Conferences/Meetings/Events

The Apollo Space Program got its message out through a wide range of targeted media and events, but there was one particular outlet that proved invaluable for building its base of fans from the get-go: *Life* magazine.

Knowing early in the manned space program that it would be stoking public interest in the astronauts' lives in a way that went beyond the scope of its mandate to provide factual information, NASA Public Affairs set up a deal with *Life* magazine that provided exclusive rights to the astronauts' personal stories. *Life*, which reached peak circulation of 8.5 million in 1969, was known for its ability to humanize celebrities through emotionally moving photojournalism. And that it did. The magazine positioned the astronauts and their families as regular middle-class people the public could relate to and cheer for. Journalist and historian David Halberstam said that President Kennedy viewed *Life* as the "most influential [media] instrument in the country" at the time and at one point intervened to allow the contract to continue. (The arrangement had become controversial, because the proceeds from the deal went directly to the astronauts as compensation for the burden it placed on them and their families and to supplement their modest government salaries.)

What the public loved about these stories was the seeming authenticity and often direct communication from the astronauts, the closest thing to Instagram at the time but delivered with the power and authority of the *Life* brand. They saw these everyday heroes grilling steaks at home, swimming in the pool with their kids, camping, and making pancakes for a son's Cub Scout troop. One issue focused just on the wives. This intimate coverage made the public feel personally *connected* to the astronauts, as evidenced by the voluminous fan mail they received on a regular basis. Neil Armstrong still had at least 70,000 letters in his possession when he died in 2012, including one handwritten letter from a ten-year-old inviting Armstrong to his house for the weekend. "If you can come, please notify me of the time, if you can," he politely wrote. Behind the scenes, however, this "authenticity" was actually carefully crafted to position the astronauts as all-American heroes, even though in reality they sometimes drank too much, fought with their spouses, or otherwise misbehaved.

The arrangement proved pivotal in turning the astronauts, and by association the Apollo Space Program, into superstars at the forefront of public awareness and admiration. It served as emotional kindling for *igniting* the "market," particularly during the early days of the program.

Social media activity, webinars, conventional media exposure, and industry presentations are standard promotional practices that your company has probably done lots of. The difference with the Apollo Method is how these are executed. First, you are espousing a provocative point of view and unique approach to solving an important problem, not hawking a product. You're rallying people around your point of view and getting the marketplace bought in on what needs to be done about the problem. No one will care that another baby stroller has hit the market, but they *will* care that babies pushed in strollers breathe up to 60 percent more particulate matter than the adults who are pushing them, why stroller height affects that, and what needs to be done about it (and they'll assume/hope you've solved the problem and want to know more).

Second, every interaction, every presentation starts with your top-line message. You should be completely consistent almost to the point of being repetitive. It takes numerous exposures for people to remember you and the message. You want to hit them with it as much as possible. Every bit of content that went out about Apollo reinforced a message of national competence and heroic dominance in space.

There was never any mistaking what Salesforce stood for. It wanted to upend the software industry, and every event, every tactic, and every piece of content it employed sent that message and contained the "No Software" red circle and slash symbol.

As I mentioned earlier, the mistake many companies make with these marketing tactics is that they take a "spray and pray" approach, covering a wide range of topics. Even if the topics closely connect to the company's overall market category or offering, they don't hang together or build on each other in any way when you put them next to each other. It's a mistake NASA is making today, because it has *so many* seemingly disconnected initiatives underway, all of which get promoted via social media and the press, that the public is having a hard time figuring out what to latch on to. As you recall with the blind-men-and-the-elephant metaphor, this completely confuses the audience as to what you're all about.

Politics have a way of sharply illustrating the incredible effectiveness of a central theme and the devastating consequences when there isn't one, lessons all businesses need to learn as well. During the 2016 election, Donald Trump never veered from the central "Make America Great Again" theme emblazoned on his red hats, a theme that energized an organic, zealous movement. Some might have viewed the red hats as kitschy and trite, but they became an iconic symbol that supported and cemented the message, and his target audience *loved* them. Even Bill Clinton acknowledged Trump's strength, warning a group of Democratic donors a full year before the election when many in even the Republican Party weren't yet taking him seriously, "He's a master brander and he['s] sensing sort of the emotional landscape of people he's selling to." Meanwhile, Hillary Clinton tried on at least a half dozen themes ("I'm with Her," "Breaking Down Barriers," and "Stronger Together," to name a few) and covered wide swaths of policy territory unrelated to the theme du jour. An analysis by *The Atlantic* concluded that "…her team's focus on micro-messaging came at the expense of thematic unity." Michael Kazin, professor of history at Georgetown University and editor of *Dissent* magazine, said in 2017, while reflecting on the election, "One of the problems that Hillary Clinton had, and one of the problems that Democrats still have, is people don't really know what we stand for."

For all content, stick to the core theme. If you need to branch off into a specific subtopic, because of the audience, it should still be presented within the context of your overarching theme.

CONVENTIONAL MEDIA, SOCIAL MEDIA INFLUENCERS, KEY BLOGGERS, AND PUNDITS

Approach your target media and, when possible, provide a back-grounding session—a briefing to discuss the trends and your point of view on what's happening, along with what your company is doing. Develop a relationship. If your story has the ABCD ingredients I discussed in the last chapter, it won't be difficult to garner attention. Journalists and bloggers love that kind of material. Meet with them as a thought leader. They don't want to hear about your company or product; they want to learn something new.

Even bloggers willing to write paid placements prefer to only cover meaty topics that enhance their reputations as sources of provocative information.

To reiterate an earlier point, only focus on social media influencers who are true thought leaders themselves and are interested in educating their audiences on new thinking and solutions in a meaningful way.

With the Apollo Method, there is a methodical approach to who you target and when. It's a bit of a game based on how blogs, publications, and social media influencers and pundits feed into one another and the foundation you need to have in place as you work your way through the target list. Your message is built around a market trend and problem. You want to prioritize based on how ready a given blog or publication is to hear it.

You may think that this is one way in which the Apollo Space Program tactics deviated, because the media was much less fragmented and more centrally controlled than today, there was no internet, there was much less noise, and Apollo already had a national platform. It didn't have to go begging for attention. But you'd be wrong. Pre-Apollo, early proponents of manned exploration in space had to work very hard to get others to see and embrace the vision, particularly those in government holding the purse strings. Without these efforts, Apollo wouldn't have come into being, as you'll see in a case study shortly. Likewise, you are likely starting as an unknown but in a wildly noisy, crowded, fragmented environment of media, blogs, podcasts, YouTube, and more. So what to do?

I'll describe how the game typically works, but it really varies by sector. Read what follows, but conduct your own analysis to see if it applies, since there are exceptions. Look to see which stories your ultimate media targets cover and track back to see what path those stories followed to get there. You can even contact a company that's gotten the kind of coverage you want and ask how they did it. (If you work with a PR firm, you'll want one with credentials in your space—one that knows how the game is played among your media targets and has those relationships.) I'll also acknowledge up front that some stories go viral right out of the gate without following the typical trajectory I describe below. Those are fortunate, serendipitous situations that you can hope for but not proactively make happen, at least usually.

Your best bet is to work your way up what I call the Media Food Chain. The more crowded and noisy your market, the more important it is to do this.

In terms of your proactive efforts, you want to start with niche media and work your way up. Yes, like everyone else, you have your media Mt. Everest—your ultimate placement, whether that's the *Wall Street Journal*, CNN, *Oprah*, or a TED Talk on the main stage—thinking that a feature placement in one of those outlets will propel you to stardom and lead prospects to come knocking on your door. Yes, that does happen on occasion, especially for innovations that the general public can easily relate to or new miracle drugs for common maladies. But it's rare for a company to just leap to this kind of exposure. And to attempt to do so will usually just burn up a load of PR budget, getting you nowhere.

Even when a company does land a cover or home page story, as one of my friend's startups did in the *Wall Street Journal*, it often doesn't do one iota of good, because there is no momentum behind it. It may lead to a short-term surge in interest and website traffic, but then you'll quickly fade back to obscurity. The story about my friend's company came out of nowhere and was a flash in the pan. It didn't stick. This was largely because there was no underlying market buzz. You want the big feature story to be a final impetus after a groundswell of support has built, not the initial one. Prospects usually need to hear and read about you numerous times before they'll remember you, be inclined to pick up the phone, or keep talking about you to each other.

Instead, your best bet is to work your way up what I call the Media Food Chain. The more crowded and noisy your market, the more important it is to do this. Let's say your story is currently a small fish. The big news websites and publications are large sharks. The way to land inside the stomach of a great white shark is to work your way up the food chain. Your aim is to get eaten by a mackerel, that's then eaten by a tuna, that's then eaten by the shark. It also turns out that the readership of each type aligns with the sequence in which you'll be going after different categories of buyers. Let's look at what I mean by this.

Innovative ideas typically work their way through a Media Food Chain. Small, edgy information outlets and influencers publish them first, where they are then discovered and consumed by increasingly large and far-reaching outlets.

Publications each have risk profiles as to what they are and aren't willing to cover, which match their readership profiles. The further down the Media Food Chain they are, the more likely they are to take risks in what they cover and be the first to start talking about a trend. This means they're more likely to be read by powerbrokers and influencers who want to keep a finger on the pulse of what's happening and by buyers who want to be the first to try new offerings.

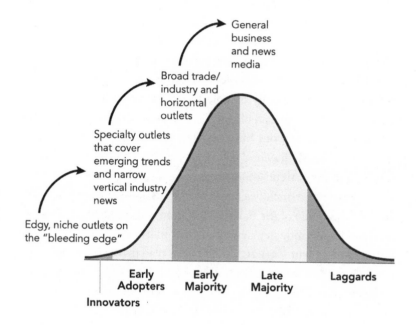

You can map the Media Food Chain in your space to Rogers' Innovation Adoption Curve to help you focus your efforts based on which of your targets they reach.

At the bottom of the Media Food Chain are small, very narrowly focused, edgy social media influencers, publications, newsletters, blogs, and forums that are the first to talk about emerging areas. For example, these are where you would have first read about the internet protocol suite (TCP/IP) in the 1970s, long before there was a World Wide Web. These appeal to buyers in the Innovator category and some of the Early Adopters, meaning they want to be the first to know about any new emerging trend in the space. Publications at the bottom of the Media Food Chain are so niche and so edgy, they have almost a cult-like following. Influential industry bloggers down here on the Media Food Chain are absolutely essential to the ecosystem. They are more than happy to cover "bleeding edge" material. They aren't bound by journalistic standards, don't have editors to answer to, have fluid editorial calendars, move quickly, and like to write about really cool stuff that turns them on—the kind of stuff that gets people's attention and makes them go "Hmmmm." If yours is a niche market, you may actually be able to ignore all traditional media/websites and focus just on bloggers, since they can be so much more effective at reaching your Innovator targets with the right message.

Next on the Media Food Chain are narrow vertical niche publications and news/trend websites that are aimed at the sector's biggest nerds, which includes Innovators plus Early Adopter buyers and perhaps some of the Early Majority. In B2B, anyone who wants to keep up with industry news and emerging trends reads these. In business-to-consumer (B2C), aficionados read them. These publications eat content found at the bottom of the Media Food Chain. The more often they have seen a company or topic popping up in edgy outlets, the more likely they are to pick up the stories. In addition to receiving direct pitches and polling their network of insiders, they mine those edgy blogs, forums, newsletters, etc. for ideas and to see what's new out there. These publications are not written for laypeople. Anyone who can read these publications without falling asleep and actually understands what they're saying is an industry expert or wannabe. They are publications like *American Banker*, *Nation's Restaurant News*, *Mission Critical* (covering data center news and trends), or *The American Lawyer*. In the consumer space, it might be publications for enthusiasts like *Tropical Fish Hobbyist*, *Nuts and Volts*, or *HockeyShot*. There are usually two or three must-read periodicals per sector. They write for audiences in the know. Your target influencers and prospects read them—people in the profession or deeply involved in the topic. These media outlets don't have to dumb anything down. You can use all the jargon you want in content for these publications, and the readers will eat it up. You can be real. The editors of these publications are hungry for leading- (but not necessarily bleeding-) edge material and are fairly accessible because, well, let's face it, they get a little lonely. They don't get approached by nearly as many people as other publications and can quickly sniff out imposters. They get very excited when they meet a true expert with a fascinating point of view.

Narrow vertical trade publications are feeders for broader trade/industry publications and also horizontal publications like *Advertising Age*, *Wired*, *Sports Illustrated*, and so on. These publications cut across a swath of related sectors. It is much more competitive to get their attention, because they are approached by so many more companies trying to get coverage. But guess where they get their ideas? Guess who they use to vet new ideas hitting the market? Yep, you guessed it—the guys below them on the Media Food Chain. They also have much lower risk tolerance. By the time these publications are writing about "new trends," industry insiders often consider the ideas old news. For that reason, they're less interesting to Innovators and Early Adopter types but of big interest to the Early Majority just now getting comfortable with a new trend.

At the top of the Media Food Chain are the general business and news media. They have the lowest risk profile. By the time they write about a trend or big market issue, it's news to people outside the industry but very mainstream and well accepted by insiders. By this point, the Late Majority and Laggards are finally adopting what were once "new" approaches. This means that if you are introducing a rather radical concept, you want a foundation of support for that idea and enough of an understanding among your base market to have it make sense by the time it hits these publications in its dumbed-down version. While there are exceptions, these writers are usually not specialists. The downside of trying to approach them too early is that you have enormous competition; they are incredibly cynical (for good reason, I might add); if you are introducing a new idea they haven't heard from anywhere else, they will be extremely skeptical, and you will have to work incredibly hard to get them to even understand what you're talking about, much less embrace it, which will take more time than you've been allotted; they'll want you to bring them success stories, proof, and additional sources, which you may not yet have; and you'll probably only get one chance, and you just blew it. For these reasons, general business and news get their ideas from publications lower on the Media Food Chain.

Here's a fascinating case study of how this helped make Apollo possible. Had one man in particular not innately understood the power of selling a vision by building a groundswell with Innovators and Early Adopters via the Media Food Chain, the masses may have never taken Kennedy's "Moon Shot" challenge seriously or been willing to pay for it. In the overall scheme of twentieth-century space exploration, Kennedy's announcement was a tipping point in itself—the moment when the hope and fantasy of space travel on the part of enthusiasts over the previous decade transformed into a sense of inevitability in the broader public consciousness.

Had one man in particular not innately understood the power of selling a vision by building a groundswell with Innovators and Early Adopters via the Media Food Chain, the masses may have never taken Kennedy's "Moon Shot" challenge seriously or been willing to pay for it.

The man's name was renowned rocket scientist Wernher von Braun, one of over 1,500 scientists, engineers, and technicians from

Nazi Germany who were secretly recruited by the US government after World War II to assist with postwar military research and who later became a pivotal member of the Apollo team.

Before von Braun's arrival in the US, a shift in popular culture had begun to occur, thanks to science fiction. Jules Verne kicked things off in 1865 with the publication of *From the Earth to the Moon*, a first imagining of a human Moon landing grounded in science and rough calculations of what it would take. H. G. Wells mentioned this novel in his own fictional *The First Men in the Moon*. Verne and Wells then both inspired the first science fiction film, *A Trip to the Moon*. All of these were read and watched mainly by kids and aficionados. Innovators in modern rocketry credited Verne's novel with igniting their imaginations as kids, while Late Majority thinkers like the *New York Times* thought the notion of rockets in outer space "absurd."

In the late 1930s and throughout the 1950s, authors like Isaac Asimov and Arthur C. Clarke wrote factually grounded space fiction drawing from their backgrounds as scientists. Ray Bradbury's ability to humanize stories turned him into a science fiction legend. These and many other writers at the time credited Verne and earlier authors of the genre for inspiring them. Westerns were still the dominant genre in books and on TV in the US, but demand for science fiction began to grow. Von Braun, who had been evangelizing a clear vision for travel not just to the Moon but also to Mars to anyone who would listen, had also been writing space fiction but had not managed to get it published.

Then a magazine editor decided to send two skeptical reporters to the First Annual Symposium on Space Travel for geeks in 1951. They were from *Collier's*, a national magazine that had once boasted over 2 million readers but was now languishing and desperate for a way to renew interest. Intrigued after hearing von Braun and other presenters, reporter Cornelius Ryan reconnected with von Braun a couple of weeks later at an Air Force convention. Over dinner and drinks, the charismatic and riveting von Braun shared his vision in detail, turning Ryan into an enthusiastic convert. Ryan went back and convinced his editor to stake the future of the publication on the topic by convening its own symposium and publishing a 1952–54 series of space-related issues written by experts like von Braun. Much of von Braun's content came from his earlier attempts at space fiction. What made these issues unique within the genre was the credibility of the authors as deep experts and the investment in groundbreaking illustrations that made readers realize just how doable it was to send humans to the Moon. While 15 percent of Americans polled in 1949 thought it possible to reach the Moon, that number rose to 38 percent by 1955. Heavily promoted with help from the authors, the event and series were a smash hit.

Reflecting on his reaction as an eleven-year-old reader, Apollo scientist Albert A. Jackson described the life-changing impact of the issue headlined, "Man on the Moon: Scientists Tell How We Can Land There in Our Lifetime," and his reaction to the spaceship illustration: "The detail! How could it be so real? I took that issue to my room…That week I must have read that issue twenty times!"

Collier's turned von Braun, both an effective salesman and maven, into a luminary spokesman, sending him on press junkets and booking him on national news programs and national talk shows, where he shared his vision for manned space travel using scale models. The series and surrounding promotions stirred up a national conversation among enthusiasts and some in the general public. But its influence didn't stop there.

Further up the Media Food Chain, Walt Disney had asked veteran animator Ward Kimball to produce some "science factual" episodes for *Disneyland*, his weekly television series and fourth-most-watched show in the country. Kimball took notice of the *Collier's* series and engaged von Braun and others to help him produce three episodes, "Man in Space" (1955), "Man and the Moon" (1955), and "Mars and Beyond" (1957). Von Braun, by now a polished on-camera presenter, captivated audiences in the first episode with his presentation of how a four-stage passenger rocket could be ready in ten years. His close collaboration with Disney animators and defense contractors resulted in realistic depictions that were scientifically accurate and convincing to viewers.

One viewer it "sold" was even further up the Media Food Chain: President Eisenhower, who watched with the rest of the country and personally called the studio the next morning to request a copy so he could share it with Pentagon officials. A few months later, Eisenhower announced that the US would launch its first satellite during 1957. Though this had been in the works, Nebraska senator Carl T. Curtis told his senatorial colleagues that Disney had played a role through "Man in Space" and had therefore done a great service for both the government and the people.

According to *Marketing the Moon* researchers and authors David Meerman Scott and Richard Jurek, in referring to US preparation for the space age at the time of *Sputnik 1*'s shocking launch, this journey up the Media Food Chain paved the way for government and public acceptance of subsequent plans to go to the Moon:

> …Walt Disney, *Collier's*, and Wernher von Braun played pivotal roles in that preparation by envisioning an optimistic future…In less than a decade, space travel had emerged from the realm of children's adventure stories and the domain of rocketry and science fiction hobbyists to the world of front-page headlines.

Bottom line: Start with the specialists, get talked about and quoted, and then work your way up. It will be a much more efficient approach, cost a lot less, and lead to more success.

Be sure to always try to offer something of value that will motivate readers to take action, such as downloading a free e-book elaborating on your point of view covered in the article. This will also help you identify interested people, build your contact database, and continue to nurture those relationships.

CONFERENCES/MEETINGS/EVENTS/PODCASTS

Industry events are an essential, efficient way to quickly gain exposure, especially in B2B, because they bring together a concentration of your target audience. And that audience is there to learn something new and get inspired.

The bad news is that many live events are "pay to play," meaning many speakers must pay their way onto the dais, either directly or via sponsorships. You thought they were up there because someone had deemed them as "special," didn't you? Nah. They had a budget.

The good news is, there are exceptions: when someone has something very fresh and provocative to say, and event organizers think their audience needs to hear it. This is where you come in. You're armed with your provocative point of view. You've been written up in the trade press. You've met with industry movers and shakers. There is a soft hum of growing buzz about what you have to say. It's very possible that your efforts to line up speaking engagements will bear fruit, even if you have no budget. Despite the bootstrapped early days of Salesforce, Marc Benioff had no trouble getting invited to speak at technology conferences because he was so willing to stir things up. Who else would have stood up in front of hundreds or even thousands of people in the software business and proudly announced that software was dead?

There is often a food chain for events similar to the one I described above for publications, which also aligns with audience profiles.

If your luminary has name recognition and is a draw—if s/he will put "butts in seats," as event organizers like to say—you also have a good chance of getting on the agenda. When I was the producer for Entrepreneurship Week at Stanford, we were especially interested in getting big-name speakers for the opening and closing events, which is typical. We cared less about the details of what they presented (as long as it was of interest to the audience, of course) and more about filling the room. The right name was going to be a hit, regardless, so we frequently invited top venture capitalists and celebrity entrepreneurs to speak. I have a client whose luminary is a big name in the wireless industry, and we have no problems getting him onto conference agendas.

If you don't have the budget, go for it anyway. You may just have to start with lower-tier events, which is fine. There is often a food chain for events similar to the one I described above for publications, which also aligns with audience profiles.

Be prepared for long lead times, because events are usually planned months, if not years, in advance. This may be where you face the steepest uphill battle, and it can be a slog. In the meantime, don't discount small groups, local chapter trade association meetings, and other such venues. Sometimes it's wise to take control and organize your own in-person events or webinars if you can involve an influencer, have some budget, and have the ability to attract the right people. Just be aware that there is a huge amount of competition for target buyers' time, and the cost and effort to get people to show up may exceed the benefits. It's usually better to initially leverage other people's audiences.

Like Al Gore, give the same stump speech as many times as possible to as many people as possible. You may have to tailor it slightly by audience, but don't deviate from the fundamental storyline. Continually refine this stump speech. Constantly improve it based on how audiences react and how your thinking evolves as you give it.

Your goal with these presentations is to have people coming up to you. They should be enthusiastically thanking you for such a provocative presentation. They should be flocking around you to ask questions, get your business card, and give you theirs. They should be visiting your website to download a free, informative piece of content that you offered during the presentation (e.g., that e-book mentioned above). And ideally, every presentation leads to invitations to address more audiences. If these things are not happening, you need to refine your presentation and approach.

Sometimes the "show don't tell" strategy is the best way to draw attention to your philosophy and unique approach. In 1909, Walter Davidson proved just how tough his new company's motorcycle was by entering and winning the 7th Annual Federation of American Motorcyclists Endurance and Reliability Contest with a perfect score of 1,000 points, thus making the Harley-Davidson case for toughness.

STEP 5

Publish Thought Leadership and Draw Attention to It

Earlier I mentioned the extraordinary volume of prepackaged stories, newsreels, and information NASA provided. This stream of information over the years set NASA apart from the secretive Soviets and positioned it as a technology leader. Just to reinforce to you how extensive and detailed its thought leadership content was, the *Apollo 11* press kit alone was 250 pages of manually typed mission specifics and hand-drawn diagrams, including a full storyboard of what would happen during the mission and a second-by-second explanation of the countdown. By providing so much technical detail, it could control the messaging, ensure the media would get the details right, and preempt thousands of inquiries. It also established credibility with science and technology thought leaders. (If you're curious, many of the vintage press kits by both Apollo and its corporate partners are available at www.apollopresskits.com.)

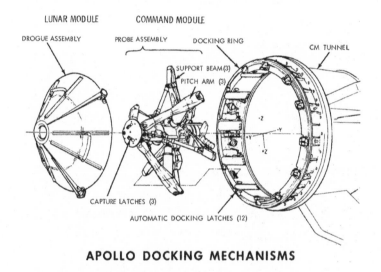

APOLLO DOCKING MECHANISMS

This diagram from the *Apollo 11* Press Kit is an example of the technical detail NASA freely shared to ensure the media could serve as an accurate information conduit to the public. *(Source: NASA, page 95)*

For reasons we talked about in chapters 2 and 3, thought leadership is absolutely critical for sustainable differentiation. It sets you apart from me-too products or services. It demonstrates that you have purpose and a commitment to eliminating the market problem you're focused on.

When others write about you, there is no control over when or how they present the message and material. The beauty of publishing your own material as bylined articles, blog posts, reports, and so forth is that you have almost complete control. You can also measure the reach and capture data about who is devouring it. More importantly, readers get to experience your expertise firsthand. It's a terrific way to build credibility, convey your point of view, and entice people to contact you.

Harley-Davidson understood this back in 1916 when it started *Enthusiast*, the world's longest continuously published motorcycle magazine, now known as *H.O.G. Magazine.*

The primary goal of content produced for the purposes of the Ignite phase is to literally lead the market's thinking around a particular issue—hence the term, "thought leadership."

Much of the activity in this step falls under the realm of what's commonly called content marketing, except there are a few rules when you're working to establish a Go-To market position:

1. Content must have an educational, intellectual (rather than blatantly promotional) bent.
2. All of the content you produce must hang together, as discussed earlier.
3. Content must be of very high quality and high value to the target audience.

The primary goal of content produced for the purposes of the **Ignite** phase is to literally *lead the market's thinking* around a particular issue—hence the name, "thought leadership." Once it becomes promotional, it's no longer thought leadership; it's sales material and belongs in the **Navigate** phase. Yes, it's possible to kill two birds with one stone by combining thought leadership and promotion in a single deliverable, and in some cases, you'll want to. And whenever possible, you still want to capture data about who is accessing the content, when, how, where, and so on. However, *this distinction in purpose is important to understand.* Once you taint something with the promotional component, audience walls go up and you diminish the power of that piece to build your company's credibility as the preeminent thought leader on that issue. It's human nature. People are wide open to ideas as long as they perceive that you are providing the information to help *them* and not you. The second they detect even a whiff of self-serving intent, they shut down.

There are many categories of material. Once again, the Apollo Method manner of executing this standard marketing technique is to stick to your theme. Here are examples of tactics you might consider (in alphabetical order and not prioritized); this is by no means a comprehensive list:

- Annual reports
- Articles authored and published by you
- Articles authored by you and published by someone else
- Assessments
- Awards and accolades won by you (with thought leadership presented during the application process)
- Awards issued to others by you
- Blogs
- Books (print and/or electronic)
- Branded content tools (e.g., a retirement planning calculator, templates)
- Case studies
- Contests/competitions
- Games/gamification
- Infographics
- Landing pages
- Licensed/syndicated content
- Messaging

- Microsites
- News releases
- Periodicals, both print and electronic (e.g., newsletters, magazines)
- Podcasts
- Presentation content distributed online or in print
- Quizzes
- Research study results and reports
- Social media posts
- Videos
- Webinars
- White papers

Online searches such as "content marketing examples" or "sample content marketing deliverables" will yield many additional, creative options. There is no shortage of possibilities, with new ones coming along every day. And that's the problem—too many options, too little budget or time. How do you choose?

The key is to efficiently deliver what will be of value to the audience and set you apart via your provocative point of view and any evidence that demonstrates its veracity. All of the content must serve three purposes:

1. Propagate your point of view to get people bought in and have the right ones self-select in
2. Help you identify who is drawn to your message
3. Generate market discussion and demand for solving the problem in the way you're prescribing (and if your approach is fresh and unique, it naturally leads people to your offering)

The other key is to find ways to most efficiently get the content in front of the largest possible pool of your powerbroker and influencer targets. There are hundreds of ways to do this, ranging from purchased or rented lists to paid-search campaigns to article placements in trade publications, to paid content syndication (services like Outbrain and Taboolah that propagate your content in other locations such as news websites). The built-in audiences and targeting capabilities of LinkedIn (for B2B), Facebook (for B2C), and niche sites make them very valuable. The challenge is that all of this can get very expensive very fast. You'll need to be extremely focused and find the best but fewest ways to reach your initial core targets that will serve as kindling to light up the rest of the market. You also want to repurpose as much of your content as possible for the various outlets. For example, a core piece of content can become a white paper, blog post, presentation, webinar recorded and then released as a podcast, long-form video and associated clips, series of Tweets and Instagram posts, and more.

Remember, you're not trying to reach your broader audience at this point. You're trying to reach and convert the core group of people that the rest of your audience respects and listens to. You want this core group to become disciples who then take your message to the masses for you.

The hard part is rising above the noise. Even credible news sites now stoop to "click bait" and celebrity gossip to generate hits. There is so much content now online that it's very challenging to be noticed. High-quality, in-depth, provocative, and very focused content is essential to reaching your targets.

Remember, you're not trying to reach your broader audience at this point. You're trying to reach and convert the core group of people that the rest of your audience respects and listens to. You want this core group to become disciples who then take your message to the masses for you.

There is a tremendous amount of material available online regarding how to develop and publish thought leadership content. Here are a few points specific to the Apollo Method approach or that address common mistakes:

- Early content should convey your overarching point of view, rather than focusing on narrow aspects—once your audience is clear on the big picture of what you stand for, you can peel the onion with articles, white papers, posts, and more that get into more detail on specific subtopics.
- Leverage other people's audiences as much as possible (e.g., via partnerships, guest blogging, bylined articles, content syndication, etc.)—it's very expensive and takes time to build your own audience and following organically, so jump-start with others' audiences.
- The same "Media Food Chain" strategy regarding publications applies to bylined article placements—build your die-hard following by starting with very focused websites, blogs, and publications.
- White papers and e-books can be very effective credibility tools for getting into more detail and providing more technical explanations on a topic.
- Beware that a blog and other social media tools are beasts you need to feed, so start these only once you know you can maintain a steady pace of activity.
- Take a highly strategic approach to your editorial calendar, rather than random ideas and brainstorms—plan the stream of content that will reach, convert, and excite your target influencers, who will then pass the message along on your behalf.
- Propagate content created by others that directly or indirectly supports your point of view.

- Your website should play a market development role in addition to the sales support role it usually plays. It can do this via the blog or in itself; make it an information hub for the industry—a place people want to come to and a place they stumble upon as they search for information related to your theme. Entice them to subscribe and keep coming back.

Some companies successfully bake thought leadership into their products as further differentiation. Online survey tool SurveyMonkey does this well. As you build a survey within its tool, it offers helpful tips and question-design aids as features within the offering itself that provide value-added expertise. The goal is to help the customer get the audience insights s/he is seeking through the survey. All of this reinforces the company's core positioning and sets its offering apart.

A common fear is that competitors will latch on to one's thought leadership and innovative ideas or that customers won't need the company or offering because you've "given too much away" through published content. Not true.

Despite all that was at stake with the Apollo program and with the Soviets watching so closely, NASA still published those thousands of detailed documents made freely available to the press. And this drove a thirst for more.

Wayne Harrison knew this all too well. He was a reporter for KMHT AM radio in rural Marshall, Texas, a station that reached just 30,000 people. He shared all of the information he could get out of NASA with his audience—tapes, packets, press kits, whatever—which generated even more demand from listeners. With no budget, he used his own vacation days to travel to Houston's Manned Spacecraft Center for the *Apollo 11* launch. He gave them firsthand, blow-by-blow coverage using a makeshift live feed by furtively running a cable down the hallway to a pay phone.

The irony is that the more thought leadership content you provide and the more informative and detailed it is, the more it generates demand for what you're offering. This is because it demonstrates enormous credibility; audiences quickly realize how complex the topic really is and how hard it is to do; the right customers would rather pay someone to jump in and get it done for them than fumble along on their own. By providing so much in-depth knowledge in advance, you've prequalified yourself/your offering, and buyers dive right into discussions of how you can help them.

The irony is that the more thought leadership content you provide and the more informative and detailed it is, the more it generates demand for what you're offering.

The power of freely sharing thought leadership as a way to *ignite* the market is well illustrated by the Stanford Technology Ventures Program (STVP). Some years ago, it started a resource section on its website and called this "Educators Corner." It was literally a corner of the STVP website that contained video clips and other teaching materials from Stanford that any professor could download and use. It became so popular that STVP expanded this corner into a separate website and started managing it like a product. STVP also added lots of new content and features such as podcasts of full lectures, the ability to download or embed videos, translation, transcription, and other popular options. Within a few years, the site had exploded in popularity and use by noneducators, with over 5,000 podcast downloads per day and users coming from over 250 countries. After various iterations since then, the site is now called eCorner and generates enormous traffic as a rich library of videos, podcasts, articles, and more (http://ecorner.stanford.edu). Bloggers frequently reference the content,

STVP receives love letters from users all over the world, and journalists contact the team on a regular basis. Users are the primary marketing engine for the site. It has played a huge role in building STVP's reputation and awareness as a Go-To worldwide, all because of STVPs generosity in freely making its thought leadership available to others.

Beware, though. The "spray and pray" caveat I mentioned earlier applies here as well. You must be sure that your central theme and raison d'être always comes through loud and clear. HubSpot, a rising Go-To in the digital marketing technology space, is all about driving "inbound marketing." It's done a lot of things right, including a seminal book on inbound marketing and building strong name recognition, and it leads some of its target sectors. It's also become a prolific publisher of useful marketing how-to content. A Google search on a given digital marketing topic is very likely to place a HubSpot article at the top. *But* it's *so* prolific that some people initially misperceive it as a *media company* rather than a provider of marketing technology because the primary exposure to its brand is through articles on all things digital marketing. Even knowing it's a technology company, the variety of topics is so wide ranging that one would be hard-pressed to tell you the scope of what its tools do just from looking across its collection of articles. Make sure your core positioning always shines through.

STEP 6

Assume a Leadership Role in Key Organizations to Set the Industry Agenda, Promote the Point of View, and Influence Others

We saw earlier how von Braun's leadership in the space fiction and space exploration subculture played a role in his ascent as a media star bearing the torch on NASA's behalf.

REI, founded by Mary and Lloyd Anderson and twenty-one of their climbing friends to advance their belief in the value of outdoor living, has spent more than twelve years working with the Outdoor Industry Association on economic-impact research. The goal, achieved in 2018, was to gain acknowledgment from influencers and policymakers that outdoor recreation is a major economic driver in the US. At the state level, it works with governors and legislators to ensure they understand the value of outdoor recreation to their local economies and quality of life for constituents. REI is also helping states establish stewardship efforts to protect their outdoor recreation resources. With environment health being a big part of outdoor life, REI has helped found several organizations such as the Sustainable Apparel Coalition. These and many other such activities have helped position it as a Go-To for outdoor living not just among the people who buy from REI but also throughout industry and government.

Here's how you can do this as an individual. I once had an educational entertainment business for children in Atlanta. I was brand new to the industry and had no contacts or network. But my goal was to become a part of the fabric of the industry, even as a complete outsider with absolutely no credentials.

The National Academy of Television Arts and Sciences (NATAS) is the major trade organization I needed to be part of. I joined the local chapter and then called to say I'd like to get involved. I explained my background and asked what the biggest problem area was—which program needed the most help. They told me it was their media literacy initiative, which was an outreach program for teaching children critical-thinking skills related to what they saw and read online and watched on television. I said, "Great. Put me on that committee."

The chairman at the time was incredibly accomplished and a genius in many different fields, but by his own admission, he didn't know much about K-12 education or child development. He also didn't have a lot of time. So I jumped in and contacted other chapters all over the country to find out what they were doing. Apparently, no one else had really asked these questions before, so I was suddenly an expert in what was going on across the national program. I found a local school that would let me come in and teach the program, which again, no one else within NATAS had ever done—taught the course firsthand. I got to know the people at Pacific Mountain Network who were spearheading this for NATAS. We issued a joint news release, and they paid to put it on the news wire and send it to their extensive contact list since I didn't have a budget. I then followed up with media to raise awareness about this terrible problem of children being exposed to sexual, violent, or otherwise controversial content without the proper critical-thinking skills to distinguish fantasy from reality. This was a bizarre message to be coming from the television industry itself, so people were intrigued. We got a lot of press, and this got the attention of the local and national Boards of Governors for NATAS. Atlanta had suddenly mobilized, and they were curious. My committee chair started bringing me to local board meetings to present what we were doing. The president decided I should be on the board and put me up for election. When I didn't get elected, he appointed me. The story continues from there, but you get the idea. In very short order, I went from being an unknown new member with no industry credentials to being on the local board and attending national meetings as a major force behind their pet outreach project, media literacy.

You can do the same thing. Identify the most important organization in your sector. Join. Find out where they need the most help and then go in and really make a difference. You'll be amazed at your rapid ascent as a leader and the kind of influence and credibility it gives you. These organizations are usually desperately hungry for help from people who bring real passion to the task. Your reputation will spread quickly, and it will become a platform for socializing your point of view.

STEP 7

Build Awareness Among Influential "Innovator" and "Early Adopter" Targets/Prospects

This is very similar to step 3, in which you were building a base of support among powerbrokers, only here you are doing this with influencers within your target accounts. This activity is shown as step 7, after powerbroker outreach, because the powerbrokers you meet with serve as channels for reaching these potential buyers and establishing credibility, especially if you have no existing brand recognition. It's the powerbrokers who will get you the meetings and do it with enough conviction to presell the prospect.

Given that your offering is likely unique and possibly on the leading edge, you want to target prospects who fit the Innovator profile—visionaries who want to be ahead of everyone else, buy new innovations first with little or no evaluation, and are willing to be guinea pigs as they help you work out the kinks—they view the early advantage as outweighing those risks. You can also introduce your point of view to select Early Adopter types—companies/buyers who jump in once the new innovation is somewhat proven but who want to be ahead of the pack. They won't be ready to buy yet, but they may be open to hearing your story and engaging in discussion.

In B2B at this stage, when trying to get those first few companies on board, you want situations where just one key person has significant decision power in the company and then shift their thinking. You want to bring them around to a new way of approaching the business problem and have them make the decision to go for it.

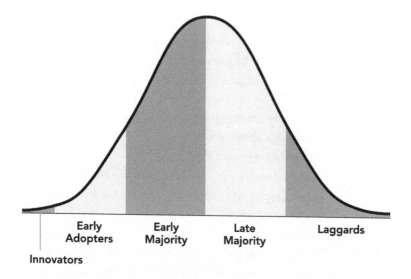

Innovators | Early Adopters | Early Majority | Late Majority | Laggards

Seven months after starting the company, the founding team at Salesforce used personal relationships to find five pilot customers who used the product for free, warts and all. The second customer it signed on was someone the product manager pitched while in line at the grocery store. This gave the team enough feedback and "proof of concept" to raise more money and eventually get the attention of the *Wall Street Journal*. Headlined, "Salesforce.com Takes the Lead In Latest Software Revolution," the article would not have happened without Benioff's provocative, overarching point of view and unique approach to solving a common, critical problem both the reporter and the audience could instantly relate to. In yet another demonstration of how one thing leads to another, that article attracted over a hundred new leads—Innovator types who "got it" and wanted in even though the product was far from being robust. (This was an exception to the Media Food Chain strategy. The Salesforce story skipped to the top of the food chain and won business despite its limited track record, because the market was so hungry for the solution.)

In complex, enterprise sales situations involving an account with multiple decision makers playing various roles throughout the sales process, it will likely be too early to quickly close a deal at this point unless the entire organization and company culture fits the Innovator profile or the Innovator has special influence. Instead, you'll start cultivating the relationship now, since it could take a while. You're seeking a sponsor within the target account who will become an evangelist on your behalf inside the organization. Your activities with these buyers will continue into the **Navigate** phase, when you will get deeper into the selling process (more discussion on this in the next chapter).

In B2C, you're focused on winning over the consumers that others listen to (e.g., social media influencers). Choose carefully. You don't want the ones who will just get paid to promote you but the ones who are true fans. You may actively sell to them, or you may give away free samples to get them on board and turn them into evangelists.

Harley-Davidson's early sales were to skilled, "tough" riders who really put the bikes to the test. In 1911, winners of seven different races, endurance contests, and hill climbs were all riding Harley-Davidson motorcycles, which gave the company enormous credibility.

Walt Disney had been incubating the idea of a clean, family-oriented theme park depicting the magical worlds from his films for years. In 1952, he formed a small company to realize the vision and entered a partnership with television network ABC to create and host an hour-long, weekly series called *Disneyland TV*. The arrangement provided benefits on two fronts: proceeds would fund the construction of the new park, but as importantly, the program became an ongoing commercial aimed squarely at his Innovator and Early Adopter targets: kids. This was the baby boomer generation, the largest in America's history, and they determined family spending on travel and entertainment during the post-World War II era of substantial disposable income. On opening day in 1955, there were

15,000 people in line by 10:00 a.m., with almost half of the country watching the celebration on TV. Within ten weeks of opening, the park had hosted 1 million visitors.

In the summer of 2011, Nextdoor, now the Go-To communications platform for over 200,000 neighborhoods in multiple countries, was just an idea. Sarah Leary and her co-founders floated their point of view and concept by a local neighborhood association that had already cobbled together its own makeshift online community tool. According to her:

> As we talked with the group, it was clear that they were interested. They loved the neighborhood map, directory, and ability to track RSVPs for neighborhood events. They were so interested, in fact, that they were concerned we were using the word "test" as we described the service. They wanted to get started right away!

Customers who fit the Innovator profile often take pride in helping companies improve their products and "get them ready for prime time." Microsoft offers a beta testing program in which customers apply to try products before they go on the market. Considered a badge of honor to participate, consumers get to help Microsoft work out the kinks. In the meantime, they become a huge source of word-of-mouth promotion about the new products.

STEP 8

Monitor, Measure, and Refine

As the saying goes, you manage what you measure. Identify the metrics that truly determine what kind of progress you're making. It's often helpful to map these to the customer journey but within the context of the powerbrokers, influencers, and early buyers you're targeting. Are they aware of you? Have they bought into the point of view? Do they understand your unique solution? Do they embrace it? Are they willing to proactively support your point of view and approach? Have they done so? What percentage of your targets have you reached? Monitoring the pipeline using categories/criteria like these will help you measure your traction.

You'll soon start to see where you are and are not getting traction. Analyze your progress and make adjustments. You may need to refine your messaging. Perhaps your approach or offering concept is not as solid as you thought and needs modifications. If your message is resonating with some people but not others, which is off base—the audience you're targeting or the offering? Sometimes we are too quick to think that it's the offering when in fact we're talking to thought leaders or prospects who don't fit the visionary Innovator profile. Instead, the people we're mistakenly talking to are Early Majority types who need more evidence and market momentum than we currently offer. During the early implementation of **Ignite**, you are not going after large numbers of people—the **Ignite** phase is all about quality over quantity. You're trying to get to the right people. So measure on that basis.

In other instances, a few forward-thinking influencers may love the concept, but in talking to more people, you may realize that the market need isn't strong or urgent enough and that you need to modify it. This often results in a pivot—a shift in positioning or the product itself in response to market feedback or readiness.

RECAP AND ACTION ITEM

Your goal is to *ignite* the market and start a movement around your point of view and solution. You'll do this by building your reputation as a major industry player and becoming closely associated with your simple, boiled-down, memorable theme.

- This theme is centered on a common, critical, and urgent business problem most companies in your target sector do or will be facing.
- You are going to frame it in a provocative and counterintuitive manner in order to attract attention and rise above the market noise.
- You are going to be completely consistent, pounding on that same theme over and over and over again. Every communication you put into the market will be built around it. This will help people develop a top-of-mind association between you and the theme.

You will focus your efforts on the most influential and powerful people in your market and the types of customers willing to buy innovative offerings before they're widely adopted, seeking to turn them into evangelists on your behalf.

The more contagious your point of view, the faster and more effectively it will spread and reach a tipping point. Your goal is to establish a groundswell, a rolling-thunder effect, so that you build and gain momentum over time that eventually takes on a life of its own.

ACTION ITEM

Complete the **Ignite** planning worksheet that follows. You can access an online tool or download the worksheet at apollomethod.com. You and your team will get optimal results by first completing the steps outlined in the chapter. However, even based on where you are and what you know today, develop a rough draft now.

Ignite

LEAD A MOVEMENT

Planning Worksheet

Profile your bullseye target market as a whole and by segment in more detail (characteristics, buyer values, culture, etc.)

_____

_____

_____

Who will your luminary be? _____

What must you do to get the internal organization on board?

_____

_____

_____

Who are your bullseye market's top ten powerbrokers and other influencers you must convert to your point of view ("large tree trunks with vast root systems")? Prioritize them.

1. _____   6. _____
2. _____   7. _____
3. _____   8. _____
4. _____   9. _____
5. _____   10. _____

What top ten outlets reach the Innovators and Early Adopters in your bullseye market: Media/podcasts/blogs? Events? Trade organizations? Other vehicles? Prioritize them.

1. _____   6. _____
2. _____   7. _____
3. _____   8. _____
4. _____   9. _____
5. _____   10. _____

What evidence will demonstrate that you are the best at what you do? What makes you truly different from the competition and substitutes?

_____

_____

_____

What handful of tangibles (e.g., content) do you need in order to ignite the market?

_____   _____

_____   _____

_____   _____

_____   _____

What are the top eight things you must do to ignite this market around your point of view (of the items above, plus partnerships, key wins, etc.)? Which three are highest priority?

1. _____   5. _____

2. _____   6. _____

3. _____   7. _____

4. _____   8. _____

What Innovator (and possibly Early Adopter) buyers will you convert to your point of view? Which could become your partner in refining the offering?

_____   _____

_____   _____

_____   _____

_____   _____

CHAPTER 7

NAVIGATE PHASE

Guide Customers along the Journey to Solving the Problem

We talked in the previous chapter about Al Gore's success years ago in sounding the alarm bells to *ignite* a movement around global warming. Why, then, did we make so little progress that scientists today are still sounding the alarm bells? Certainly people must have gotten the message by that point. Gore had a clear point of view, backed by sound science and strong emotional impact. He brought the topic to the forefront of social consciousness across the US and possibly the world. He even won the Nobel Peace Prize. What happened?

He didn't offer a solution.

Al Gore was clear in his setup of the problem and what needed to be done about it, but he didn't offer audiences a specific approach. He stopped short of implementation. And implementation, of course, is where the rubber meets the road. You are nowhere without it.

Yes, Gore's talk convinced me that as a society we had to do something about this. But I didn't walk out with the actions I should personally take. The problem seemed so big and my potential impact so small that it seemed my personal role was inconsequential. That was wrong, of course. Surely, there are many actions I and others could have taken then to have cumulative impact. Gore got everyone fired up about the problem but missed the opportunity to mobilize them. What he needed as the final piece of his talk was an action plan each person, each family, each community could implement. He needed to offer a specific approach and have a mechanism in place to help all of us get it done. For example, he could have challenged every person in the US to use one less set of plastic utensils per month, stating that this one small action alone would result in the equivalent of taking 26,000 cars off the road every year. He could have had some organizations lined up in advance to help individuals and institutions along a journey to do their part in slowing or stopping global warming. He could have encouraged people to join a particular organization he'd lead for a centralized push toward the goal. People would have signed up in droves.

Implementation, of course, is where the rubber meets the road. You are nowhere without it.

Unless you have a solution, your point of view is just rhetoric. The underlying strategy of the **Navigate** phase is to start working with the *right* types of early customers, gain market traction, and importantly, deliver and *get paid well* for high-value outcomes rather than mere products or services.

A *key distinction* from business as usual is that in **Navigate**, you sell and price your offering based on the value you provide rather than the product or service itself—value that customers are happy to pay more for.

OVERVIEW

The **Navigate** phase is all about walking your talk. In **Launch** and **Ignite**, you tell the world what you're all about, but **Navigate** is where you win customer business and deliver on your promises. We call it **Navigate**, because you are leading customers along the journey toward a solution to their problem, culminating in meaningful, ideally measurable, results customers are willing to pay a premium for, because they are so valuable. If you can't deliver remarkable value to customers by truly solving their problems, you're not doing your job. You're also not generating high-margin revenue. And you don't have a long, bright future ahead of you. The key is to develop your offerings, create partnerships, assemble a team of rainmakers and delivery people, win clients, and execute for them.

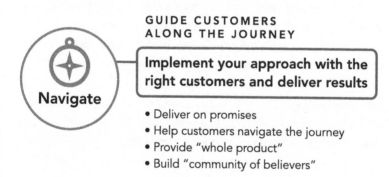

GUIDE CUSTOMERS ALONG THE JOURNEY

Implement your approach with the right customers and deliver results

- Deliver on promises
- Help customers navigate the journey
- Provide "whole product"
- Build "community of believers"

The goal is customer impact. Salesforce doesn't just drop software in your lap (in the form of a cloud-based tool). It offers access to a cadre of implementation experts who can help you set your business up on its platform or convert your existing data and processes over. It provides an entire ecosystem of add-on products and services directly and through partners, which add value to the platform based on your unique needs. It offers community with other users, should you wish to get advice or adopt best practices. It offers an entire "Success Cloud" to accelerate and assist with getting maximum value from its products through coaching, administrative assistants you can delegate tasks to, training, and more. Every day, it offers dozens of free online events and training sessions aimed at helping customers achieve business results using its products.

Harley-Davidson would be nowhere without loud, heavy, go-the-distance motorcycles that live up to its reputation among the rebels and rebel wannabes it targets and that justify premium pricing; marketing outreach that gets customers to walk through the door; its network of over 1,500 dealers staffed with salespeople who sell customers on not just a motorcycle but a lifestyle; and most of all, its rabid and loyal customer community.

The **Navigate** phase is the crux of the business, where you generate your revenue and high margins. By providing superior, bundled value and keeping costs modest, you are able to price your offerings at high margins that feel like a bargain to customers.

Like Al Gore, with the right **Launch** and **Ignite** execution, you might do a great job of building a market perception as a Go-To, but you won't be able to sustain it without delivering on your promises with real, paying customers and genuine experience in the trenches. And, of course, you won't build a sustainable business and margins that enable investments in your future growth.

By providing superior, bundled value and keeping costs modest, you are able to price your offerings at high margins that feel like a bargain to customers.

NAVIGATE Toward Results

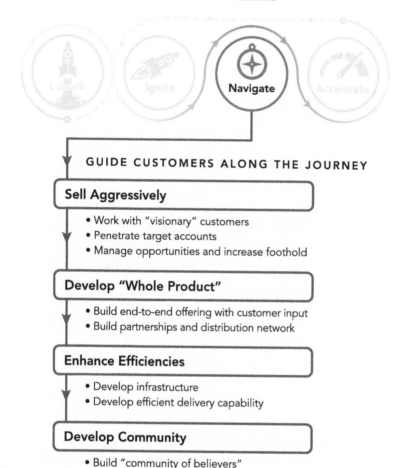

The biggest change in the **Navigate** phase to what most companies already do is the emphasis on delivering and pricing for results and outcomes rather than functions, features, and capabilities. Part of the way you accomplish this is by bundling various products and/or services so that customers can't get into apples-to-apples comparisons to your competitors. You want them to fix their attention on the results you're promising. A simple example is the five-year maintenance package that car dealerships offer. Customers are really buying peace of mind. They know that for at least the next five years, they won't have to pay much, if anything, out of pocket for maintenance and repairs. They have no idea as to what the piecemeal costs break down into. They just know that for one price, they are set for five years. In order to keep you focused on this distinction, I'm going to hereafter refer to your offerings as *solutions*, rather than products or services.

The biggest change in the Navigate phase to what most companies already do is the emphasis on delivering and pricing for results and outcomes rather than functions, features, and capabilities.

When you arrive at a Disney theme park, you're not paying the premium they charge just so you can jump onto some cool rides. You're paying for an utterly unique day (or more) of delight immersed in your favorite childhood films at "the happiest place on Earth" in an atmosphere that no other theme park can emulate. It's a bundled offering. You're paying for a complete, fantasy experience that begins before you even go through the gate, starting with a beautifully landscaped photo op and status as a "guest," not a customer. Cast members (as park workers are called) randomly bestow Magic Moments upon unsuspecting guests, such as a free ride photograph. Disney characters pose with and trade collectable pins with guests. The surroundings come straight out of your favorite Disney movie sets and are perfectly manicured; trash barely touches the ground before being scooped up by a cast member; ubiquitous music keeps the mood light; and a mobile app lets guests make or change ride reservations, monitor wait times, and order food. There are shows, movies, rides, shops, jaw-dropping parades, and in case you didn't get enough during the day, a fireworks show at night. Should you choose to stay on-site at a Disney resort, the magic continues around the clock.

In addition to this bundled-solution and pricing approach, two other key differences with the **Navigate** phase are the emphasis on rainmakers as opposed to just salespeople, and the role of fostering a "community of believers" among your customers. We'll cover both of these in a bit more detail shortly.

Otherwise, the **Navigate** phase encompasses what most businesses already do but with refinements that result in more effective demand generation and greater impact on clients. The scope of **Navigate** is very broad, and there are dozens of books, methods, and other sources of information that cover each step of this phase and the subtopics within it. *I don't cover the basics in this chapter; instead, I'll focus on special twists you need for each and lessons from interviews, other extensive research, and my own school of hard knocks.*

Two other key differences with the Navigate phase are the emphasis on rainmakers as opposed to just salespeople, and the role of fostering a "community of believers" among your customers.

In traditional terms, the **Navigate** phase encompasses running the business. It covers standard functions such as:

- Demand generation and field marketing (building on what you're doing in **Ignite**)
- Business development and sales
- Solution creation, pricing, marketing, and management

- Solution delivery
- Business operations

Here is what you are trying to achieve during **Navigate**:

- Get your first customers, who collaborate to help you design, build, and possibly even market the solution.
- Find partners who help you develop and market the solution.
- Develop a bundled solution with value-based pricing that offers healthy contribution margins.
- Actively take your solution to market, still focusing on Innovators and Early Adopters until it begins to catch on with the Early Majority.
- Implement demand generation and sales enablement programs to support direct selling activity and speed the sales cycle.
- Carefully manage your sales resources and hold them accountable.
- Help customers realize tangible benefits by implementing your solution and ensuring success.
- Position the company to scale as needed to support growth.
- Develop a community.

The steps are:

1. Develop an integrated operating plan.
2. Develop sales support materials, teams, and processes.
3. Sell your solution to a few select "visionary" customers and begin to implement and refine it.
4. Establish a fully developed, end-to-end solution ("whole product") that is value priced and uses internal and/or external resources, products, services, etc.

5. Target prospects, pursue and develop relationships, and begin to market and sell the solution more broadly.
6. Build an efficient solution delivery capability (customer service, recruiting, enculturation, training, distribution channels, partners, methodologies, etc.).
7. Carefully manage opportunities and increase your foothold in key accounts.
8. Establish an industry "community of believers."
9. Expand your organization's infrastructure in order to scale.
10. Monitor, measure, and refine.

We'll get into the details shortly. As with the other phases, execution of the **Navigate** phase is going to be iterative. Even in large companies, the key drivers are usually funding and staffing—what you can reasonably expect to achieve with available resources. For example, large or small, in year one you may only be able to execute a few essentials, such as a minimum viable solution, some basic digital marketing activities for demand generation, and a key marketing partner who helps you target just one geographic market. In year two, you build on those to also develop some sales tools, version 2.0 of your solution, and partners who help you reach additional markets. And so on.

While the Apollo Space Program was not a for-profit venture, it certainly still had to execute the **Navigate** phase flawlessly and deliver a return to its investors, the American taxpayers—It had to deliver on the promise of putting a human on the Moon and constantly prove the value of doing so. It was effectively a bundled offering with a price tag tied to a result. Every **Navigate** step applied, in its own way, to Apollo. For starters, it was an enormously complex undertaking that required extraordinary operational planning and coordination. NASA had 10,200 employees and 36,500 contractors when Kennedy arrived in the White House in January 1961. By the end of 1962, it had ramped up to 23,700 employees and 115,000 contractors. By the mid-1960s, Apollo had 20,000 corporate partners, engaged dozens of universities, involved 34,000 NASA employees, and 375,000 outside contractors, and had teams in hundreds of locations across the country, plus some overseas.

Apollo was in constant fundraising and selling mode. Its "venture capitalists" were members of Congress, and NASA had to tirelessly ensure the funding would continue at the levels needed to achieve the goal. That funding was never a given. There was frequent debate throughout the 1960s as to the value of the program and whether to cut the budgets or change the priorities. Rarely was more than 50 percent of the public in favor of the program cost, though 80 percent favored the concept when not considering its expense. Congress, and therefore NASA, were accountable to their "customers," which were the American public. It also operated under three different presidential administrations and could have therefore been wiped off the map at any moment. In addition to political lobbying, NASA used the media and especially the marketing departments of its corporate partners to constantly "sell" the program to American citizens. Dozens of campaigns by companies like Del Monte, Omega, Ford, and General Foods touted their affiliation with Apollo and stirred public interest with ad copy like, "Everybody who's been to the Moon is eating Stouffer's."

Meanwhile, of course, NASA had to develop more than just innovative product in the form of rockets and spacecraft; there were other "whole product" elements involved, such as satellite communications, mission control, launch infrastructure, massive computing resources, and research efforts such as the sheer physics of landing an object on the Moon and getting it back into lunar orbit. NASA was responsible for the full end-to-end solution, so to speak, even though it was depending heavily on outside partners. Like any company, NASA had to build an efficient supply chain and "delivery capability" by recruiting and training thousands of people, working with its partners like Boeing, Lockheed, and Ford, and establishing methodologies that would ensure high-quality output. The complexity was mind-numbing. The *Saturn v* rocket alone had more than 3 million parts such as nuts, bolts, washers, circuit boards, and transistors. The command and service module had almost 2 million parts. The lunar module had 1 million parts, and weight was such a sensitive factor that NASA paid prime contractor Grumman (now Northrop Grumman) a $50,000 bonus *for every pound* of weight it could design out of the vehicle—that's over $383,000 per pound in today's dollars.

Execution of the Apollo Space Program—what it took to put a human being on the moon for the first time—was extraordinarily complex. *(Image: NASA)*

Apollo was a manufacturing operation building spacecraft and other equipment. It was a services organization helping astronauts use sophisticated simulators to practice space rendezvous and orbital docking. It was a training boot camp teaching astronauts about geology, how to collect soil samples in bulky space suits, how to move in zero gravity, how to operate the spacecraft, and even how to survive in the jungle and desert in case an ocean landing didn't go as planned. Teams of experts trained them in grueling walk-throughs of every aspect of each mission and every possible contingency.

NASA had to develop more than just innovative product in the form of rockets and spacecraft; there were other "whole product" elements involved.

It wasn't always smooth sailing. While preparing for the *Apollo 1* mission, three astronauts died (story covered in step 6). Congress was often on the fence about funding. *Apollo 8* had to make a last-minute change and fly to the Moon without the lunar module, because that was behind schedule and not ready. This was a big risk, because that module was meant to be a life raft had something gone wrong, as later happened to *Apollo 13*. As author Jeffrey Kruger puts it in describing *Apollo 8*, the first time humans flew to the Moon:

> Well, of course, the crisis points are in the planning, the crisis points are all in the work that had to be done to make sure the hardware and the software worked, and the crisis points are in all of those maneuvers: the liftoff, the trans-lunar injection (TLI)—the leaving Earth—the LOI—the lunar orbit insertion. All of those critical moments are crisis points, even though

they all worked. Every single thing was a crisis point because it had never been done before.

As part of its **Navigate** phase, Apollo built two communities of believers, both of which were essential to its public support and continued funding. First, there were members of the media. NASA Public Affairs and corporate partners fostered a deep sense of community among reporters by developing personal relationships with them, helping them bond with each other, feeding them detailed information they would need in order to educate the public, and conducting a two-day symposium to teach them the details of how the lunar module would actually land on the Moon. The other community was the American public. To generate excitement and sell the program, NASA deployed astronauts to give talks at civic organizations and schools. It created and distributed educational documentaries. Members of Congress frequently asked them to come talk to constituents—senators and representatives voting in favor of the massive budgets needed their taxpayers to understand the value of the program through personal interaction.

As the operation scaled, so did the infrastructure. NASA had a small Washington, DC, headquarters and three research centers in 1960. As Apollo ramped up, it expanded its existing research centers and added three new facilities: Houston, Cape Canaveral, and Mississippi.

And to "monitor, measure, and refine," NASA had detailed processes in place. One could write a book just on this topic, but they included technical reviews every step of the way; quarterly program operating plans that rolled up from field operations to track expenditures and keep them on track; quality assurance teams and elaborate program management, schedules, and key performance indicators. For example, during the review of failings that led to the *Apollo 1* fire you'll read about in step 6, NASA had precise metrics to look back on, such as Engineering Orders (design changes): 113

that had not been implemented at the time of command module delivery, 623 submitted subsequent to delivery of the module, and 22 not recorded at all.

Apollo was a massive program. What about smaller companies or even startups? Does all of this apply? Yes. It's just a matter of scale. Regardless of size, **Navigate** is by far the most challenging phase, not just for Apollo but also for any company, especially startups. Can you deliver a product or service customers will pay for? Will they come back for more? Can you generate revenues quickly enough and at high enough margins to sustain you? Can you build a loyal customer base?

In a talk at Stanford, Elon Musk reflected on how tenuous both SpaceX and Tesla were in 2008:

> ...when we started SpaceX and Tesla, I mean, I really thought the probability of success was very low. I mean it wasn't like I thought, "Oh, it will definitely be successful." I thought it would be maybe 10 percent likely. Yeah. And we came very close to both companies not succeeding in 2008. We'd had three failures of the SpaceX rocket. So we were zero for three. We had the crazy financial recession, like the Great Recession. The Tesla financing round had fallen apart, because it's pretty hard to raise money for a startup car company if GM and Chrysler are going bankrupt...
>
> And fortunately, at the end of 2008, the fourth launch— which was the last launch we had money for—worked for SpaceX. And then we closed the Tesla financing round, as you know, Christmas Eve, 2008—last hour of the last day that was possible.

Again, this chapter covers a very broad, complex scope of activity in the typical business. It's not feasible to cover it in-depth in a single chapter. Also, be aware that, while the steps below are presented as a sequence, in reality many involve parallel efforts. Or the sequence may be different for you, based on your circumstances, available resources, or market. Or there may be some components that you should not do at all until others are in place. It's critical that you know your market and execute the minimum required to achieve the goals. Keep your efforts as strategic, streamlined, and focused as possible, and then build on success from there.

STEP 1

Develop an Integrated Operating Plan

NASA administrator (CEO equivalent) James Webb often said that Apollo's success hinged more on proper management than anything else. The technological challenge was within reach. It was the orchestration of the myriad functions, partners, and projects that was critical. To that end, Apollo pioneered an integrated program management approach that exerted centralized control over design, engineering, procurement, testing, construction, manufacturing, spare parts, logistics, training, and operations. *Science* magazine acknowledged the role of this approach in 1968 when it wrote:

> It may turn out that [the space program's] most valuable spin-off of all will be human rather than technological: better knowledge of how to plan, coordinate, and monitor the multitudinous and varied activities of the organizations required to accomplish great social undertakings.

A mistake that many companies make is that they develop their go-to-market, solution development, and operating plans in silos.

Sometimes even the sales and marketing teams don't work in lock-step. Instead, you want to coordinate across all functions. Let your list of target prospects be the key driver—what are you going to sell and deliver to whom and how will you do that most efficiently? The plan needs to cover a specific time frame, include business objectives (desired outcomes), specific tactics, deadlines, person responsible for each, investment budgets, and financial estimates.

Fortune magazine senior editor Adam Lashinsky, who researched and wrote the book *Inside Apple*, says that Apple very carefully integrates every aspect of its business, including design, marketing, product management, manufacturing, engineering, and all other functions, "in a highly regimented, milestone-oriented, planned-out way." And in keeping with its raison d'être, design takes precedence. "At Apple, it would be preposterous for a financial person to tell a designer, 'Oh, we can't do that because it's too expensive.'"

Attesting to importance of tight integration between functions, Pixar Animation Studios co-founder and former president of both Pixar and Walt Disney Animation Studios Ed Catmull told an audience of Stanford students in 2014 that "for me the model is that you know you are an integrated company if you can't draw a line between the technical and the creative."

Your plan should address each of the steps below and answer the following questions, which the rest of the chapter helps you do:

- Who are we going to target?
- What should the customer journey look like, and how will we keep them as customers for life?
- How are we going to get them into the sales funnel and move them through it?
- What are we going to sell them?
- What intellectual property and other offering components do we need to develop?

- How are we going to deliver our offering to these customers and help them achieve results?
- How will we create and build our community of believers?
- What will our organizational and infrastructure needs be and how will we put those in place?
- What are our key success indicators and how will we capture, measure, and respond to those?

Be sure that your plan is fairly straightforward and that everyone's goals are aligned. For example, this is where it's important to ensure field marketing and sales are in sync so that both are working in concert to make the sales funnel "fill and flow." It's not just marketing's job to get prospects into the funnel, and it's not just sales' job to move them through it. It must be a team effort, especially in B2B companies.

Marketing and operations have to also be in sync. Butterball has operated the Turkey Talk Line for consumers every November and December for nearly forty years, during which over fifty experts handle more than 100,000 calls regarding every turkey thawing and cooking question you can imagine. That's in addition to texts and emails. Now, what if the Butterball marketing team were to plan a campaign to encourage dramatically more calls to the hotline? Just hire more call center workers, you might say. Wrong. Staffing the Turkey Talk Line is serious business. First, one must have a four-year degree in a food-related discipline just to apply. Second, applicants are accepted by referral only. Third, all hotline operators must go through extensive, on-site training. While a sudden surge in calls would delight the marketing team, it would wreak havoc on the operations team without plenty of advanced planning. No team in a company should operate in a vacuum.

As you begin to implement the plan, you have more control over some outcomes than others. It's easy to declare a deadline for an email campaign, but you can rarely control how quickly a prospect enters and moves through the sales funnel. Regardless, you need objectives and schedules, since there will be so many dependencies in your plan. And you need to be ready to adjust quickly as realities set in. If sales are coming through more slowly than expected, for example, you'll need to know what investments to cut back on until revenues will support them.

On that note, assume sales cycles are going to be three to five times longer than you think and then plan accordingly, especially when it comes to hiring and other spending. *Rarely* does market adoption occur as quickly as you expect it to. *Rarely* do deals close as quickly as you think they will. Prospects are not operating on your time frame; they're operating on their own. And any number of factors can delay a booked sale. In enterprise sales, even after the deal closes, actual implementation often drags out as well because of dependencies on the customer, even when the customer is seemingly in a hurry to achieve results.

STEP 2

Develop Early-Stage Sales Support Materials, Teams, and Processes

In a perfect world, there is a solution prototyping, design, planning, and development process that builds on what was done during the **Launch** phase. It may involve figuring out the solution specifications, positioning, messaging, value proposition, and other necessary inputs to subsequent marketing deliverables. In large enterprises, there are planning documents and blueprint sales support materials that articulate the competitive situation, elevator pitch, etc., which get debated, tested, and refined. The various stakeholders across departments weigh in and finally come to an agreement on how this solution will be articulated and presented to the market. These inputs then form the basis for final-version sales and marketing materials that are rolled out to sales teams in the field. And, in theory, this step actually comes after you have created the offering with your visionary customers.

But reality is very different.

What I have found in practice is that most companies do not have the patience to go through these initial planning activities in a thoughtful or methodical way. Or the market is moving or changing too fast to allow it. Or companies don't involve customers enough in the design and prototyping phases to ensure that what they're creating is what customers will want.

Often, there is pressure to start selling right away, especially when sales cycles are long, which means sales teams will want at least some marketing deliverables immediately. So what happens is that those early-draft marketing materials become a mechanism for crystallizing the solution's marketing story (critiquing it through the eyes of the buyer) and as a way to refine the solution roadmap. This is especially true for solutions that are too broad and/or complex to prototype (e.g., many complex enterprise solutions that involve a combination of products and services).

I was once helping a provider of data analytics software and services roll out a new offering that would help large banks grow their credit card businesses. It was a very complex solution with a price tag of about $40 million—not something to easily prototype or demo. Instead, we developed sales and marketing materials in partnership with both the solution team and account representatives who would be taking the story to their clients, tailoring the materials as needed. After each presentation they gave, we obtained a detailed debriefing on how the meeting went and the customer's feedback to then refine the story for the next account they'd be approaching. The solution team also incorporated each round of feedback into the solution roadmap and plans.

This isn't ideal and can be less efficient, but it can work. The key is to get customer feedback early and often to see what does and doesn't resonate, just as you did during **Launch** and **Ignite**.

And there is a benefit to this approach. Regardless of how objective the solution/product management team tries to remain, it's almost impossible for them not to take on an insider's bias toward the product and story that they have now fallen in love with. By asking a marketer to work on the market-facing materials and by engaging salespeople in the process, even before the solution is fully baked, you'll uncover weaknesses in the story and product positioning. For example, you may discover that the value proposition doesn't sound as strong as you thought it did. You may realize that the elevator statement doesn't sound as unique and compelling in a one-on-one customer situation as it did when you were talking to influencers who aren't living in the trenches of the business problem.

In the previous banking example, we soon learned that the story was too specialized and complex for account representatives to comfortably deliver. We ended up training subject matter experts to accompany account reps to client meetings and co-deliver the presentation, a strategy I share in the upcoming "SWAT Team" section.

The key is to get customer feedback early and often to see what does and doesn't resonate, just as you did during Launch and Ignite.

Through this process, you may even discover an entirely different market that's more ready to buy than the one you originally targeted. When Apple introduced the Macintosh 128 in 1984, it didn't take off with the intended consumer and business word-processing markets and was even somewhat panned; but it did come to dominate desktop publishing, graphic design, and education, markets that valued its high resolution, unique graphical user interface, and ease of use. Apple listened to feedback from those markets and introduced the then-revolutionary LaserWriter laser printer and PageMaker software to fire up what became the desktop publishing revolution, changing personal computing forever. For the first time, people could instantly produce their own professional-grade publications without using manual graphic layout techniques and a physical print shop.

In the early stages of rolling out a new solution, it may be premature and inefficient to try to set up formalized tools and processes for demand generation purposes—digital marketing initiatives typically geared toward building a database of opt-in "leads," moving them through the sales funnel with drip campaigns (a steady stream of information and interactions designed to engage prospects), and other such activities. You'll get to some of this in step 5, but other programs often come later, unless you are already set up with this capability and can mine an existing customer base for opportunities related to your new solution. In most cases during this early stage, you will focus on activities that accelerate the sales process with a relative handful of innovative customers/prospects who are biting at the bit to solve the problem you focus on. The other "mass" traditional and digital marketing activities come once you've got some market momentum and early customer successes to point to.

SALES ENABLEMENT PLANNING

You may think of Twitter as a B2C company, but it also has an expansive enterprise sales function serving *Fortune 500* companies, marketing agencies, and partners, helped by over 1,200 sales reps. When a new solution comes out, the company needs to arm those people to talk to clients about it and sing from the same songbook.

It does this through sales enablement, the process of enabling, or equipping, a sales team to take an offering to customers. This can include content, content management, training, coaching, and other means. There are any number of essential marketing and sales support materials you may need, but you want to start with the fewest possible. This is because you probably have limited resources and everything could change anyway as you learn what does and doesn't resonate. The fewer deliverables that have to be redone, the better.

Tactics will vary by industry and situation, but do as much as possible through your website, only creating additional deliverables that the website can't provide. (Many companies still produce product spec sheets for sales team use, for example, when they are actually redundant with what you can and should provide on the website.)

Start by taking a hard look at what the market and organization truly needs. Salespeople will sometimes ask for collateral or leave-behinds, but ensure they'll be necessary and effective before producing. Some salespeople use these as crutches, and you're not concerned with the "typical" salesperson right now. You want to engage rainmakers (more on them later) and ask them, "What's the minimum you need in order to sell this?" Think through the sales cycle and customer journey, focusing first on items you need in order to target the right prospects, get them into the sales funnel, get the initial meeting, and then conduct the initial meeting. Items needed for later in the process, like proposal and contract templates, can wait.

The key guideline here is just-in-time materials creation. Only create what's needed to get those first customers into the top of the sales funnel and begin to move them through it. You will save a lot of time and money. I've learned this lesson the hard way by producing elaborate sets of sales enablement tools, only to have to redo them once we started getting market feedback. We would have been better off with just enough to have the first customer conversations and then refine and expand from there, like in the previous banking example.

A formalized plan done in advance will help keep the team focused, because great opportunities and suggestions are going to come at you from every direction—your CEO, your board, your sales teams, your solution teams, outside firms, etc.—and the list of possibilities will far outstrip your budget or execution capacity. The following usually suffice as a start, in order of priority:

- Basic Sales Enablement materials and activities (see next section)
- SWAT team of subject matter experts who do the real selling in concert with a sales rep, who knows the specific account
- Website content
- Demo/trial/samples
- One-stop marketing support
- Basic sales process and operations
- Basic field marketing and business development processes

Each of these is a big topic in itself, so I'll just touch on a few practical tips related to each.

SALES TEAM ENABLEMENT

In his book *Selling Outer Space: Kennedy, the Media and Funding for Project Apollo, 1961–1963*, James L. Kauffman describes some of the ways NASA equipped key program representatives to "sell" the program to Congress and the public:

> Besides working with the astronauts, NASA took great pains to prepare its officials for questions about its programs, especially those officials who spoke before congressional appropriations and authorization committees...NASA not only

coached officials on how to testify at congressional hearings but also provided material describing and justifying its programs directly to the committees. The volume of material grew steadily, so that by 1963, [NASA director] Webb submitted...four volumes of "justification books"...

In this step, you prepare the salesforce to take the offering to market, whether that's just you or legions of sales representatives.

This effort can take many forms. You usually need some internally focused materials and possibly training activities to teach your sales team about the offering; get them excited about its potential at their accounts or with their customers; help them understand who is a candidate for it and how to sell it; and make them effective representatives at their accounts.

Less is more here, especially if your offering is just one of many that a given sales team represents at their accounts. Large, multi-product enterprises such as Oracle, IBM, Conagra, Pepsi, large advertising and marketing firms, etc., have dozens, if not hundreds, of potential products and solutions to offer any given account. These companies' account reps are expected to be familiar enough with the various offerings to pitch them to clients, but an account rep can grasp and remember only so much. You need to offer concise information that is easy to digest and speaks to their core interest: how does it solve my customer's problem, what's the return on investment, and what's in it for me? The following set of materials will often be enough, at least in the beginning:

- A one- to two-page cheat sheet
  - Elevator pitch (one-sentence version of why/what/how)
  - Market problem (problem, who it affects, why, size of problem)
  - Point of view (short summary with link to manifesto)

- Message platform (three sentences on why/what/how)
- Target markets
- Solution description
- Solution infographic
- Key components
- Value proposition (quantified, if possible)
- Use cases, success stories, testimonials, and ROI
- Delivery model
- Buyer personas and qualifying questions
- Expected objections/concerns and suggested responses
- Competitive overview
- Win-loss analysis
- Frequently asked questions
- Internal support resources
- Overview presentation and/or call scripts (for internal use)
- "What It Is and How to Sell It" training session
- Executive presentation (if you need more than what's covered in your stump speech)

The following page has a cheat sheet example. You can get the free template at apollomethod.com.

SWAT TEAM

In the early stages of any offering, especially a solution that is results-oriented and innovative, it's best to designate a small "SWAT team" of experts who actually do most of the presenting during the early stages of the consultative selling process, particularly to Innovators and Early Adopters. This team consists of one or more people with deep, credible expertise in the solution who move from opportunity to opportunity to consistently tell the story.

Facing pushback on the Apollo Space Program shortly after it was rolled out, NASA's SWAT team included Webb and his deputy

Solution Cheat Sheet: (insert solution name)

Elevator Pitch	Market Problem	Point of View

Message Platform	Target Markets	

Solution Description	Solution Infographic	Key Components

Value Proposition	Use Cases/Success Stories/Testimonials and ROI	

Delivery Model		

Buyer Personas and Qualifying Questions	Expected Objections/Concerns and Suggested Responses	

Competitive Overview	Win/Loss Analysis

Frequently Asked Questions	Internal Support Resources

Sample Solution Cheat Sheet Format—see apollomethod.com for an electronic template. *(Source: Apollo Method for Market Dominance)* administrator, Hugh L. Dryden. Between them, they delivered 128 presentations in just eighteen months. NASA took "great care in presenting a consistent, coherent image of the agency and Project Apollo."

Realistically, even your best account executives are not going to be effective messengers of this overarching point of view and your unique approach. They know their customers really, really well. But they usually don't have the overall market vision or the requisite depth of expertise on the cross-market business problem (such that the client will learn something new); and they usually don't have deep functional or technical expertise related to the solution, which means they won't have necessary confidence, conviction, or credibility when talking to clients. You need someone who can walk in and be prescriptive, with authority on the topic, saying to clients, "Here's what we're seeing in the market and what you're going to face, if you aren't already. And here's what you need to do about it." This is especially true when selling to senior executives. The account salespeople won't be able to get into the details of the business issues or counter objections. They *are* experts in the account or territory. Their job is to prequalify opportunities, get the meetings, and bring the SWAT team in to deliver the message and do the selling. Together, the salesperson and the SWAT team member strategize in preparing for the meeting, conduct the meeting, and determine how to follow up.

You need someone who can walk in and be prescriptive, with authority on the topic, saying to clients, "Here's what we're seeing in the market and what you're going to face, if you aren't already. And here's what you need to do about it."

I mentioned Al Burgess, head of Accenture's Communications Industry Group (as it was known in its early days). He was *the* expert in the firm on trends, challenges, and opportunities facing the communications industry at the time, particularly with regard to billing and customer service. When he started the business unit, Accenture executives in various offices had some relationships at major accounts around the world but little expertise. They didn't feel confident approaching the chief information officer (CIO) of a *Fortune* 50 company for a meeting of their own, but they did feel comfortable offering up an expert who could hold his own with the CIO. So Burgess had a standing offer to the field: if you could get a meeting with a senior executive, he would get on a plane and show up to present to them. The strategy proved highly effective. His goal for the new business unit was to reach $150 million in sales by year three, and the business blew right past that, routinely booking deals valued at $30 million and up with customers who would have previously not given Accenture the time of day. As a one-person SWAT team, Burgess walked in as their peer with incredibly deep expertise, able to go toe-to-toe with extremely high-level executives with substantial buying power. He offered an opinionated, prescriptive point of view on the problem that the executives had not previously considered and a solution whose ROI eclipsed the cost. From there, the local Accenture executive would continue to nurture the relationship and close new business.

An added benefit of keeping the sales executives (or account relationship executives) out of this subject matter expert role is that they can continue to play the role of client advocate—looking out for the client's best interests throughout these early conversations.

The lead person here is usually the luminary who is the face of the company in the **Ignite** phase. In a startup, this is probably a founder or CEO. In a more established company, it may be the chief subject matter expert, solution manager, or solution marketing lead. Some companies have a dedicated "presales" role that serves this purpose. It's best to have someone who is equivalent to your target in stature and position. CEO buyers want to deal with CEO sellers. Vice president buyers want to deal with at least vice president sellers, and so on. But the real key is that you provide a central point of expertise for this thought leadership presentation activity, particularly early on, rather than expecting generic salespeople with only broad, surface knowledge to effectively educate the customer, elicit the right information from them, and connect dots between the customer's needs and how the solution will address them. This will ensure consistent representation of your offering, more effective customer interactions, and higher quality.

This person (or team) is going to deliver the stump speech you developed during the **Launch** phase as the first step in the selling process. You will likely follow these conversations with the executive presentation referenced above. It takes the message to the next level of detail, going into more depth on the solution and is tailored to the prospect's situation.

An exception to this SWAT team approach may be consumer situations in which it's not feasible to meet personally with prospects. But some companies still manage to employ this strategy in a cost-effective manner. In 1995, acne remedy company Proactiv did this by putting Drs. Kathy Fields and Katie Rodan in an infomercial sharing their expertise and prescriptive advice, which led to explosive growth. An updated version of this is a video presentation of your luminary on the website, YouTube, or other online channels. Apple stores offer yet another approach. When you walk in, someone greets you, asks you what you need, and then directs you to a person with the right expertise. Any salesperson can help you with the basics, but they'll direct you to a specialist for more complex needs.

WEBSITE

The big trap with the website at this stage is that companies try to have it speak to the *future* customer base instead of the *immediate* customer base.

The immediate customer base is Innovators and Early Adopters in your core target segment who know they have the problem, feel the daily pain of the problem, and are actively seeking a solution. Speak directly to the needs of people who already get it. You're not yet trying to appeal to the future customer—the tougher sells—the people who need to be convinced they have a problem. Those come later after significant market traction. Something is off about who you're targeting if you're having to do too much education about the problem itself.

Here's an example of discovering who to really home in on with your website and associated sales and marketing efforts. In the early days of Salesforce, Rob Acker left Oracle to help Salesforce build a lead generation team and an account management team. He looked at the data and noticed something interesting. Marc Benioff tells the story like this:

> After tracking every metric, Rob noticed the success we were experiencing with small companies (businesses with fewer than 30 employees). He approached me with the idea to ramp up our efforts to specifically target the very small business market, which he found to be progressive in its support of new technology: "There's a huge opportunity," he said. "We're thinking this isn't profitable, but this might be a goldmine..."
>
> I mentioned my concerns to Rob, and he responded with conviction that he believed this was the right idea. He had research to support his claim...
>
> It turned out to be a very good decision...The close rates were higher, and the sales time and cost of sale were low. We experienced phenomenal growth in this area and expanded from four sales reps to 20 reps in just six months.

Remember to have the website do as much of the sales and marketing for you as possible. The goal right now is to offer content and tools on the website that make those "Ding! Ding! Ding!" bells go off inside the heads of the right prospects. You want them to quickly self-select in and each raise their hand to say, "Hey! I'm over here, and I've been looking for what you've got!"

DEMO/TRIAL/SAMPLE

Demonstrations, product trials, and samples are particularly valuable when you are selling something that a customer can't truly experience or try out until after the sale. There are many examples all around us, so you can witness the value firsthand and think about how to apply it to your situation. Auto dealers allow you to test-drive their cars. Numerous online services allow free trials of their software or provide a free version from which you later upgrade for a monthly subscription fee. Retailers like Costco allow food brands to offer free samples. When complex enterprise software companies can't offer free samples or trials, they may offer demonstrations. One enterprise analytics software provider I know of runs a predictive analysis on an actual data file provided by the prospect in order to show them what the product can do. Again, aim these for now at the "I need it ASAP" buyers, not the "Hmm, I never thought about that before but interesting..." buyers.

A key distinction here that most people forget is that the demo/trial/sample doesn't do the selling. *It's a prop and only a prop.* The real selling happens as the salesperson sitting next to you during a test drive finds out what else you're looking at, points out differences, and ensures you're visualizing owning the car of your dreams. When you walk by a Costco Vitamix demonstration, what you see is a well-thought-out *production*, complete with props, microphone, and fresh fruits and vegetables. What you experience is a *performance*, with the representative educating you nonstop on healthy nutrition throughout a lengthy presentation as he or she blends items you didn't think it possible to blend, like a whole orange, peel and all. And tens of thousands of people a day stand by listening to those demonstrations just so they can finally taste the crazy but enticing concoction the rep is whipping up. And then *lots* of people plunk down $500 and up for a blender—a *blender*—so they can go home and re-create that concoction and others in order to adopt a healthier lifestyle. Even a technology demo on a website or in person must be aimed at "selling the sizzle, not the steak," as the old adage goes.

A key distinction here that most people forget is that the demo/ trial/sample doesn't do the selling. It's a prop and only a prop.

Demos, free trials, and samples can get expensive if personal interaction or custom preparation is necessary. So you want to pre-qualify prospects to the extent possible before you engage. And you want to design the demo or trial version of the offering to focus on outcomes so it elicits a "Wow, I've *got* to have that." Too often, teams take a very internal view when designing demos or trial experiences. Be sure to get external market and customer input so that they have the intended impact.

Homepage "explainer videos" are a great way to hook people and help them self-select in or out. Some clients prefer this anyway, since they don't have to schedule a set time or feel the pressure of a live interaction. Include a call-to-action enticement at the end for a more in-depth live demo, meeting, white paper, and so on.

In a pure services environment, such as accounting, where a "demo" is not necessarily applicable, your expertise, thought leadership materials, and free consultations serve as demos—the white papers and articles you created in the **Ignite** phase offer "free samples" of your expertise. In conversations with prospects, you provide samples by freely sharing your knowledge in meetings with prospects. The same applies when selling complex business solutions that might be hard to demonstrate.

ONE-STOP MARKETING SUPPORT

In addition to the SWAT team of experts, it's really important to offer one-stop marketing support for the organization, especially as you start to scale. This means you offer a help desk, of sorts, to assist the sales team and save them the trouble of fishing around for the right information or not knowing it exists in the first place. Many organizations offer an online repository of sales enablement materials, but human support is vital as well. Until artificial intelligence catches up, a human is uniquely capable of the kind of lateral thinking that can cross-pollinate activities across the organization and connect people who may be able to help each other or whose activities are synergistic. Maybe two teams are pursuing very similar opportunities at different accounts and can join efforts to gain efficiencies.

I talked earlier about how NASA's small public affairs team filled this role and provided in-depth technical documents such as the thick *Apollo Spacecraft News Reference* to support the media and the communications arms of their many contractors. Both the team and a repository of materials served as invaluable resources.

It's interesting that even those of us who think we know what we're talking about can so often break our own rules and come to deeply regret it later. I always felt that our emphasis on a centralized sales support function for the Communications Industry Group (CIG) was a huge part of its success. We essentially provided a call center that anyone in the field could contact at any time to be coached through a sales opportunity, directed to sales enablement materials, obtain competitive intelligence, or just ask a question. At first, this was one person who performed this role in addition to many other tasks, but even as the business grew, there was always one phone number and one-stop shopping for all things sales related. Yet, somehow, I failed to implement this at a managed-services startup where I was chief marketing officer, and it cost us.

STEP 3

Begin to Implement With Select "Visionary" Clients

Anytime you are introducing an innovation to the market, you are probably going to deal with the Innovation Adoption Curve I discussed in chapter 6. As I've said, your first few customers are going to be Innovators and Early Adopters. These are individuals or companies that like to be at the front end and experiment for competitive advantage or personal prestige. Even though Tesla Roadster test drive models were starting to fall apart and make odd noises by the end of its Santa Monica launch party in 2006, the company collected 127 orders at $100,000 each up front for the initial special-edition cars. "The [test-drive] cars were destroyed," according to Tesla co-founder and CTO J. B. Straubel. In Musk's own words, the early Roadster "was completely unsafe...broke down all the time, [and] didn't really work." Innovator customers waited nearly two years to get their cars—and still loved them, flaws and all.

Another reason Innovators buy is that the problem is so profound that time is of the essence. They believe the benefits of an imperfect offering far outweigh the risk of being one of your guinea pigs. To minimize this risk, they'll be partners with you in developing the solution, including how to maximize value and price it. They will tolerate imperfection in exchange for solving their problem sooner rather than later. This will give you an opportunity to work out the kinks. Geoffrey Moore discusses this in detail in *Crossing the Chasm*, where you can read more about it.

At one company I worked with, our first few "visionary" customers were huge consumer packaged goods companies, like Procter & Gamble and Conagra. As early as 2002, we were helping them use advanced digital marketing techniques and sophisticated analytics to help them market directly to consumers in a very targeted, precise fashion long before their competitors started doing this. They were so involved in the development and evolution of our solution that they were essentially part of the solution development team. This is very common in business services situations, particularly in IT. It rarely makes sense to develop a prototype or solution in "the lab." They are too complex, and you need rapid, iterative product development with real-time input and feedback from customers in order to get them right.

This approach is now becoming more mainstream, helped along by methodologies like Design Thinking by David Kelley, Customer Development by Steve Blank, and Lean Startup by Eric Ries. They encourage customer involvement in practices like rapid prototyping that enable designers to experiment and get immediate feedback, involving the user in the design process far more than in the past.

The solution development process with these customers is going to be sloppy, iterative, and sometimes inefficient, largely because you are feeling your way along through the dark to an extent. If you think of NASA as the visionary customer to the prime contractors like North American Aviation, which oversaw development of the lunar command module, you can imagine how integral the customer collaboration was. These early customers are your opportunity to make sure you get it right. You work with them as you continue your **Ignite** and **Navigate** efforts so that by the time the broader market is embracing your solution, you are ready for prime time. Tesla used the limited-run Roadster as a learning experience to gear up for the Model S production vehicle for the mass market. And there were many lessons learned. In the Roadster's first year alone, Tesla had to recall 75 percent of those sold, sending technicians to people's homes to repair loosened bolts essential for handling. There were other problems and other recalls. Nonetheless, the Model S was the top-selling plug-in electric car globally in 2015 and 2016.

One big pitfall you want to be mindful of is to make sure you are developing a solution that will be in demand by the broader market within a reasonable time frame. What I've seen time and time again is that a company sells a large, complex solution to the first three big customers and assumes it has a hit on its hands, when in reality, it's something only those first three visionary customers are indeed ready for, or they are the only ones who will ever want or need it.

Through your **Ignite** efforts, you've been getting broader market feedback to ensure this doesn't happen to you. But be careful not to fall into this trap.

STEP 4

Establish an End-To-End Solution ("Whole Product") that Is Value Priced and Uses Internal and/or External Resources, Products, Services, and So Forth

How often does a vandalized car help the police identify and capture the perpetrator? On April 9, 2019, model Jed Franklin was at Levi Strauss headquarters for a fitting in downtown San Francisco when he received an alert on his Tesla phone app telling him something was up. Thanks to a recent software update that had installed Sentry Mode in the car, the on-board cameras started rolling when Sentry sensed trouble. Video that Franklin later posted online shows a white Honda Civic pull up and parallel park immediately in front of Franklin's car. The license plate is clearly visible. A man then gets out of the passenger side, crouches, and sneaks toward the Tesla. A different camera angle shows him crouching next to the Tesla's rear passenger window and punch the window out with his elbow. He quickly peers in and reaches, then returns to the Civic, and off they go. The whole encounter takes less than one minute. Franklin later wrote that they didn't get anything, saying, "I guess he didn't need a child booster seat or empty grocery bags." Local police circulated the video and were able to identify and arrest the vandal on second-degree burglary and a parole violation. (If interested, you may be able to find the fascinating video by searching for "Tesla records its own break-in.")

In creating a high-performance electric car and to overcome the hesitation many upscale buyers had about electric vehicles, Tesla realized it would need to provide more than just a car. It needed to provide a unique, "end-to-end solution"—a vehicle that gets increasingly smarter over time through software updates, a network of Superchargers, navigation to these Superchargers, as well as nearby amenities you can use while you wait for your vehicle to charge, and a mobile app that can control some of the car's functions remotely. Unlike other auto companies that charge a fee to update navigation system maps, Tesla performs automatic software updates that go beyond navigation updates to actually add new features. One user noted that a few weeks after buying his Model 3, a software update added heated rear seats. Tesla also later issued updates to his car that improved braking distance. As part of its value-added approach, Tesla has rejected the automotive industry dealership model in order to control the entire customer experience—it sells and maintains cars itself, putting showrooms in shopping centers rather than stand-alone lots and making cars to order. It also constantly collects enormous troves of data via the sundry sensors in each car that educate Tesla not only on how to improve vehicle performance but also what's happening around the vehicle—other cars, buildings, pedestrians, road signs, you name it. This data goes via cellular network into the cloud, where it's analyzed incessantly for current and future purposes, like self-driving technology. If, for example, a driver is forced to suddenly brake hard, Tesla combines the data from cameras, the steering wheel, and the pedals to understand the circumstances and use the insights at a future time.

Geoffrey Moore talks about Bill Davidow's concept of "whole product" for high-tech companies in *Crossing the Chasm*, and it's an important concept here as well. "Whole product" is the notion that customers adopt products more readily when they are "ready to use," regardless of how many different manufacturers and partner agreements are involved on your part to make that happen. An example he offers is the personal computer (PC). When these arrived on the market, you had to be a tech whiz to buy and use a PC. You had to buy the PC itself, an operating system, application software, a monitor, etc. You had to load all of the software onto the computer and go through a bunch of machinations to get it to all work together. Market adoption was slow. When manufacturers got smart and started selling PCs preloaded with an operating system, all hardware, and some basic applications, sales took off. All a buyer had to do was pull it out of the box, turn it on, and start using it. No technical expertise was required.

This is especially important when selling solutions. You need to provide everything (or ready access to everything) it takes to deliver a valuable outcome. You aren't just dropping a product on the buyer's desk and leaving the rest up to them. You are their partner in achieving an important result. And you are taking responsibility by bringing together all of the ingredients and people required to achieve it, whether provided by your company, a partner, a supplier, or even the customer. You have to start from the customer perspective—the customer or business problem—and provide a blend of products and services from both inside and outside your organization.

You are their partner in achieving an important result.

The original Tesla founders, who knew nothing about the car business, were drawn to it once they realized almost everything on a car is outsourced and that manufacturers really only keep engine design, assembly, marketing, and financing in-house. The founders figured they could design a groundbreaking battery and rely on manufacturing partners for almost everything else. (As it turned out, once they got underway, they had to design and build a lot more from scratch than planned in order to provide a truly distinctive solution.)

The Apollo Space Program, on the other hand, relied heavily on its contractors and staffed mainly for things like research, program management, quality assurance, astronaut training, and mission execution. Numerous universities and 20,000 corporations such as Boeing, Grumman, RCA, Honeywell, IBM, General Electric, Lockheed, Sperry Rand, Omega, and Raytheon manufactured rockets, engines, components, and equipment; they conducted trajectory design and analysis and enabled Earth-to-Moon communications; they fed the astronauts in space, provided their watches and tape recorders, and made their suits. The complexity and scope of work was mind-boggling, and a vast spiderweb of public-private partnerships made it possible.

Jerry Seelig, an executive vice president of Lockheed Electronics Company in 1968, said recently, "It would have been almost impossible for NASA to achieve the mission given to it by the administration without reaching out to the aerospace industry and others."

Solutions don't have to be complex in order to be effective and of high value. Salesforce intentionally *launched* with a very stripped-down CRM system that was purely aimed at salespeople, a major reason it gained traction so quickly. It was easy to understand, had a very clear and simple value proposition aimed at a specific audience ("Hey, salesperson, you'll close more business and make more money using this"), and was infinitely easier and less costly to implement and use than its competitors. It wasn't until five years later that Salesforce broadened into a robust platform upon which developers could create custom applications.

The Proactiv Solution acne kit I mentioned earlier is a great consumer example—different components that work together to solve a problem. The Dollar Shave Club starter shaving kit comes with a razor and cartridges, a prep scrub, shaving cream, and aftershave—all of what you need to get going.

STEP 5

Target Prospects, Pursue and Develop Relationships, and Begin to Sell the Solution

Many, many books have been written on how to sell, how to establish and run sales organizations, and how to target and penetrate accounts. And there are even more on how to plan a spectacular customer journey and keep customers happy. You'll find a sampling at apollomethod.com. Here are a few practical tips to augment what they talk about.

RAINMAKERS

"If you want a track team to win the high jump, you find one person who can jump seven feet, not several people who can each jump one foot."

—Frederick E. Terman, former Stanford University dean and professor, and "Father of Silicon Valley"

Regardless of all of the strategic and marketing advice I'm giving in this book, the one ingredient you can't do without is rainmakers— these are people who have a gift for finding and closing deals. You must have rainmakers from the very beginning. These need to be well-connected, consultative salespeople who are masterful at gaining entry to an account, understanding the customer's needs, and selling them on the solution. In a purely online model, this may be a marketing person who is exceptional at driving inbound demand to the website. Either way, rainmakers are the kind of people who can sell anything to anyone. The best ones are often incredibly creative, a little unconventional, and humble (ironically); they don't see obstacles, only opportunity. They don't need collateral or other selling tools, though they are often highly collaborative and effectively draw on the expertise around them. They pursue customers on the strength of their knowledge, confidence, and problem-solving and people skills. This is a special breed of person who just makes it happen. In addition to the SWAT team members being rainmakers, you want account representatives who have these characteristics. In the early days of the Communications Industry Group at Accenture, a single partner closed $160 million (in today's dollars) in services at just one client; another closed over $80 million at another client; yet another closed over $20 million at a third client. Don't get me wrong, each had a supporting team who assisted and shared in the credit. But by providing leadership and by forging personal relationships with the most senior decision makers at their clients, those three people were responsible for more than half of the business unit's revenues one year.

In a startup, the founder/CEO should be a rainmaker; if s/he doesn't possess those qualities, you need someone on the team who does. Marc Benioff was a rainmaker at Oracle and brought those skills to Salesforce to get it off the ground. Michael Dubin, Dollar Shave Club founder, drove $3.5 million in sales in its first year by writing and performing in a humorous viral video that generated 12,000 orders within forty-eight hours of going live. He knew just what to say and how to say it.

You need these people early on, because they need to be out there selling while you're getting your marketing, offering, and delivery act together. Remember, there usually isn't time or money to do these phases completely sequentially. In the real world, they need to be done concurrently and are iterative.

During the early days, you must be ruthless with the sales team. The biggest mistake I've seen companies make in this area time and time again is that they hang on to weak salespeople way too long. There are the types who are always "on the verge of a huge deal. Just give me a couple more months to close it!" Or the ones who "don't have the right tools—if I just had better collateral or [fill in the blank], I could close some deals." Then there are the ones who look to everyone else to provide them with leads and just view their job as getting contracts signed. That model might work in some businesses, but in a relationship-intensive business, you need people who are skilled at going out and generating their own leads and opportunities and moving them through the sales funnel quickly.

TARGET CUSTOMER LIST

This is another huge mistake a lot of companies make. They don't research and develop a list of target customers they are going to proactively pursue. Companies selling to enterprises should have a list of target accounts by name. As I mentioned earlier, the initial Accenture Communications Industry Group target list was composed of just thirty companies, each of which held at least $200 million in revenue potential for us. Other companies should have a (short) list of well-defined target personas—very detailed profiles of the ideal companies or individuals you want to sell to. Dollar Shave Club initially targeted young men who wanted a cheap, reliable, no-frills shaving experience without having to ask an attendant to open a locked case or remember to buy them in the first place; and who preferred to shop online and have product delivered to their door. It may sound general, but if you unpack all of that, you'll find a quite specific psychographic profile, and the founder's early marketing efforts spoke directly to those people in their own language using a distinctive, dry-witted tone they could relate to. He was, after all, one of them.

If you don't get specific, your sales and marketing efforts will be scattershot, even in a narrowly defined market. The sales team has no guidance on who to be pursuing. They'll go after anything that moves and dilute your sales efforts. The marketing team needs guidance on who to be reaching with direct marketing efforts and more broad-based efforts like social and traditional media outreach. Otherwise, sales and marketing activity will be all over the place with no synergy between efforts or companies.

If you don't get specific, your sales and marketing efforts will be scattershot, even in a narrowly defined market.

If your offering requires a complex sale to enterprises (meaning you need to work multiple relationships across a large account versus a single decision maker who buys on the spot), you want to employ what many today refer to as "account-based marketing" but with a few twists. I won't get into general education about this approach—there are numerous articles and books on this topic (again, see apollomethod.com for some suggestions). But here are a few specific pointers. (If you have a simple sales model or sell directly to consumers, you can adapt this strategy by targeting some very, very narrow and specific microsegments with obvious gathering spots on places like certain Facebook groups, online and offline organizations, and so forth. Where I discuss "company" below, you can substitute in microsegments.)

First, do some research on the bullseye segment of your Target Market Dartboard. Develop a list of target companies based on the profiles you created during the **Launch** phase. Plot the companies on the Innovation Adoption Curve as a way to prioritize who you'll target first. For example, if you are targeting the hospital sector in a set of major metropolitan areas, there are probably certain hospitals that gravitate toward innovation ahead of others. While your strategy may eventually call for 100 percent penetration of a list of, say, eighty hospitals that meet your criteria, it may be that you proactively target only twenty at first—the twenty that are "Innovators," "Early Adopters" and the "Early Majority." You may decide to include all eighty in your low-cost content marketing outreach but pursue only twenty through direct selling activity at present.

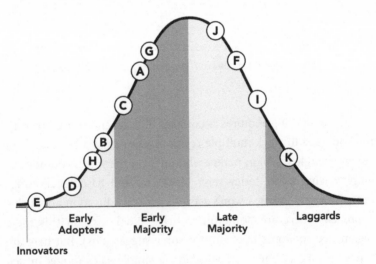

Here is an example of how you can further prioritize your target segments and buyers by plotting each major account or segment (as represented by a letter) on Rogers' Innovation Adoption Curve. This will help you focus your early efforts on targets most likely to buy first.

After that, define buyer personas for each of the types of people who will influence buying decisions at these accounts or as consumers. Also segment based on how you'll most efficiently reach clusters of prospects. This list may be somewhat dynamic, but try to make it as stable as possible. You want your efforts to build on themselves over time and not be wasted on someone who is here today, gone tomorrow.

The Apollo analogue to all of this was the program's strategic targeting of members of the science community, Congress, and the public at large to ensure continued funding and support for the program. In *Selling Outer Space*, James Kauffman describes one such targeted effort:

> In late 1963, for example, the astronauts and their wives traveled to Washington to receive an award in a White House ceremony. Coincidentally, the ceremony took place on the exact day the House conducted crucial debates on NASA's appropriation bill. Conveniently, chairman George Mills (D., Calif.) invited the astronauts and their wives to visit the House chamber during the actual floor debates.

Enterprise sales cycles can be long, and that's if you catch a buyer at the point when they actually need what you have to sell. You want to be on their radar screen over a period of time so that by the time it occurs to them that they need your help, they've heard *about* you numerous times, heard *from* you numerous times, and know you provide what they need.

We were really lucky with Accenture's Communications Industry Group (CIG), since there were only roughly thirty major communications service providers at the time, though they fell on different points of the Innovation Adoption Curve. Our proactive efforts were completely focused on about eight of these at first, even though each was extremely complex, political, and a market unto itself. Still, it made our job very easy. We did more general outreach to the other twenty-two companies.

What do you do when that's not the case—when there are thousands of companies in your space? How do you select them and *how many* do you select? You want enough but not too many, or your efforts will be too dispersed. The answer is at least a white paper in itself, but here is a very simplified approach. You identify a set of targets and conduct an integrated sales and marketing campaign to qualify them and get them into the sales funnel. This requires tight coordination between sales and marketing. The process begins with reverse engineering your sales funnel (or projected sales funnel) statistics. Calculate backward how much revenue needs to be in the funnel at any given stage and the number of prospects that equates to. This will tell you how many potential customers you'll have to target to meet your ultimate revenue goals. (You'll find an automated tool that does this at apollomethod.com if you'd like to just plug your numbers in and calculate how many targets you need to pursue to meet your revenue goals.)

1. Build a revenue model for the next two to three years that lays out growth goals. Be realistic based on how quickly you can scale.
2. Calculate how many customer contracts you will need in order to generate that revenue based on an average deal size you're aiming for or expect.
3. Based on your win (or close) rates (percentage of sales-qualified leads that turn into paying customers), calculate how many companies you will need at the very top of the sales funnel in order for the right number to filter down and become revenue-generating contracts. This is the number you'll need in your target list—let's say it's

one hundred. (If you don't have a history to go on, ask around within your network in order to estimate—but be pessimistic.)

4. Research the target company list you developed above and narrow down (or scale up) to the number you arrived at in step 3—in this case, you'd choose the one hundred highest-probability targets.

5. Identify, at minimum, the top three to five executives who are prospective buyers and fit the Innovator or Early Adopter profile; obtain their contact information.

6. Create a CRM database that both sales and marketing can use to track contact with these individuals and companies, filling in as much information about each target as you can.

INTEGRATED SALES AND MARKETING

Now it's time for outreach. On the sales side, assign chunks of this list to each salesperson, who now owns the relationships with that set of companies. It's their job to lead the charge on gaining entry into each and ultimately turning it into a customer. They must figure out each company's "readiness" for your solution and know the company inside and out. They should introduce themselves, orchestrate briefings, and stay in constant contact with that company with help from marketing. For example, a first step might be to send a well-researched and highly personalized introductory email based on a warm introduction through a mutual contact. They may send a copy of your e-book or other useful information. If appropriate, they may ask for a brief meeting to get reactions and feedback. At minimum, the goal is to get the target to engage in some way and, ideally, get permission to stay in touch—an opt-in essentially. The salesperson should record all contacts in the CRM.

Meanwhile, the marketing organization augments direct selling efforts by putting an appropriate and highly useful stream ("drip") of relationship nurturing communications in front of the prospects via email, social media, regular mail, briefing events, webinars, and other "content marketing" tactics designed to engage them or at least keep you top of mind. These should leverage and build on all of the content generated during the **Ignite** phase and be of great value to the audience. Marketing also conducts inbound activities designed to attract the right people to the website and encourage engagement there through valuable offers, such as a free analysis tool, a list of tips, a diagnostic, information, etc. that encourage visitors to opt in. (You might hear these referred to as "lead magnets." I don't care for that term, because it sounds transactional and manipulative. Instead, your goal is to nurture and develop a lasting, trust-based relationship through ongoing value.) You may also want to set up an inside sales function aimed at initiating relationships through calling campaigns and such.

The key with the marketing activity is to do a deep up-front analysis of these target buyers and what drives them. Figure out the vital few tactics that will get their attention and motivate them to act.

The overall goal here is to narrow your efforts but get enough prospects into the top of the funnel. You then move them through the buying process as a complement to direct sales activity. You want to establish credibility, raise top-of-mind awareness, encourage prospects to engage in a dialogue, and grease the skids for selling efforts.

The key with the marketing activity is to do a deep up-front analysis of these target buyers and what drives them. Figure out the vital few tactics that will get their attention and motivate them to act.

I don't like to refer to any of this activity as "lead generation," because, again, it sets up a transactional mindset in which you're mainly after the "deal." No. You are *not* mainly after the deal. You are aiming for an extremely valuable, win-win relationship, so you should be in a problem-solving, lifetime-partnership mindset. Your goal is to initiate and nurture relationships of trust and long-term, mutual benefit that eventually lead to high-margin revenue streams. All content should center on problem solving related to your core point of view and solution.

Your proactive sales and direct marketing efforts will focus on this carefully selected target company list. However, opportunities with other companies not on this list may come along. Great! If they are good fits and meet your criteria, go for it. But plan to actively invest in the companies on your target list and regard these as your "qualified prospects."

Be sure to start investing in these sales and marketing activities early. This is a marathon, not a sprint. Buyers aren't on your timeline, and most of what you sell will be a matter of being in the right place at the right time. You want to be top of mind by the time they're ready to buy, and that is a process. It doesn't happen overnight.

A big mistake I've made and have also seen at many other companies is waiting too long to start filling the funnel. Sales teams then become frantic, expecting marketing to snap its fingers and fill the funnel for them. No, this has to be a coordinated and complementary partnership between sales and marketing with a long-term view.

For complex enterprise solutions, marketing activity supports and complements sales outreach and personal relationship building. In B2C and non-enterprise B2B situations targeting thousands or even *millions* of customers, the sheer volume will require that you rely more heavily on marketing activity and less on the direct selling. You'll make even heavier use of sophisticated analytics and digital marketing techniques.

SALES AND MARKETING CHANNELS

I mentioned earlier how NASA used the marketing departments of its contractors as channels for reaching and "selling" the value of the program, but it also relied on other channels. For example, in partnership with the *Cleveland Plain Dealer*, it hosted the Space Science Fair, a ten-day event for Cleveland citizens that included many attractions such as exhibits, movies, presentations, and programs for kids and schools.

It's very expensive, very hard, and very slow to develop market awareness and grow a customer base from scratch. If you don't have built-in sales and marketing channels, you need to develop them. In a section below, I talk about working with partners that provide the parts of your solution that you don't have. In addition, identify partners that have already penetrated your target accounts and whose offerings complement yours. Offer revenue-sharing incentives for them to introduce you into the account. Because you are so focused, it's easier to find fellow vendors whose offerings don't overlap with yours. This gives you an advantage over me-toos, who are so broad that they're essentially in competition with everyone.

A year after launching, Amazon initiated its enormously successful affiliate marketing program in 1996, offering a 5–15 percent commission on sales generated through online referral links. Consumer brands often find success leveraging social media influencers as channels. An important channel in the information technology sector is "value-added resellers," who add components or services to an existing product and then sell it to the end user. Salesforce offers AppExchange, a marketplace of add-ons that third parties create for its core product. In addition to adding value to Salesforce offerings, the store serves as an important sales and marketing channel. In a September 2018 article to partners, Salesforce wrote, "During our second quarter earnings call, the message was loud and clear: if Salesforce is on a rocketship ride, partners are the fuel helping us keep pace."

Sales and marketing channels are where startups are at a huge disadvantage, especially when targeting enterprises. It's much easier to be a business unit within a large matrix organization, like a vertical solution offering within IBM. Your company likely has account teams and relationships with many of your targets. If this is the case, much of your initial selling is internal. You need to sell them on how your offering benefits their customer and work through them to gain entry to accounts. This is where the SWAT team is valuable— salespeople sell what they know. If they don't feel expert enough, they won't introduce the offering. Knowing that your SWAT team is ready to do the heavy lifting, they'll be more inclined to pursue an introductory meeting.

If you aren't part of a large company and are selling to large enterprises, it's critical to develop partner relationships early on in which the partner has a strong incentive to take your product to market, using your luminary and provocative point of view as a door opener.

STEP 6

Build an Efficient Solution Delivery Capability (Customer Service, Recruiting, Enculturation, Training, Distribution Channels, Partners, Methodologies, etc.)

Unlike a typical product, a solution is not always something that you just plop on a customer's doorstep with a pleasant, "Adios. Enjoy!" Your role in implementation of the solution is a big part of the value you bring and what helps set you apart. It's also an opportunity to cement your relationship with that customer. Remember, you want customers for life. Therefore, you had better be able to deliver *results*.

A fervent emphasis on the customer experience is crucial. Again, many excellent books and articles address this topic. But it's surprising as to how many companies never take a deep look at what would make for an outstanding experience and how to provide that.

Throughout its nearly one-hundred-year history, Vitamix has maintained an incredible bond with customers, which isn't an accident. Holly Hacker, the company's director of direct sales and customer experience, explains:

> Customer experience is something that we take very seriously as it relates to serving our customers and making sure that once they get a Vitamix, that it's going to be part of their family for potentially a generation or more...In about 2013 and '14 we did a study to understand the [customer] journey. And so we went through the lifecycle and said, "What are the steps that people go through and where are the key moments of truth that, if we get that right, they will continue on that journey and ultimately become raving fans?"

She describes an example of where the company fouled up but turned a problem into a brand loyalty opportunity, saying, "We got very, very busy during the holiday time period [and] ran out of certain models. So we actually took the time and made outbound calls to 700 customers and either upgraded them into a nicer model or, if they really needed to have it, we put them on an escalated list... Everybody got something and they were satisfied."

When a merchant uses Amazon fulfillment services, it gets a complete solution. It doesn't have to put the pieces together itself—Amazon handles everything from collecting payments and pulling items from shelves to boxing and shipping them. The merchant gets an end result—its item arrives at the customer's location as promised.

Products and/or services can be enormously expensive to provide unless you consciously design in efficiencies. You want to be sure you look for ways to get the best leverage from your most skilled people and develop tools that will reduce effort, lower risk for you and the customer, and allow you to scale.

A huge part of Amazon's success is its efficient operations at more than 175 fulfillment centers occupying 150 million square feet of space. In 2001, Jeff Wilke became CEO of Amazon's consumer business and brought best practices he learned from his days in the manufacturing industry to Amazon's warehousing and distribution operation. To gear up for one-day shipping, his team rewrote software, reconfigured warehouses, and implemented lean manufacturing techniques under an umbrella effort called FastTrack. They reduced the order-to-shipping time frame from twenty-four hours to a mere three hours.

"I would have the managers of the facilities at the end of each day send me an email to describe why we missed each shipment that missed," Wilke said. "Every single one of them. We did that for almost a year to make sure that the processes worked and then we were confident launching it externally."

In 2012, the company introduced robots that work alongside employees at twenty-six of these centers. Over 100,000 devices move bins, boxes, and pallets, further improving workflow, safety, and efficiency.

If there is a manufacturing component to your solution, you have to consider supply chain issues and balance cost savings against quality. If there is a service component, you have to ensure you can maintain quality as you grow. How does a graphic design firm ensure it can provide repeatable processes and teach each new designer to deliver consistent output? You need to be very clear on what it takes to fully implement your solution in terms of skills, processes, methodology, and tools. Then you need to create them yourself or line them up through partners.

When managing innovation or a highly creative pursuit, you may have to evaluate how to balance efficiency and effectiveness. When Pixar was acquired by Disney in 2006, its president, Ed

Catmull, became president of Walt Disney Animation Studios as well. Though he could have gained efficiencies by merging the two operations, he recognized they were completely different entities and kept them separate.

He also needed to figure out why Disney Animation was floundering after huge successes like *The Little Mermaid* and *The Lion King* in the 1990s. What he observed was that corporate process experts had taken control of the production approach in order to reduce costs and gain efficiencies, but the result was one bad film after another. As Catmull has described:

> When I got there, above the director they had three levels of people who were giving mandatory notes [changes]. None of them had ever made a film before. So that's the first thing to go. You go to the director, "You don't listen to any of their notes. You don't have to take our notes either." And that was a rather shocking thing for [the Disney production team]...

Instead, the Pixar team trained the Disney team on its "brain trust" approach in which anyone can offer direct and honest input to the director, but the director maintains complete decision-making control. Immediately after that, the same team that had been cranking out duds produced the hits *Tangled*, *Wreck-It Ralph*, and *Frozen*, the highest-grossing animated film to date.

Remember, your overall goals here are to:

1. Ensure that your customer realizes significant results/outcomes.
2. Create a positive customer experience while appropriately managing expectations.
3. Appropriately reduce your costs.
4. Position yourself to scale.

To do this, you need a high-functioning team, strong operating practices and processes, and a proper focus on the customer.

The more your business relies on human talent, the more important training and enculturation are (helping employees understand and embody the company culture). Go-To management consulting firm McKinsey & Company spends at least $10,000 per consultant and researcher per year on training. Accenture, the Go-To provider of technology consulting and outsourcing services, spends about $1 billion per year on training. From very early on, Marc Benioff wanted employees to embody an "Aloha spirit" of respect and compassion toward others, so Hawaiian shirts became an informal uniform in the early days as just one of many means of building the Salesforce culture.

At NASA, the Apollo Program culture underlying all efforts throughout the decade was, "We've never done this before, but let's try," according to Norman Crabill, who led the effort to identify potential landing sites on the Moon. He said this was due, in part, to Kennedy's influence.

On December 23, 1935, Walt Disney wrote an eight-page letter to Don Graham, who taught art classes for Disney animators at the Chouinard Art Institute, where the company's training program was based. The letter listed Walt Disney's criteria of a skilled animator. He also spelled out a formalized and rigorous approach to preparing animators for the kind of comedy and emotional connection Disney wanted his films to convey, saying:

> ...the animator should know what creates laughter—why do things appeal to people as being funny...I am convinced that there is a scientific approach to this business, and I think we shouldn't give up until we have found out all we can about how to teach these young [people] the business.

The studio proceeded to make history with *Snow White and the Seven Dwarfs*, *Pinocchio*, *Fantasia*, and *Dumbo*, just as a start.

In the extreme, a failure to properly orchestrate all of the moving parts of your operation, including proper internal communication and coordination across your own organization and that of key partners can lead to catastrophic outcomes, which Apollo experienced firsthand in preparation for its very first manned mission. On January 27, 1967, three astronauts piled into the compact *Apollo 1* spacecraft for a routine launchpad test. With a tiny, errant spark, the airtight compartment of pure oxygen became a "raging inferno" within seconds, killing trapped inhabitants Gus Grissom, Ed White, and Roger Chaffee. It was an emotionally devastating and morale-destroying blow. With unvarnished introspection and external reviews, the program acknowledged many mistakes and lessons to be learned, including with design, development, assembly, and testing of spacecraft. Many within NASA, including Grissom himself, had been convinced all along that the spacecraft was not ready for prime time. Word has it that just days before, he presciently plucked a lemon from his yard and hung it on the flight simulator. Post-accident, there were lots of changes. No more pure oxygen in the spacecraft. No flammable materials. Hatches must open out, not in. And so on.

Underlying all was the importance of communication, both within NASA and among its nearly half-million contractors. As coauthors David Meerman Scott and Richard Jurek state in their book *Marketing the Moon*, the review concluded that "...the power structure within NASA was a contributing factor to the disaster and that good communications were crucial to the success of the Apollo program." Still reeling and exhausted from the devastation just three weeks after the accident, a NASA program manager involved in the review implored an audience of internal officials and executives from partner contractors:

Somehow, we have to reach a degree of sophistication in the motivational area that I have yet to see. It's got to get the in-line people in the organization feeling responsible, to get them to really understand their job, to get them feeling they're a part of the thread that leads right up to the launch.

As Scott and Jurek write, "Long hours, close friendships, and shared goals had forged a closely integrated community of NASA employees, contractors, and the press during the [pre-Apollo] Mercury and Gemini years." This had initially extended into Apollo but gradually became lost as the program grew exponentially. "Immediately after the trauma, everyone was painfully aware just how easily and how quickly things could go wrong."

It would be eighteen months before NASA sent the next human into space following massive design and operational changes. But the effort paid off. No more lives were lost, despite the enormous risks and the fact that NASA was attempting something that had never been done before.

STEP 7

Carefully Manage Opportunities and Increase Your Foothold in Key Accounts

This step is where you strengthen your position within current accounts, if selling to enterprises, or within microsegments. You also break into additional new accounts and increase your market penetration. Naturally, this is the lifeblood of the company. It doesn't matter how great your solution is unless someone is buying it.

For the purposes of this discussion (which is more enterprise-sales-oriented), I'll define "opportunity management" as the process of managing the quality and quantity of active sales "opportunities" (a prospect that is interested in buying) and also moving that opportunity through the sales pipeline to a signed contract in a timely manner. During **Navigate**, when you are just getting off the ground with your solution, you want to be sure you are focusing your efforts on the kinds of companies that are ready for what you're offering. You were careful about this when you developed your target list, but now that there are multiple deals in the pipeline, you need to keep a critical eye on which ones will and won't really go anywhere.

This is where you strengthen your position within current accounts, if selling to enterprises, or within microsegments. You also break into additional new accounts and increase your market penetration.

This is critical. Most likely, you have limited sales and marketing resources and need to prioritize how you allocate them. You certainly don't want them wasted on deals that will never happen while you miss other, more lucrative opportunities.

Typically, companies use estimates of how likely a deal is to close and when in order to project revenues and manage the business. Many companies use a weighting technique in which a probability is assigned to a deal based on where it is in the sales pipeline (for example, a company might give a rating of 25 percent if a qualified prospect has expressed an active interest; then 50 percent, 75 percent, on up to 95 percent, which often means you have a verbal agreement and just need to sign a contract). The flaw here is that deals are usually all or nothing—they close or they don't. And in reality, a collection of deals in the same stage of the pipeline don't have the same probability of happening—many factors come into play.

Another big mistake companies make here is that they aren't ruthless enough in managing this pipeline, holding salespeople accountable for the accuracy of their projections, and wiping deals off the list that don't belong there at all. Their pipeline reports are full of a lot of hope, not genuine deal flow on its way to closing. This means they are wasting their time chasing opportunities that aren't opportunities at all. Worse, these bad projections are disastrous for the business. If you can't project when you'll close deals, you can't project when you'll generate revenue. You also kill your credibility with investors, your board, and other stakeholders watching your financials.

Another big mistake companies make here is that they aren't ruthless enough in managing this pipeline, holding salespeople accountable for the accuracy of their projections, and wiping deals off the list that don't belong there at all. Their pipeline reports are full of a lot of hope, not genuine deal flow on its way to closing.

Try a little experiment. Take the bottom 50 percent of your sales performers. Look at their current sales pipeline. How many of those "95 percent probability" prospects have been sitting there "on the verge of closing" for six months when you normally have a four-month sales cycle? Go back to some of their old pipeline reports and compare their projections at the time to what eventually actually happened. How many of those projections were accurate? How good a job is that salesperson doing of being realistic about what will and won't close? Let go of your chronic offenders.

Then do a similar analysis of your overall pipeline. Analyze how accurate earlier forecasts ended up being. If the results are bad, spiff up your monitoring, become more vigilant, and possibly rethink your approach to pipeline reporting. Consider modifying your model (or sales forecasting tool) to incorporate at least two more factors that determine an opportunity's weighted revenue value at any given stage of the pipeline: the salesperson's historical close (or conversion) rate—that person's track record for closing deals—and the opportunity's conversion probability, which is the likelihood that a particular deal will close. You might standardize that with a checklist based on past experience, such as whether it's an active or new account, how complicated the politics are, the financial health of the company, etc.

The same general principal applies to B2C and non-enterprise B2B sales forecasting: analyze the historical accuracy of your forecasts, figure out where the flaws have been, and build in more precision and accuracy moving forward.

It's essential that you get sales and revenue forecasting right. This one area can make or break your cash flow, profitability, investor support, and overall credibility.

STEP 8

Establish Industry "Community of Believers"

Rock stars have them. Entertainment celebrities have them. Now it's time for you to have one: a fan club. Ideally, they're fans of your point of view and offering. If it's too early in the game for that, they're fans of your point of view. They feel you are onto something and want to be part of it. They want an inside track. And they are proactive, involved people who want to weigh in and help shape the direction of the industry. Think of them as ambassadors for your company.

In 1983, during a rough patch in the company's history and finances that we'll talk about later, Harley-Davidson formed the Harley Owner's Group (H.O.G.) with a mere fifty members, growing to 33,000 members within the first year. With little money to spend on marketing, the company viewed the club as a grassroots mechanism for reconnecting with loyal customers, but the power of the community far exceeded Harley-Davidson's expectations. Now there are over 1 million members in 1,400 chapters worldwide. A valuable group, members typically spend 30 percent more than other Harley owners, mostly on merchandise, vacations, and events. By requiring every chapter to have a dealer sponsor, the company has forged tight relationships between dealers and local customers, but member volunteers run the chapters. The company sponsors rallies around the world that often attract 25,000 people, bringing new bikes in for members to try out. The company solicits feedback on all aspects of its products and customer experience at the events, which then drives product decisions. Club member enthusiasm is unbounded, which is evident in photos on its blog showcasing members and their bikes at the many H.O.G. events around the world.

Rock stars have them. Entertainment celebrities have them. Now it's time for you to have one: a fan club.

There is huge power in community, and you want to harness this as part of your marketing, client and prospect relations, and even ongoing market intelligence. You want them to interact with you and with each other.

During the Apollo program, a few entities sprung up to foster a tight community among members of the press, NASA Public Affairs, and marketers representing its various contractors. The Escape Velocity Press Club was a private, invitation-only club where members socialized and bonded. The club was so influential that it was where NASA used a gala celebrating the anniversary of Alan

Shepard's historic Mercury flight to declare that the mourning period for *Apollo 1* was over. With the deceased astronauts' wives and other astronauts in attendance, the goal was to rekindle enthusiasm for the program among the press, and by extension, among the public. Apollo public affairs officer Bob Button described the event, saying:

> This was the social event of the decade at the Manned Spacecraft Center, and people left that place full of new energy and enthusiasm for getting America back into space and on route to the Moon. The hiatus was officially over.

There were also the contractor-run Joint Industry Press Center (JIPC) in Houston and the Apollo Contractors Information Center in Florida, which offered places for people to pick up press materials, grab a drink, and socialize. These three organizations were key to creating a sense of joint ownership by the press, contractors, and NASA in Apollo's public acceptance and success.

What you want to do is gather and build a community of believers in your point of view and, ideally, the solution you've developed. In technology, software and product user groups may come to mind, but those often intentionally operate independently of the company they're associated with. Instead, you should be the glue that brings your community together and holds it together, with the members as your partners in continuing to evolve the point of view and solution. Run the community online, but also hold live events to allow people to make personal connections.

Like Apple has done, make your community
"the party everyone wants to be at."

Airbnb does this with the Airbnb Open conference for hosts and guests. Apple does this with its annual developers conference. At Accenture, we created the Global Communications Forum (GCF), an invitation-only gathering of the world's senior executives from throughout the communications industry, which continued for over twenty years. From the start, the GCF was a combination of education, networking, and an emotional connection to our brand (through fun bonding experiences like golf, elegant dinners, and deep-sea fishing). It also became a safe place for the most senior executives from different companies to meet and share ideas with their peers without raising suspicions of impending mergers or acquisitions. It became a powerful sales and marketing initiative for us with year-round interactions.

Like Apple has done, make your community "the party everyone wants to be at." Make people feel like part of an exclusive club. Give them special perks. Most of all, be sure to listen very carefully to what they have to say. If all goes well, they will be a gold mine of information, leads, and business. They will become your ambassadors, evangelizing and generating word of mouth on your behalf. Your goal is to grow this community, deepen the loyalty that members feel to you, and as they say in politics, solidify the base.

STEP 9

Expand Your Organization's Infrastructure in Order to Scale

Eventually, you are going to need to hire more people, expand your facilities and technology infrastructure, automate some activities you've gotten by doing manually, and so on. The biggest challenge here, as Stephen Covey says in his book *The 7 Habits of Highly*

Effective People, is to not let the urgent tasks keep you from doing the important tasks. Urgent tasks at this stage might be things like getting proposals out the door and managing the quality of delivery activities in progress. Important items that are less urgent but still critical might include things like setting up a recruiting engine or rethinking your sales compensation model.

The key is to achieve just the right balance between keeping things efficient without overinvesting or investing before you really need to. It's like buying new shoes for growing children when you barely have enough to pay the electric bill. You don't want to buy new shoes before you have to, so you wait until the child's toes are just starting to touch the tip of their old shoes. Even then, you try to optimize the next size you buy so they last as long as possible without being so big that the children will trip over themselves until growing into their new shoes.

Jeff Bezos initially operated Amazon out of a garage, boxing and labeling packages manually. Over time, the company has steadily increased the size and number of its facilities. Within three years, it had 373,000 square feet of space. By the end of 2018, the company leased or owned 288 *million* square feet of space.

Many of us have learned the perils of overinvesting in fancy infrastructure too soon after living through several boom and bust cycles. Heavy overhead has killed a lot of companies during eras when demand dropped and companies couldn't scale back quickly enough. I was with one company that lost over $80 million in booked revenue backlog almost overnight, because our clients were suddenly going out of business due to a recession. Having invested in the infrastructure we would need to support the services we had sold, we were saddled with all kinds of obligations we couldn't get out of—office leases, recruitment and severance packages for executives, ad spending contracts, and other obligations.

Always be ready for the blips. Silicon Valley learned its lesson and was ready when the 2008 recession hit. Venture capitalists called their portfolio companies in for meetings in advance and told them to cut back to the bone. The warning was: "There may not be any more money on the horizon, so run yourself as leanly as possible."

For an excellent, well-researched book on the key success factors for scaling a business while maintaining quality, read *Scaling Up Excellence: Getting to More Without Settling for Less* by Robert Sutton and Huggy Rao. You'll find many practical tips and interesting stories derived from interviews with senior executives.

STEP 10

Monitor, Measure, and Refine

Amazon has always built measurements around the company's Go-To status, which Jeff Bezos said from the beginning was the company's key driver. In his 1997 letter to shareholders the year Amazon went public, he wrote:

> Our decisions have consistently reflected this focus. We first measure ourselves in terms of the metrics most indicative of our market leadership: customer and revenue growth, the degree to which our customers continue to purchase from us on a repeat basis, and the strength of our brand. We have invested and will continue to invest aggressively to expand and leverage our customer base, brand, and infrastructure as we move to establish an enduring franchise.

As in **Ignite**, you want to set up measurement processes that are meaningful and truly indicate how you are progressing against your goals. Three of the most critical measurement areas during **Navigate** are:

1. Filling the sales funnel (turning targets into active opportunities)
2. Managing the sales pipeline stages to turn active opportunities into closed deals (booked sales)
3. Delivering the solution and associated outcomes that result in realized revenue—the quality of your work for customers; as you gain traction, customer-related metrics become critical

In early 1997, Bezos conducted a company retreat and announced that Amazon would have a "culture of metrics." Bezos then led a group brainstorming session on what metrics would most help Amazon improve its performance. In the 2004 book, *Amazonia: Five Years at the Epicenter of the Dot.com Juggernaut,* author and former Amazon employee James Marcus summarizes some of the dialogue:

> "First, we figure out which things we'd like to measure on the site," [Bezos] told us. "For example, let's say we want a metric for customer enjoyment. How could we calculate that?"
>
> There was silence. Then somebody ventured: "How much time each customer spends on the site?"
>
> "Not specific enough," Jeff said.
>
> "How about the average number of minutes each customer spends on the site per session?" someone else suggested. "If that goes up, they're having a blast."
>
> "But how do we factor in purchase?" I said, feeling proud of myself. "Is that a measure of enjoyment?"
>
> "I think we need to consider frequency of visits, too," said a dark-haired woman I didn't recognize. "Lot of folks are still accessing the web with those creepy-crawly modems. Four short visits from them might be just as good as one visit from a guy with a T-1. Maybe better."

"Good point," Jeff said. "And anyway, enjoyment is just the start. In the end, we should be measuring customer ecstasy."

It's interesting to see a window into the early days of Amazon when it was still figuring things out and just how carefully it thought through the use of metrics before the availability of today's sophisticated data analytics technologies. This should serve as inspiration for how you can also explore measures of success for your business, whether large or small.

You also want to track progress on solution development and hiring and managing people. Determine your key measures of success, keep them fairly simple as a start, and monitor. Adjust your plans and actions as needed. The key is to watch closely, hold people accountable, and respond quickly when something isn't working.

RECAP AND ACTION ITEM

The **Navigate** phase is where you deliver on your promises and walk the talk. Your goal is to take clients on a journey toward solving their problem and leave them so thrilled that they are willing to pay handsomely for the valuable end results you deliver and, ideally, start promoting you to others. The **Navigate** phase encompasses sales and marketing, solution development and delivery, and operations.

Starting with visionary customers who "get it," **Navigate** is where you begin to gain real traction in the market. You get your solution out there and deliver meaningful impact with it. Meanwhile, you also seek to improve efficiencies and drive costs down, which in addition to value-based prices, offers you very healthy margins. You gain selling efficiencies by using rainmakers and a SWAT team approach in which solution specialists support your generalist account managers and sales teams. You develop a carefully curated and prioritized list of target accounts or microsegments and focus your proactive sales and marketing efforts on that list. You gain operating efficiencies by looking for ways to reduce the overall cost to you of providing the solution.

You cement your position as a market leader through an industry "community of believers" who become ambassadors for your point of view and approach. You expand your infrastructure at an appropriate pace, and importantly, you measure progress and adjust accordingly.

Don't get lost in the weeds, though. The objective is to help customers *navigate* their way to such a valuable *outcome* that they are willing to pay a premium to get it.

ACTION ITEM

Complete the following **Navigate** planning worksheet. As always, you can access an online tool or download the worksheet for this exercise at apollomethod.com. Again, it's ideal if you and your team first complete the steps outlined in the chapter. If you haven't done that, take a first cut anyway based on where you are now.

Navigate

Planning Worksheet

CUSTOMERS AND SALES

What minimal sales enablement materials or SWAT team members will you need?

_____   _____

_____   _____

Who will your rainmaker(s) be?

_____

What is the profile of your early target buyers? (characteristics, locations, buyer personas, buyer values, structure & culture, etc.)

_____

_____

Of the above, what are the top three types of ideal customer, situation, deal? (Define as buyer personas, if useful)

1. _____
2. _____
3. _____

What three sales and marketing tactics will be most effective in getting them into the funnel?

1. _____
2. _____
3. _____

What customer service approach will you need for your targets?

_____

_____

What sales and distribution channels do you have or must you build? (e.g., account teams, third-party relationships, etc.)

_____

_____

_____

SOLUTION

What must happen to build out the offering?

_____

_____

What pieces are you prepared to offer right away?

_____ _____

_____ _____

What is the process for delivering the solution to customers?

_____

_____

What key partners will you need? _____

_____

What will make the delivery process most efficient?

_____ _____

_____ _____

COMMUNITY

Through what vehicle will you establish an industry "community of believers"? _____

OPERATIONS

How will you track and measure success?

_____

_____

What additional infrastructure/processes do you need?

_____

_____

What people do you need? How will you recruit, enculturate, and train them?

_____

_____

CHAPTER 8

ACCELERATE PHASE

Stay Ahead of Market Changes and Competition

"Even if you're on the right track, you'll get run over if you just sit there."

—Will Rogers

Once the first real crowdfunding site, ArtistShare, saw some success in 2003–2005, others started to quickly sprout up: Indigogo in 2008, Kickstarter in 2009. Now there are at least twenty.

When the iPhone came out in 2007, it was revolutionary. Within no time, however, every other major phone manufacturer had something similar on the market.

In the classic science fiction film *Invasion of the Body Snatchers*, pods grown from alien spores invade people's bodies when they fall asleep and become soulless, robot-like clones devoid of emotion. Regardless of how unique you are when you *launch* and begin to establish market dominance, me-toos are always going to be coming after you. If you aren't careful, they'll clone you. And just like those body snatchers, they'll have none of the passion and deep, deep expertise you bring to the table. Yet no one will be able to tell the difference between you and the clone. You'll be a commodity all over again.

No matter how solid your Go-To status may be, it's going to be crucial to always watch your back and stay ahead of the pack.

As if that weren't threat enough, market conditions change continuously and even abruptly, sometimes in your favor and sometimes not. Suzuki was a leading producer of Japanese weaving looms until the cotton market collapsed in 1951, at which point the company shifted its focus to motor vehicles. Regulations, technology, industry trends, politics, and many other factors are going to constantly jostle you around. You can never stand still. You are going to have to constantly watch what's going on around you, study the horizon, and adjust accordingly. Competitors, clients, and substitutes are likely to force you to *accelerate* your pace and possibly even shift course if you want to own the market.

No matter how solid your Go-To status may be, it's going to be crucial to always watch your back and stay ahead of the pack.

The fundamental strategy underlying the **Accelerate** phase is to pick up speed, scale your business and further penetrate the market, monitor what's going on around you, and anticipate market changes. And if you don't, your business will die. Witness Blockbuster.

Blockbuster was the Go-To for video rental and a market darling when it went public in 1999 with a market capitalization of

$4.8 billion. However, unbeknownst to it, there was a storm brewing on the horizon. Two years prior, software entrepreneur Reed Hastings had returned a copy of *Apollo 13* (coincidentally) to his local Blockbuster store six weeks late and incurred a late fee of $40, which enraged him. It turns out that these customer penalties were a significant part of Blockbuster's revenues and margins. Realizing that DVDs could just as easily be mailed, Hastings vowed to start a mail-order DVD rental service that promised no late fees. The service took off. Meanwhile, Blockbuster carried on with business as usual, even as Netflix began its monthly subscription service. In 2000, Blockbuster declined several opportunities to buy Netflix for a mere $50 million and turned down a proposed partnership. Former Netflix CFO Barry McCarthy described a meeting with Blockbuster's then-CEO to a Stanford University student-led podcast:

> I remembered getting on a plane, I think sometime in 2000, with Reed [Hastings] and [Netflix co-founder] Marc Randolph and flying down to Dallas, Texas, and meeting with John Antioco. Reed had the chutzpah to propose to them that we run their brand online and that they run [our] brand in the stores and they just about laughed us out of their office. At least initially, they thought we were a very small niche business. Gradually over time, as we grew our market, his thinking evolved, but initially they ignored us and that was much to our advantage.

Blockbuster's failure to anticipate market trends and respond quickly enough destroyed it. Within six years, the company had lost all but $500 million in market cap and had a mere 2 million subscribers to Netflix's 6 million. And it got worse from there. A year later, the board fired the CEO pushing streaming (the same one who had laughed Netflix out of the room) in favor of a lieutenant with doubts about online subscriptions who favored short-term profits over investments in the streaming model. Even as Netflix, Amazon, and others gained traction with streaming, the company's board and new CEO just could not see where the market was going and even reintroduced the unpopular late fees it had scrapped a few years earlier. When the Great Recession hit in 2008, the company's massive debt became a pair of cement shoes. Weighed down by $900 million in debt and a half billion in net losses, Blockbuster declared bankruptcy in 2010 with a market cap at that point of just $24 million.

OVERVIEW

Having grown up sailing on the Chesapeake Bay since I was nine years old, I thought of myself as fairly skilled when I moved to the San Francisco Bay Area. My first time sailing there was with a client. Over the course of just a couple of hours, we experienced no wind, raging wind of over 25 knots/hour, sunshine, flat water, six-foot swells, temperatures ranging from 75°F down to 25°F with the windchill factor, and blinding fog. The conditions changed by the minute with almost no notice. I was caught completely off guard (silly me had not even brought a jacket), but my client wasn't. He had sailed these waters many times and knew the possibilities. He didn't know exactly when they would hit, but he was on alert for when they did, ready to adjust the sails or do whatever else was needed to keep us safe and moving forward.

On a sailboat, you must make constant adjustments to the rigging, sails, and even your body position to optimize and leverage the relationship of your boat to the wind and maximize your speed. The wind and weather are there. You can either let them toss you around uncontrollably, or you can harness them to your advantage.

This is what the **Accelerate** phase is all about. And remember how I said earlier that the four phases of the Apollo Method aren't necessarily sequential? **Accelerate** may come in the midst of your journey, requiring a midcourse correction. Startups call this a pivot—a fundamental shift in who they're targeting or what they're offering. Twitter was the result of a pivot by podcasting company Odeo. PayPal pivoted at least twice (some say five times) from cryptography and wireless payments to its ultimate web-based payment system model. You'll see later in this chapter that Kennedy almost pushed the Apollo Space Program itself into a major pivot just as it was gearing up!

REFRESH THE VISION AND PICK UP SPEED

Adjust to market changes and strengthen your position

Accelerate

- Build loyalty
- Constantly monitor the market
- Stay ahead

In many ways, **Accelerate** is a rinse and repeat of the prior phases, but you are out to accomplish several key things. The bottom line, though, is that you need to adapt:

- Fix what's not working.
- Broaden your market presence and strengthen customer loyalty.
- Broaden your offerings.
- Anticipate market trends and additional competition.

The Apollo Space Program initially had a singular goal of getting a person to the Moon and then home again. In the parlance of this book, NASA's plan was to use the **Launch, Ignite,** and **Navigate** phases to get us to the Moon the first time and then **Accelerate** with ten more Moon landings for further exploration. This would, NASA believed, maximize the value of the country's $25+ billion investment in lunar exploration at that point ($112 billion in 2018 dollars) and continue to demonstrate dominance in space in case the

ACCELERATE to Stay Ahead

Soviets decided to step it up. In fact, the Soviets did so, launching the first piloted orbital space station in 1971. To maintain the US lead, President Johnson even had a follow-up program planned as early as 1966 called the Apollo Applications Program (AAP), which would be two-week missions exploring the surface of the Moon. Astronauts would live in "camper" landers, wear "hard-shell" space suits, fly lunar vehicles, drive long distances, and even do some deep drilling beneath the Moon's surface.

Indeed, the Apollo program did continue. As an analog to expanding its "market presence and offerings," six more Apollo missions occurring between 1969 and 1972 had a vastly broadened scope beyond just landing and coming home: explore other sections of the Moon, be able to make precise landings, stay for multiple days, drive for miles along the Moon's surface in a rover, and collect a total of 842 pounds of geologic samples.

By the early 1970s, however, market forces were shifting US priorities. The costly Vietnam War, a huge federal budget deficit, and the declaration of space dominance were making continued Moon exploration investments more difficult to defend. In addition, efforts were afoot to demonstrate détente with the Soviets. President Richard Nixon decided to bring the program to a conclusion and shift NASA's priorities to less expensive reusable spacecraft.

Therefore, as a fitting and powerfully symbolic conclusion to the program in 1975, an *Apollo* command and service module (the mother ship that took astronauts into lunar orbit and brought them back to Earth) rendezvoused with a Soviet *Soyuz* capsule, and the US and Soviet mission commanders exchanged the first international handshake in space through a hatch joining the two spacecraft.

"...this last Apollo flight ends one era and launches a new one."
—*Aerospace* magazine

Some have argued that the Apollo Space Program fizzled, but in reality, the post-*Apollo 11* missions were just the beginning of continued dominance in space exploration. Not resting on its laurels, NASA has "anticipated market trends and competition" and continuously adapted with groundbreaking initiatives extending far beyond the Moon, such as Cassini (study of Saturn), Juno (study of Jupiter), the New Horizons probe (study of Pluto), the Hubble Space Telescope, Voyager (study of interstellar space), Kepler (discovery of new planets), and the Mars rovers. And it has continued Kennedy's original primary objective of demonstrating that space can be a domain of freedom and international cooperation. Many of the aforementioned efforts, along with the International Space Station, involve numerous partners from numerous countries.

The Apollo Space Program came to an end in name only. As *Aerospace* magazine said at the time, "…this last Apollo flight ends one era and launches a new one." In practice, it was just the beginning of a new phase of space exploration.

As you work to achieve market dominance and maintain that position over time, here are the steps you'll take in the **Accelerate** phase:

1. Analyze your current status and take corrective actions.
2. Increase your foothold in existing accounts.
3. Lead and expand your "community of believers."
4. Penetrate the Early Majority and beyond.
5. Monitor the market and adjust the strategy as needed.
6. Update your point of view and solution as needed.
7. Continuously adapt to and stay ahead of your changing market.
8. Carefully broaden while maintaining your Go-To status.

STEP 1

Analyze Your Current Status
and Take Corrective Actions

In 2008, Steve Jobs was fuming. MobileMe, Apple's precursor to iCloud, was a paid-subscription service that synced items like calendars, contacts, photos, and such across Apple devices. Jobs called the product team into an auditorium and made a simple inquiry: "Can anyone tell me what MobileMe is supposed to do?" Upon hearing an engineer's response, Jobs said, "So why the f*** doesn't it do that?"

There were many problems. It was difficult to sign up for the service. When trying to switch over to the new service, users experienced a delay that put their devices out of sync. There were service outages that would even kick users off the site. And there was much market confusion about what the service even was. After many efforts to improve it, Jobs decided to kill it in 2012. Some of the functionality was absorbed by iCloud, and some went away altogether.

By this point, you have been driving toward Go-To status for a particular market problem and unique approach to solving it. Are you there? Are you at a point where the market is seeking you out and you are considered the first name that comes to mind? Do you meet all or most of the criteria we discussed in chapter 2? If not, step back and do an analysis to figure out where you are weak or where you went wrong.

There are many obstacles along the road to success. As we saw earlier, Tesla almost didn't make it. LEGO has hit rough patches and had to recover. Walt Disney's company nearly folded on many occasions as he pursued his goals.

Harley-Davidson had been going through a rough patch when it sustained the first losses in the company's seventy-eight-year history and a workforce reduction of 40 percent in 1981. During the previous decade-plus, it had gone from an undisputed monopoly of the large-motorcycle market to just a 30 percent share. Blaming cheap Japanese imports, it had worked to get tariffs imposed. But there was more to the story than it wanted to admit. Chief executive Vaugh Beals said, "We realized the problem was us, not them." After a tough self-assessment, the company revamped its product line, instituted a more efficient production process that dramatically improved quality, created its H.O.G. community, and deepened its connection with dealers through training and support. By 2007, the company had posted record sales and profits for twenty consecutive years, was the world's most profitable motorcycle company, and was considered one of America's most successful manufacturing companies and brands.

Perhaps you haven't been able to get to the right influencers. Maybe your **Ignite** activity hasn't been focused enough. Or maybe your solution isn't distinctive enough in an obvious, compelling way. Perhaps you are going after too broad a market—you haven't gotten specific enough to stand out and gain traction.

There are any number of reasons you may not be catching fire the way you had hoped. Step back through the methodology in the preceding chapters and see where you need some course corrections.

It may be that you have accomplished the basics but simply need to take everything to the next level. I've been involved in initiatives where we only had the resources for the first couple of years to take merely a rough, first pass through **Launch**, **Ignite**, and **Navigate**, like an artist sketching out what she intends to paint. Then over the following few years, we went back through the phases again. Having initially tested and gained some support for the point of view and approach and having generated some profitable revenues, we were able to more confidently promote our point of view to a wider audience of influencers and build out a more robust offering. We filled in the painting.

Netflix started by mailing rented DVDs and became the Go-To in that domain before moving into streaming third-party content. It then became the Go-To there, before moving into producing and streaming original content.

And finally, identify your strengths and do more to capitalize on them. In talking about how LinkedIn grew from 13 to 175 million users, former LinkedIn executive Elliot Shmukler said that LinkedIn analyzed growth channels in 2008 and realized that the homepage was driving 40 percent of new signups, whereas email invitations drove only 4 percent. The company increased its focus on driving organic homepage visits and making it as easy as possible for people to sign up. Within four months, there were as many new signups through homepage improvements as there were during a full two-year period following email improvements.

STEP 2

Increase Your Foothold in Existing Accounts

Existing customers are, of course, the lifeblood of your company. You have to keep them happy. You also want to cross-sell your other offerings and radiate within your accounts, meaning spread out and look for opportunities in other parts of the customer organization. I don't have to cite research and statistics to remind you of how much cheaper it is to sell to a current customer than break into a new one. You already know this. But this is an area that many companies forget to fully exploit.

Often, it takes a different kind of person
to radiate within an account.

What happens is that companies get fixated on generating leads and penetrating new accounts. The company assigns "salespeople" to find new customers and puts "account management" or "customer success" people on existing customers. They might be good at upselling or encouraging scope increases and related projects. The risk is that they usually become consumed with doing work rather than expanding your presence within the account. If someone is heads down in projects and focused on delivering against deadlines, they are not likely to raise their head up and look around for completely new opportunities in other parts of the account. They are not going to have the luxury of developing new relationships, which takes time, is an unpredictable process, and requires an entirely different frame of mind. Often, it takes a different kind of person to radiate within an account.

Years ago, I heard about a great example of this difference in personalities in action with two of my colleagues. "Stuart," a senior executive in Washington, DC, at a major consulting firm, was overseeing a lot of work at a major communications service provider. He was a brilliant technical guy and also very skilled at managing complex technology implementation projects. He was teamed up with "Ray," a business development executive at the firm who was assigned to help Stuart radiate within the account. Ray was a very seasoned former IBM marketing representative. They were a great team. Ray would walk the halls, develop relationships with client executives, and be on the lookout for opportunities. He would set up meetings and then bring Stuart in to dazzle the executives with expertise and close deals.

One day, a very interesting incident occurred, and it was fascinating to see how differently each of them reacted to it. They were on a trip to Chicago to take the chief information officer (CIO) of a huge account on a tour of the consulting firm's innovation center and stoke his imagination with possibilities for the future. They got back to O'Hare airport for their return to DC, and a snowstorm suddenly grounded their flight. Stuart and Ray each jumped on the phone. Stuart, the technical expert, was calling airlines to try to get himself, Ray, and the client home that night. He didn't want the client to get mad about being stuck. Ray, the business development guy, was on the phone to book a limo, dinner reservations at the best restaurant in Chicago, and three hotel rooms. Stuart's first thought had been, "Oh no!" Ray's first thought had been, "All right! A captive audience!" And what happened? They spent the night in Chicago, bonded over an extravagant dinner the client would never forget, and arrived in DC the next day having all become best buddies. Much business soon followed.

Another pitfall is that account executives often fall short in cross-selling the company's other offerings. Their focus on service or product implementation means they are usually experts in a particular area and aren't comfortable selling outside their area of expertise. They may have the best intentions, but their lack of confidence in other product or service lines becomes an inhibitor. They're also often not good at recognizing opportunities for new solutions and feeding those back to the part of the organization responsible for that. To get around this, assign business development people to this task like the consulting firm above did. That person's job is to become an expert in an account's business and enough of an expert in your full portfolio of solutions to recognize an opportunity when s/he sees it and draw in the right subject matter experts (SWAT team) to help pursue it.

What you want at this point is an account team that will treat the account like a market unto itself. You could even implement a micro-version of the Apollo Method within the account. You would take all of the same steps, starting with an analysis, and tailor the messaging, **Ignite** activity, solution, etc. to the account's specific situation. It's just very important that all of this cascade from and be driven by the company's higher-level strategy, positioning, offerings, etc. You will only be working against yourself to invest in serious account-level marketing that doesn't fit within the overall objectives for establishing the company as a Go-To. Every proactive investment should have strategic value.

For a consumer business, Amazon Prime is a great example of a key cross-sell and upsell strategy with existing customers. Perks like free, expedited shipping and streaming content have hooked at least 100 million customers into a paid, annual subscription, and those customers tend to spend 30 percent more than non-Prime customers, with a renewal rate of 90 percent.

Take a hard look at how you're doing in this area. There is probably a lot of money sitting on the table right in front of you if you just put the right people and programs in place to go after it.

STEP 3

Lead and Expand Your "Community of Believers"

Maintain a very close relationship with your community of believers. Conduct events, such as global customer conferences, that bring people together.

It's impossible to overstate the power of community for a brand, especially when you successfully get customers proselytizing to other customers on your behalf. When you first establish your community of believers during the **Navigate** phase, you want to orchestrate or at least curate it yourself in order to gain traction and build momentum. However, the goal is for it to eventually take on a life of its own, even if you're still deeply involved.

Let's take Apple. There are a number of forums in which Apple users, developers, and other members of the Apple ecosystem interact with each other, often with no Apple involvement. When Apple decided to retire the MobileMe service, which included publicly available hosted content like websites, photos, and videos, a group of volunteers named the Archive Team emerged to preserve 272 terabytes of content provided by 380,000 MobileMe users. This kind of engagement occurs mostly online and at conferences. But it's astonishing to see how actively involved people are. I recently bought a new Mac and was having some migration issues. I got answers to every question I had by searching online. In one forum, I read a post in which someone was offering to go to their local Apple store to help a user in another part of the world resolve their issue.

Another example of a company successfully leading and expanding its community of believers is Salesforce. In 2003, the company kicked off its Dreamforce user conference with 1,300 people in attendance. In 2019, there were 170,000 registered attendees representing at least one hundred countries. There were over 2,700 sessions and workshops, which was more than twice the number of *attendees* the first year. There was such a shortage of accommodations in 2015 that the company had to bring in a cruise ship to provide additional housing. I had the misfortune of flying out of the San Francisco International Airport on the last day of Dreamforce one year and nearly missed my flight due to the unprecedented ticketing and security lines. Salesforce has successfully positioned itself at the center of a vast ecosystem of companies and users who now play a huge role in expanding the company's reach and influence.

STEP 4

Penetrate the Early Majority and Beyond

This is where fruits of your labor with **Launch**, **Ignite**, and **Navigate** start coming together to create momentum for you in the marketplace. Now that you have wider market recognition as the Go-To in your space and have numerous success stories under your belt, targets that are a little slower to adopt new approaches and are more risk averse will be comfortable responding to your marketing outreach and call to action. Evidence and testimonials that your approach is effective will appeal to them. They may not be the first on board with a new approach, but this Early Majority segment is among the largest and more lucrative. If you haven't done so already, now is the time to identify who these companies are and start going after them.

Salesforce gained significant traction out of the gate with small companies and had 3,000 business customers within two years of launching. Morgan Stanley named it the fastest-growing CRM company at the time. A few months later, Salesforce began targeting its "Early Majority" market, introducing its Enterprise Edition aimed at large companies. Revenues quadrupled within a year.

It may be a set of companies in your original target sector that, culturally, are only now ready to take action. Or it may be an industry sector in the next ring from the bullseye in your Target Market Dartboard.

LinkedIn's Innovator market consisted of high-profile Silicon Valley executives who were friends of the founders and then those friends' immediate colleagues. Then it gained traction more broadly in the San Francisco Bay Area tech scene, its Early Adopter market, which then expanded through that network to the information technology sector nationally. At that point, LinkedIn loosened its requirements and changed some features to help the site take off with the Early Majority, which were nontechnology sales and marketing executives and recruiters who valued networking.

The same dynamic occurs in the consumer space. Facebook's Innovator market was, first, Harvard students and then that initial group of eight universities I mentioned earlier. The Early Adopters were students from any college or university, then their friends. The Early Majority were friends of friends and siblings and other teen-agers, followed by parents, relatives, and so on.

Later, your next batch of customers, the more conservative "Late Majority," will start to realize they had better get on the bandwagon. Only start expending resources on them when you see some movement. (A signal is when you start to see issues related to your point of view start to surface in general business publications.)

Eventually, the laggards will get on board as well. But let these come to you. They are the last to adopt innovation, are usually highly price sensitive, and are typically not worth proactively pursuing.

STEP 5

Monitor the Market and Adjust the Strategy as Needed

One of my great-great-grandfathers was a buggy painter (think horse-drawn carriages) in the early 1900s who failed to adapt his career as the automobile came along and wound up out of work for almost a decade. Rather than change, he allowed his career to completely evaporate.

That part of our family lore has always stuck with me, and in many a meeting, I've cautioned executives not to be the buggy painter.

Beyond Blockbuster, the corporate graveyard is littered with companies that didn't anticipate competition or market changes and adapt quickly enough. Kodak, Xerox, record companies, news-papers, bookstores, and many others underestimated the digital revolution. They failed to anticipate players like Amazon and Apple coming out of left field and decimating their businesses.

Apple is widely touted for its dominance in several markets, record-setting market cap, and phenomenal growth; but in 1997, it was on the verge of collapse. It was losing money; had not gained mainstream enterprise traction, losing it to Microsoft's operating system and applications; had products that cannibalized each other and had lots of others that distracted from the core business; and had lost sight of its core mission. Steve Jobs came back to the company through the acquisition of his firm, NeXT, and later became CEO. He immediately ruthlessly attacked sacred cows, even some he had encouraged before his original departure—like his outright hate for Microsoft. In the spirit of "if you can't beat 'em, join 'em," Jobs did a 180-degree turn by signing a five-year deal that would make Office a more integral part of the Mac's appeal to business users. He said:

> If we want to move forward and see Apple healthy and prospering again, we have to let go of a few things here. We have to let go of this notion that for Apple to win, Microsoft has to lose.

At one point, he sat the team down and said, "You know what's wrong with this company? The products *suck*—there's no sex in them." He dramatically changed Apple's product strategy, including slashing and refocusing product lines and canceling pet projects. He also got back to basics by introducing the colorful iMac in 1998, which sold 800,000 units within five months and helped put Apple back in the black. For the first time in three years, it posted a profit in 1998. A year later, net income grew 95 percent and the stock price increased 140 percent.

Even if you start out in Launch with the most brilliant strategy possible, you have to keep watch and be prepared to make a strategic shift at any time.

After fighting back from a Great Recession dip and peaking in 2014, Harley-Davidson stock has been on the decline in recent years, mostly because of a major demographic shift that's largely out of the company's control: its primary market of baby boomers is aging out, and younger buyers want "ease of transportation" that fits their modest budgets rather than a rebel image and heavy bike at a premium price—in other words, the opposite of what Harley-Davidson currently stands for. In 2018, the company issued a 2027 growth strategy to "build the next generation of riders globally." It involves new products, including the company's first electric motorcycle, for new markets and segments; new channels; and a framework for strengthening dealers and the customer experience. The big question remains: will the company succeed in revving back up?

Even if you start out in **Launch** with the most brilliant strategy possible, you have to keep watch and be prepared to make a strategic shift at any time. More than ever, we live in a highly dynamic world in which anything can happen, whether it be a new technology, new regulations, a sudden economic downturn, a terrorist attack...there are infinite possibilities. More typically, however, you will notice a trend that seems to build over time and either open up new opportunities or present new challenges. Be on the lookout at all times.

ASSIGN SOMEONE TO WATCH THE HORIZON

Until relatively recently, "strategy" was left to the CEO (or senior business unit leader) with support from other executives. On the rise, however, is a chief strategy role, as seen at companies like Airbnb, Salesforce, and Uber, because of the pace of change they face. Even when companies don't officially declare the job title, there is someone in the organization driving this function. A chief strategy officer (CSO) for a twenty-two-hospital system in Utah explained the need for a senior strategy person and removing them from day-to-day operations to watch the horizon:

The thing that's changed the most…that has elevated strategy work is the rapidity with which the world around us is changing. Some of it is purposeful change in a consistent direction, but much is turbulent in that it goes one way one day and another the next, and figuring out the correct path is significantly more challenging than when I started.

Your business is probably also moving at 500 miles per hour. That's too fast to have the same person piloting the company and responsible for hour-by-hour decisions to also be watching the horizon and doing long-term planning. Your pilot needs a navigator who knows the destination, keeps a big-picture view of market changes, can plot the course, and determines when to change direction. While your top leadership will always ultimately determine the strategy, you need to designate a person (or team, if you're a large organization) who drives the process on an ongoing basis. The job is to continuously monitor the market and competition, assess/anticipate market trends, and identify needed adjustments to the strategy. This person/team should not be in operations and subject to the short-term financial performance pressures that the operating team is driving toward. Instead, this team should be able to keep a long-term view without having to sacrifice it for short-term results. This is how companies get caught off guard. It's like having everyone on the soccer team play offense, with no one positioned to defend against the player making a fast break in a drive down the field.

If you operate in a cyclical industry, you want to learn the patterns that indicate that an upward or downward shift is about to occur. For example, in real estate markets, a definite sign that things have overheated is condo conversions. This means that buying activity is so feverish and prices are so high that the return on capital from rents is very low. It's more lucrative to sell multifamily units than to rent them. People in the real estate industry know this. When the market hits that peak point, a downturn is on the way. No one can know when, but the smart ones see the signals, prepare, and are in a position to actually capitalize on the downturn.

It's important to identify and watch for these leading indicators in your own sectors. For some, it's oil prices. It may be housing starts, cutbacks or increases in the use of contingent workers, or number of initial public offerings (IPOs). In technology, one signal is a slowdown in marketing job openings after a heated period of hiring. Know your market signals and be ready.

Also be sure to watch the direct competition and competitive alternatives that customers have. If you've really hit on something with your market dominance strategy, the market will fill up with me-toos.

STEP 6

Update Your Point of View and Solution as Needed

Just as you can't stand still in the context of your marketplace, you can't stand still with regard to your point of view and solution. You must constantly be interacting with the market and obtaining feedback on your point of view and offerings. The more dynamic your market, the more you may need to update and reissue your point of view.

If you did your work during **Launch** and decided to focus on a complicated problem driven by an emerging trend with huge potential, your point of view is probably pretty stable and won't require much of an overhaul for quite a while. But the devil is usually in the details and implementation, so your solution will require constant tweaking.

In the twenty years since its founding, Salesforce has gone through a dramatic evolution from that first stripped-down offering focused on small-business sales teams to now offering a vast array of cloud-based solutions covering the entire sales, marketing, and customer interaction spectrum. And while the "End of Software" theme is still applicable in that Salesforce encourages companies to operate in the cloud as much as possible, the company now focuses the message on its users and developers through its off-shoot Trailblazers theme, which is now ubiquitous throughout Salesforce's current Ignite activity. In 2019, chief marketing officer Stephanie Buscemi said, "The premise behind the two [themes] is the same." However, gone is the "No Software" logo, since it's less relevant today, now that software-as-a-service and cloud computing have gone mainstream.

My point of view on what companies need to do in order to achieve sustainable differentiation hasn't fundamentally changed in well over a decade. The fundamentals of the Apollo Method haven't changed. However, the nuances, details, and certain aspects of implementation for the Apollo Method have certainly changed dramatically. The internet, ready availability of analytic services, campaign management tools, and other capabilities have completely transformed media relations, direct marketing, the ability to interact with a community of believers, and so on. Some of the tactics of what should happen in **Launch**, **Ignite**, **Navigate**, and **Accelerate** have changed quite a bit over time, even if the fundamental strategies and steps have remained the same.

Ditto what I said above about the competition. As I discussed in chapter 3, a Go-To maintains a healthy paranoia and doesn't take its success for granted. It will be easy for others to talk the talk, but you need to be sure they can't walk the walk at all like you. Always be several steps ahead with your solution. Always evaluate your solution very critically and look for ways in which others can mimic or even leapfrog you. Then *accelerate* to stay out in front, which takes us to the next step.

STEP 7

Continuously Adapt to and Stay Ahead of Your Changing Market

The famed race car driver Richard Petty was once asked how fast he intended to go to win a 500-mile race at the Ontario Motor Speedway. His response was, "That all depends on how fast the car in second plans to go."

Assume you are aiming for first and that there are dozens of competitors coming after you, even if there aren't—yet. Always keep your eye on where the market is going and be prepared to shift course accordingly. Always have a contingency plan. Be ready for a variety of scenarios.

About thirty months into the Apollo Space Program and a year before the next election, Kennedy got bad news during a private meeting with NASA chief James Webb: even if Kennedy was reelected, the US would not get to the Moon until the year he was out of office. Here is an excerpt of the recorded exchange:

> [Kennedy] If I get reelected, we're not going to the Moon in our period, are we?
>
> [Webb] No. No. You're not going. We're not going...It's just going to take longer than that. This is a tough job. A real tough job.
>
> [Kennedy] Do you think the manned landing on the Moon's a good idea?
>
> [Webb] I predict you're not going to be sorry—ever—that you did this.

Kennedy was already torn about the politics of such a large, sustained investment going into an election year, especially given that tensions with the Soviets had warmed. Two days later, Kennedy shocked NASA, Congress, and the world with a United Nations speech proposing that the US and Soviet Union do the Moon landing together.

Many pushed back, and he was preparing to reverse his position yet again, reaffirming the country's commitment to achieving the Moon mission, in the speech he was on his way to deliver when he was shot.

This is just one example, actually, of the many uncertainties NASA, Apollo, and the post-Apollo US space program have had to continually monitor and adapt to—changing White House administrations and policies, changing public opinion and financial support for space exploration, and now, competition from private industry such as SpaceX, Virgin Galactic, Blue Origin, and more.

Apple has never stood still, moving from hardware into software and streaming services. Amazon clearly constantly adapts to market changes and trends.

Watch the trends impacting your industry. Colleges and universities worldwide, including top schools, are carefully studying online learning trends, realizing that this will dramatically impact the future of higher education. Any sector that is car related is looking at the potential impact of self-driving technology, including auto manufacturers and suppliers, insurance providers, ridesharing and taxis, gas stations, convenience stores, parking garages, and government transportation agencies. YouTube and streaming services are cutting into pay-TV sector revenues—about 33 million people in the US canceled their cable subscriptions in 2018, which was 32.8 percent more than in 2017. Golf has lost 5 million participants in the US since 2008. Millennials are driving changes across numerous industries, avoiding processed foods, often preferring to rent rather than own even luxury goods, and choosing bargain retailers over higher-end department stores while climbing out from under student debt.

As a cautionary tale, Siebel Systems was the Go-To for salesforce automation software in the 1990s (expanding then to customer relationship management [CRM]). Within five years of its founding in 1993, it had become a force to be reckoned with: nearly $2 billion a year in revenues, 8,000 employees, and a market cap of $30 billion. No competitor could touch it. Then the 2001 recession hit. By that point, Siebel had placed a major bet through an acquisition that doubled its size and then couldn't retrench quickly enough. Like many major companies, the recession had caught it off guard. Climbing out of that hole, Siebel successfully transitioned some of its offerings to the cloud to adapt to customer needs and upstarts at the time, like Salesforce. But it was too late. In 2005, Oracle was able to acquire Siebel for just $5.85 billion while Salesforce went on to become the juggernaut it is today.

STEP 8

Carefully Broaden While Maintaining Your Go-To Status

I mentioned earlier how Salesforce started with a narrow focus on salesforce automation and then broadened into CRM and marketing. Once you become a Go-To, you can strategically and carefully broaden into additional, adjacent markets—"adjacent" being the pivotal word. It's crucial that all markets you are serving are complementary so that you don't dilute your resources and for the reasons I discussed in chapter 1. This may mean selling a broader set of solutions to the same customers, the same solutions to a broader set of customers, or leveraging some other core strength to sell new solutions to new customers. It's essential that you do this, of course, so that you don't have all of your eggs in one basket. But only do it after you have secured a firm beachhead.

Amazon has successfully done all three. Once establishing its dominance in books, Amazon began to offer additional products to its customers, starting with music (still sold on CDs at the time). It then leveraged its heavy holiday shopping traffic to expand into popular holiday categories such as home improvement products, software, video games, and gifts. It also made acquisitions that gave it access to large new pools of customers. As of 2015, Amazon had expanded to offer almost anything you can think of and was ranked as the ninth largest retailer in the US, surpassing Walmart in market value.

But that's not all. In the background, Amazon was also quietly becoming the Go-To player in cloud computing (remote data storage and processing). Having built a sophisticated data center infrastructure and software platform for enabling other businesses to integrate with Amazon's retail systems, Amazon began leveraging this core strength as a service to address an unmet need in the market. According to research firm Gartner, this not-so-little side business AWS had a whopping 51 percent market share in 2017. By 2018, it had become a $26 billion business and the Go-To cloud infrastructure provider, towering over Microsoft, IBM, Oracle, and many others. (Get the full story at apollomethod.com.)

Tenneco's journey, on the other hand, is an illustration of what not to do. Ultimately building the largest natural gas pipeline network in the United States, Tenneco became the Go-To for gas transmission in the 1940s and '50s. It then acquired oil companies in the 1950s and an oil and minerals company in 1980. These made sense.

Then Tenneco got itself into trouble. There was a trend in the '70s for companies to "diversify" into far-flung businesses that had nothing to do with their core offerings. Tenneco jumped onto this bandwagon, making more than a dozen other acquisitions of capital-intensive businesses that didn't blend in with the core business. These included Newport News Shipbuilding, J. I. Case (farm and construction machinery manufacturing), a British chemical company, automotive parts companies, insurance companies, and the Ecko houseware brand companies. At one point, Tenneco was even the largest dried nuts and fruits processor, owning brands such as House of Almonds and Morrow's Nut House; it owned four distribution centers, a confectionary production plant, and dozens of retail stores nationwide.

I witnessed all of this firsthand. My dad began his career as a civil engineer at the shipyard, helping to design aircraft carriers before taking other executive positions there. And I had several summer internships in the engineering logistics department responsible for restocking spare parts inventories on ships in for repair; I also spent a summer with the public relations department. Even as a young child, I remember my dad bringing almonds back with him from business trips to Bakersfield and thinking it made no sense for a company that owned a shipyard to also be in the nut business.

And it didn't. By the 1980s, Tenneco was fighting off shareholder efforts to sell off its various subsidiaries and was viewed as a takeover target. It did divest some divisions and start to refocus. But when a new CEO arrived in 1991, he had to take such drastic actions through layoffs, divestitures, and dividend reductions that *Businessweek* magazine labeled him "a tough boss for tough times." Within three years, the company went from $2 billion in losses over a two-year period to a positive net income of $426 million and a reduction in its debt-to-capitalization ratio from 70 percent to 49.3 percent.

The company eventually evolved into a manufacturer and supplier of automotive parts with expansion plans centered on adjacent markets. The new strategy was effective, as evidenced by a steady growth in its stock price. From late 2001 to early 2017, the stock climbed from less than $2 per share to over $67 per share. Tenneco won awards from accounting firm PwC for delivering the highest shareholder return among automotive suppliers during the mid-aughts. But the story is not over yet. Now facing rising materials costs, automotive industry headwinds, and the integration of a major acquisition, it remains to be seen as to how effectively Tenneco will weather new storms.

Once you get to the top, you have to figure out how to stay at the top. No one is ever safe.

RECAP AND ACTION ITEM

The **Accelerate** phase is all about refreshing the vision and picking up speed to stay ahead of market changes and competition. You are operating in constantly changing conditions and must therefore constantly adapt and course correct. Adjust your vision, strategy, point of view, solution, and operations as needed, starting with an honest assessment of your current situation. Meanwhile, strengthen and expand customer relationships, break into the Early Majority, and broaden to other segments as appropriate. Continue to provide leadership across the market and grow your community of believers to further solidify your position as a market influencer and Go-To. Above all, maintain a healthy paranoia, because no matter how firmly established you are as a Go-To, the market will inevitably fill with me-toos.

Jeff Bezos put it best in the company's IPO filing in 1997 when he first shared his "Day 1" philosophy. His belief is that a company should always operate as if it's Day 1 and that:

> Day 2 is stasis. Followed by irrelevance. Followed by excruciating, painful decline. Followed by death. And that is why it's always Day 1…An established company might harvest Day 2 for decades, but the final result would still come.

In a recent letter on this concept, he said:

The outside world can push you into Day 2 if you won't or can't embrace powerful trends quickly. If you fight them, you're probably fighting the future. Embrace them and you have a tailwind.

ACTION ITEM

Complete the following **Accelerate** planning worksheet. As always, you can access an online tool or download the worksheet for this exercise at apollomethod.com. Again, it's ideal if you and your team first complete the steps outlined in the chapter. If you haven't done that, take a first cut anyway based on where you are now.

**REFRESH THE VISION
AND PICK UP SPEED**

Planning Worksheet

What course corrections do you need right now? What isn't going well and needs to be fixed?

_____

_____

How might you cross-sell and upsell within existing accounts?

_____

_____

What will you do to lead and expand your "community of believers"?

_____

_____

Are you and the market ready for broader penetration into more pragmatic Early Majority clients, now that you have traction and success stories? What will it take and who will you target?

_____

_____

_____

_____

_____

How will you constantly monitor the market and quickly adjust the strategy as needed? How will you ensure you can stay ahead of the curve?

_____

_____

_____

ACCELERATE PLANNING WORKSHEET *(cont'd)*

What is happening with the competition?

_____

_____

_____

How are market trends already impacting your market, point of view, strategy, and solution?

_____

_____

_____

_____

Is the point of view still valid? Does it need refinement? How will you test the revisions?

_____

_____

_____

_____

Do you need to reissue the point of view and/or adapt the solution?

_____

_____

_____

_____

Are you ready to broaden to the next rings of your Target Market Dartboard or other adjacent markets? Do you need to revise your targeting strategy? What will you target next?

_____   _____

_____   _____

_____   _____

_____   _____

CHAPTER 9

YOUR ONE-PAGE FLIGHT PLAN

The preceding detail is all well and good, but wow, this is a lot to take on. You may be feeling overwhelmed by the amount of work involved. Where do you begin? Let's get you started with a simple one-page flight plan and the option of a 30-day challenge. This will give you quick wins.

I've put together my share of extensive plans that could each fill a binder (or more). But it's a lot less overwhelming to start with just enough to fit on one page—think of it as the outer layer of the onion. You can always peel additional layers as needed. The Apollo Method is essentially your strategy. Now you just need to tailor it to your circumstances and identify the tactical activities you'll take to start implementing it. By boiling your plan down to one page, you are forced to focus on the "vital few" actions needed to get you going. Very few organizations can take on the full scope of the Apollo

Method program in a single stroke of effort. Most likely, you'll do this in stages.

To create your one-page flight plan, bring together the summary planning worksheets you filled out at the end of chapters 5–8. If you've done the work prescribed in the preceding chapters and if you know your market well, perhaps they were easy to fill out. If your market is complex or changing by the day, this was and may continue to be a challenging exercise. If you haven't done them yet at all, now is the time.

If you're stuck somewhere, skip it for now and come back to it. Or fill it in based on where you are now and refine later. Some areas may warrant more research or analysis. It's okay to work it like a jigsaw puzzle, filling in as you can. By boiling it all down on worksheets like this, however, you can avoid analysis paralysis and get started.

Either way, this one-page flight plan is a shortcut compared to what people typically do. Your answers should be concise—by the time you're done, you'll be able to fit it all on one sheet, as shown in the illustration that follows. (You'll find a more legible version, an online tool, and a printable template at apollomethod.com.)

In the preceding chapters, we covered a lot of detail regarding each phase of the Apollo Method for Market Dominance. But in the end, it's rather straightforward, because any organization has mindshare to execute only so much at a time.

NOW CRITIQUE IT

Once assembled, what you have in your hands is a blueprint for pursuing market dominance. Take a holistic look at the document to see whether it hangs together, makes sense, and seems appropriate. If you feel the template itself is missing a few things, add them, even if it means tailoring the template. Make this work for your situation and business. (And tell me about it at apollomethod.com—I read every comment personally and would love to know how you needed to tailor it for your situation.)

Apollo Method for Market Dominance
One-Page Flight Plan Worksheet

This image is merely for illustration purposes. A legible worksheet to print or download and an online tool are available at apollomethod.com.

Next, go through each item in the plan and rate on a scale of 1–5 how close you think it is to really being distinctive and ready for prime time. For example, does the point of view reflect the status quo versus being fresh and unique? Give it a "1." Is the offering unique but still a product or service rather than a *complete solution* that delivers a result? Give it a "3." And so on. Now you know your strengths and weaknesses, what you can play up, and what you need to fix.

SOCIALIZE IT

Start socializing it with key stakeholders, starting with internal stakeholders. Have them poke holes in it and play devil's advocate. Have them play the prosecutor and you the defendant. Get some feedback and reactions. Improvements based on these conversations will only strengthen it and serve as good practice for starting to implement the feedback cycles called for within the Apollo Method phases themselves. Industry analysts and pundits can be very helpful here.

Consider it a living document that you will update and improve as you go along. Each conversation will teach you something. By the time you're done getting buy-in throughout the organization and from others you depend upon, you will have enormous insights and confidence in your plan.

START EXECUTING

Now that you have a strategic game plan, convert this into a tactical action plan—a work plan—that lays out projects and subprojects, individual tasks and assignments, dependencies, start/end/due dates, and budgets. Create a Gantt chart that visually represents the time frame of each task and what the overlaps are. You can do this in a spreadsheet or use a project management tool. There is an example at apollomethod.com and also a simple spreadsheet template you can use as a starting point. For anyone unfamiliar with project management techniques, Gantt charts, and best practices, there are links to a few resources.

TAKE THE 30-DAY CHALLENGE

If even your work plan seems overwhelming and you still need help getting some quick wins, start with an easy 30-day challenge. I've posted this at apollomethod.com. It's extremely specific with daily assignments. Even incremental improvements in your messaging, positioning, value proposition, and execution will make a big difference.

COMMON PITFALLS AND HOW TO AVOID THEM

In many ways, this material is very easy to talk about and very hard to execute, even without any major obstacles. But there are indeed common obstacles that can completely derail a company's efforts to become the Go-To, and they often originate from within. Here are four common ones and how to avoid or overcome them.

- **Too many "entrepreneurs," each taking the organization in a different direction:** This is a very common problem in services organizations in particular. Obtain participation and input into the process of deciding what *one* direction you are going to head in, and either have everyone on board or have someone bow out. At Apple, there came a point where co-founders Steve Jobs and Steve Wozniak were no longer in sync, so Wozniak chose to reduce his involvement, saying the company had "been going in the wrong direction for the last five years."

- **Not everyone on the team being completely clear on the vision and Go-To goal:** Communicate, communicate, communicate internally. And train. Even before you take your message outside, it's imperative that every person in the organization know the song and be able to sing it. We heard earlier from Marc Benioff about how he discovered his team wasn't in sync on what Salesforce was and what it stood for and why it was so important to fix that with training and communications.

- **A Go-To position you think is unique, compelling, and focused enough, but isn't:** Once you think you have it, test, test, test. Try to shoot holes in it. Invite others to do so as well, especially customers, prospects, and market influencers. Clearly, the US had not staked out an adequate space race Go-To position as of the late '50s, considering the Soviets kept trumping US accomplishments, thus prompting Kennedy's mandate to figure out what would do so.

- **Going to market too early:** As they say, you only have one chance to make a good first impression, and frequently companies start selling "vaporware" before they know for a fact that they can deliver on their promises. You don't have to have everything fully fleshed out—you can still go to market with a minimum viable offering. The pivotal word, though, is *viable*. If you're not a certain amount of ready, you are going to, at a minimum, hurt your credibility and, even worse, tank completely.

A case in point was the infamous Iomega "Click of Death."

In its quest to expand into the consumer market and become the leading external storage provider in the late 1990s, Iomega rushed to market with the well-priced Zip Drive, a groundbreaking device that used high-capacity miniature disks, invaluable for backups and porting large files from one device to another. (This was still the Dark Ages, when consumers used slow, dial-up internet access and long before the availability of flash drives or high-capacity external hard drives priced for the average person.) The product was a huge hit. But there was a problem. Some users started hearing a strange click emanating from their drives. This meant that the drive head had become misaligned and was no longer capable of reading disks. But that wasn't all. The misaligned drive head would then permanently damage any disk put into it. But wait, there's more! If you were to put that damaged disk into a different, properly functioning drive, the damaged disk would throw off the alignment of the healthy drive, which would then damage other disks and so on. It was viral. Losing their backups and precious files, users dubbed the flaw the "Click of Death," and word spread rapidly. Iomega never quite recovered and was eventually absorbed by another company.

Remember how in school, it only took one D to drag your whole grade point average down, and it took forever to claw your way back to where it was? It's the same with a reputation.

Even if you do all of this right, there will be other pitfalls to avoid at every turn. We've looked at many examples of Go-To companies throughout this book that have, to date, achieved the goal of sustained differentiation and growth. But they, too, face daily challenges, and the situation for them could turn on a dime if they don't continuously innovate, adapt, and stay ahead.

STUFF HAPPENS

The four phases of the Apollo Method for Market Dominance that so effectively helped the United States win the space race in the 1960s continues to help both large and small companies dominate as the Go-To brands in their markets. By applying these principles and techniques, you can significantly enhance your own chances of succeeding against all odds. But be aware that it can't possibly rule out all odds. Sometimes bad things happen to good businesses.

On September 10, 2001, many businesses were in the ring, leaning heavily on the ropes as they struggled to pull their bloodied, battered bodies back up after several knockout punches over the previous eighteen months of the dot-com market crash that had throttled capital markets and company bottom lines. The next day, a terrorist act shattered the United States' sense of security. It was one of the darkest days the country had ever seen. Economically speaking, it was a catastrophic blow that put many businesses back down for the count.

Seven years later, in a matter of days in September 2008, without warning, all but two of the most vaunted independent investment banking firms either went under or sold themselves in a fire sale; Fannie Mae and Freddie Mac announced they were insolvent; and the Federal Reserve was forced to provide an $85 billion bailout loan to AIG, a leading insurance firm that would have otherwise declared bankruptcy and roiled global markets beyond repair. Credit was suddenly almost completely unavailable. The US, and to a large extent the world, economy was in crisis.

No amount of market analysis, planning, or foresight could have anticipated those two events or many others past, present, and future. All you can do is manage your business, monitor your market as closely as possible, and do everything in your power to minimize your risk and maximize your odds of success.

Thankfully, these catastrophic events are far and few between. And even during those dark times, there is opportunity to create new businesses and solutions to market problems. Disney released its first full-length animated feature, *Snow White and the Seven Dwarfs*, in the midst of the Great Depression, which was embraced by a country in dire need of uplifting entertainment. Both Electronic Arts and Adobe were founded during a deep recession in the early 1980s. Apple launched the iPod less than sixty days after 9/11. Financial technology and lending company Kabbage launched smack in the middle of the Great Recession and had revenues of $200 million in 2017. Salesforce took off like a rocket during both the dot-com and Great Recession crises. Kickstarter and Instagram both launched during the global financial crisis recovery. Netflix rolled out its new streaming service in 2009 during the peak of the Great Recession and *gained* 3 million new customers.

DIFFERENTIATE TO DOMINATE

The overarching goal of the Apollo Method for Market Dominance is to help you build a platform as the Go-To brand. It will help you achieve *sustainable differentiation* in your crowded market(s). This will lead to *sustainably higher gross margins* through healthy pricing and lower costs. These higher margins, in turn, will allow you to invest in your future, fueling *sustainable, profitable growth*. Most of all, the Apollo Method for Market Dominance provides a blueprint for ensuring that you deliver remarkable value and results to customers in ways that dramatically improve their lives and/or businesses. Success for your customers will lead to success for you.

The method boils down to:

- **Launch:** Develop a unique and prescriptive point of view on a common, critical, and urgent market problem and a unique, results-oriented solution; and then launch yourself into the market to declare ownership.
- **Ignite:** Start and continuously ignite a movement in the marketplace around your point of view and approach, beginning with powerbrokers and visionary early customers.

- **Navigate:** Walk your talk, deliver on your promises, and help customers navigate the journey to solving their problem with a complete, results-oriented solution customers are willing to pay a premium for.
- **Accelerate:** Continuously adapt and accelerate to stay ahead of the pack as me-too copycats emerge and market conditions change.

Stay in continuous orbit (a state of continuous improvement) as you repeatedly cycle back through the four phases of the Apollo Method for Market Dominance to achieve sustainable market leadership and healthy pricing as the Go-To brand.

Even today, almost sixty years after its inception, the successful Apollo Space Program remains one of the most powerful examples of human achievement in the face of competition and radical change. By applying valuable lessons from the efficacy of the Apollo Space Program as a focused, unified effort aimed at a specific and tangible outcome, any of us can win a business space race. Apollo serves as a dramatic role model, encouraging companies to take a focused, methodical approach. Declare the goal of market dominance in a very specific market space and rally the resources of all stakeholders around that goal. As proven by the Apollo Space Program, dominance is a process—a long-term initiative that requires courage, investment, structure, and persistence.

My hope is that this book has inspired you to declare your own moonshot by aiming to *be the Go-To* in your market and has given you some tools for a swift, relatively safe journey to the top.

May you win your own space race.

AUTHOR'S NOTE

Whatever you do, act now. Please put even just one task from your one-page plan or elsewhere in this book into use immediately. Ideas are meaningless without action. And implementing the activities in this book *will* have a meaningful financial and brand reputation impact on your business. You'll be amazed.

- **Free Online Companion Course:** To solidify what you've learned, take the book's free companion course online at *apollomethod.com*. This is a self-paced, self-study program that includes bonus and supplemental materials to help you get results more quickly.

- **Reviews and Notes:** If you enjoyed the book, I hope you'll write a review on Amazon, Goodreads, or other online resources and send me a note. I read every review and personally respond to every note. I'm always a sponge for stories, your experiences, and any suggestions or new ideas this content may spark. I'd love to hear from you! *theresa@apollomethod.com*.

- **Additional Resources:** There were *many* additional stories, in-depth case studies, examples, and concepts arising from my research that I just couldn't fit into the book, so check *apollomethod.com* for those, along with the many Apollo Method templates and tools I mentioned along the way. I'll answer all questions you send in a running FAQ on the site. You'll also find bonus material and recommended reading.

- **Community:** If you'd like to interact with others who are working to implement the Apollo Method at their companies, visit *apollomethod.com* to join the community for idea sharing and support. I also encourage you to form local meetup groups and let me know about them so I can support your efforts.

- **Bulk Orders:** For discounts on bulk orders of twenty or more copies for your company, team, club, meetup group, etc., contact *inquiry@apollomethod.com*.

Thank you for joining the journey. Now go Be the Go-To!

ACKNOWLEDGMENTS

The Apollo Method for Market Dominance is the culmination of direct work experience with amazing colleagues and clients, hundreds of formal interviews with executives in the field, and other extensive research. But it really all started with Al Burgess, who was my boss at Accenture and allowed me to be his partner in crime in starting and growing the Communications Industry Group, where I essentially got my MBA. Al has an ingenious strategic mind, and businesses everywhere would be so much better off if we could just bottle and sell the way he thinks. At a time when I wasn't quite finding my place within the company, he saw my potential to bring out-of-the-box creativity into an organization that had not yet fully embraced it and gave me free reign to be wildly entrepreneurial. Most of all, despite my being young and still green, he included me in every high-level meeting with the company's most senior leadership, mentored and guided me through many political land mines, and pushed me to my limits in ways that have been invaluable ever since. He was and still is the embodiment of a true leader, and I will always be eternally grateful for what I learned from him and all that he has done for me.

Our team included many brilliant partners, managers, and staff around the world, along with a stellar marketing team composed of Faye Shannon, Belinda Deyton, Lois Colborn, and Deb Kalaritis, to name just a few of the fabulous people I had the privilege of working with. I also thank Skip Battle, Jim Murphy, and Michael Krauss for what I learned watching their inspirational leadership of the umbrella global brand and for their support whenever Al and I ruffled a few feathers trying something new. All of these people contributed directly and indirectly to the ideas in this book.

I am enormously grateful to Tina Seelig, Tom Byers, and Kathy Eisenhardt for giving me exciting opportunities to contribute to the Stanford Technology Venture Program's status as a Go-To brand. I also want to thank Bob Sutton for being so inspirational and wonderful to work with. Likewise, I am incredibly appreciative of the opportunity to engage with both the Graduate School of Business and the Department of Management Science and Engineering (MS&E) in the School of Engineering at Stanford University. In particular, I thank Melinda McGee, the entire faculty, and the marvelous staff that keeps the MS&E department humming. And no one keeps me on my toes and up on the latest trends like the incredible students of the Stanford Marketing Group, which I've had the privilege of helping for over a decade now.

During a hiatus in the writing of this book, marketers Richard Jurek and David Meerman Scott published their meticulously researched book, *Marketing the Moon: The Selling of the Apollo Lunar Program*, which turned out to be a gold mine of fabulous stories in support of my thesis. They also generously provided supplemental information and pointed me in crucial new directions by phone and email. It was wonderful to meet two more people who share my passion for what the Apollo Space Program can teach us.

Likewise, I appreciate the firsthand insights that former NASA employees, contractors, and members of the Apollo Space Program team shared with me. Among them were Apollo astronaut Dick Gordon (RIP), Norman Crabill, Jerry Seelig, Joe Young, and his late wife, Kathy Young, who was among the very first female programmers to work at NASA. And while it may sound crazy, I want to send a heartfelt thanks to Tom Hanks, Ron Howard, Brian Grazer, and Michael Bostick for creating the stunning HBO miniseries *From the Earth to the Moon*. It was while watching this that I came to viscerally understand the full extent of the parallel between the Apollo Space Program and what it takes to become a Go-To brand. The emotional impact of that series energized me to get the Apollo Method for Market Dominance out into the world.

When I first developed this material, I ran it by trusted friends and colleagues and used it with clients I knew would give me unvarnished reactions and help me improve it. Among the hundreds I'm grateful to are Robin Johnston, Tina Seelig, Kay Young, Peggy Burke, Jane Weston, Jane Lombard, Janet Strauss, Michele Barry, Tina Smith, Loren Eskenazi, Susan Anderson, Craig Stevens, Marilyn Schlitz, Tom Byers, Paula Courtney, Paul Walker, Rosemary Moore, Tom Kosnik, Steve Blank, Jane McCracken, Joan Vogel, Patti Stevens, John Oltman, Gresh Brebach, Wendy Goodyear, Bridget Taylor, Curtis Mills, Gary Stevens, Mary Gatch, Laura Heinrich, Liz Greer, Ellen Gustafson, Patti Johnson, Kathleen Marvin, Scott Mize, Feather Hickox, Judy Watson, Suzanne Beisner, Joanne Burgess, Mayla Clark, Sandra Ewers, Michaela Zuckova, Elias Awad, Leslie Kelly, Susan Harrington, plus many I am somehow forgetting to name but will post to apollomethod.com in gratitude for their enormous contributions. I also want to thank Sandy Schmidt and the late John Gwin, the beloved marketing professors who inspired my career choice.

Books are team efforts, and this one's initial glimmer of hope for success came about because literary agent Matt Wagner was the first to see its potential. His early support led me to go for it. Many of the people I've named above have reviewed and commented on drafts, offering marvelous feedback, for which I'm so grateful. I also thank my editor, Hal Clifford, and publishing manager, Natalie Aboudaoud, for the marvelous guidance, prodding, and assistance, which were the ultimate reasons it got done.

Many of the people I've named above are also close personal friends, and I can't begin to thank them enough for all of the encouragement they've offered over the years this methodology and book have been taking shape. I am so fortunate to call you my friends.

Naturally, I want to thank my amazing parents and siblings, who have all been incredible role models for what it means to be a kind, loving, and generous human being. I am also blessed with a large, loving, fun, and supportive extended family.

Finally and with highest gratitude, I thank my beloved husband, Michael, for having the patience of a saint to help me get through this project, critique many drafts, keep me laughing, and frequently hold down the fort at home. And then there are my daughters, who cannot begin to know the depth of my love, even though I tell them about one hundred times a day. Everything I do is for you, girls.

SELECT NOTES

This is a thoroughly researched book containing over 450 citations. For comprehensive, annotated endnotes, visit *apollomethod.com*.

PROLOGUE

Roger Launius, "*Sputnik* and the Origins of the Space Age," nasa.gov, accessed November 11, 2019, https://history.nasa.gov/sputnik/sputorig.html.

"*Sputnik*: 'Intellectual Earthquake' That Led to *Apollo 11*," Agence France-Presse, September 30, 2007, http://www.spacedaily.com/2006/070930005912.gy10716s.html.

"May 25, 1961: JFK's Moon Shot Speech to Congress," Space.com, May 25, 2011, https://www.space.com/11772-president-kennedy-historic-speech-moon-space.html.

David Scott and Richard Jurek, *Marketing the Moon: The Selling of the Apollo Lunar Program*, (Cambridge, MA: MIT Press, 2014).

CHAPTER 1

"Win/Loss Trend Analysis," OmniTech Consulting Group, Inc., April 25, 1998, internal company document, used with permission.

Andrew Holmes and John Ryan, "Commoditization—Coming to a Company Near You," *International Journal of Business and Management* 3, no. 12 (December 2008): 3.

David Chau, "Amazon on Track to Dominate Australian Retail within Seven Years, despite a Shaky Start," Text, *ABC News, December 26, 2018,* https://www.abc.net.au/news/2018-12-26/amazon-dominate-retail-within-years-slow-start/10667884.

Joan Capelin, "Confronting Commoditization," August 9, 2013, https://www.di.net/articles/confronting-commoditization/.

CHAPTER 2

Michael Cabanatuan, "A-maze-ing/ His Reputation on the Line, Contractor Finishes Repair Early, and I-580 Opens," *SFGate,* May 25, 2007, https://www.sfgate.com/bayarea/article/A-MAZE-ING-His-reputation-on-the-line-2592154.php.

Clint Myers, Phone Interview with Theresa Lina, September 25, 2019.

Kevin Kelleher, "Amazon Is Still Executing Bezos's 1997 Plan," *VentureBeat,* May 15, 2017, https://venturebeat.com/2017/05/15/amazon-is-still-executing-bezoss-1997-plan/.

Stephen Diorio, "The Financial Power of Brand Preference," *Forbes,* January 22, 2019, https://www.forbes.com/sites/forbesinsights/2019/01/22/the-financial-power-of-brand-preference/.

"Brand Strategy That Shifts Demand: Less Buzz, More Economics," *Bain,* November 14, 2012, https://www.bain.com/insights/brand-strategy-that-shifts-demand/.

Eugene Kim, "Amazon Is Growing Its Gross Profit at a Staggering Rate," CNBC, May 14, 2018, https://www.cnbc.com/2018/05/14/amazon-gross-profit-growth-bigger-than-top-five-retailers-combined.html.

CHAPTER 3

Space.com, "JFK Moon Speech."

Al Ries, *Focus: The Future of Your Company Depends on It* (New York: HarperBusiness, 1996), viii.

Andrew S. Grove, *Only the Paranoid Survive: How to Exploit the Crisis Points That Challenge Every Company* (New York: Crown, 2010), 151.

David Robertson and Bill Breen, *Brick by Brick: How LEGO Rewrote the Rules of Innovation and Conquered the Global Toy Industry* (New York: Crown, 2013).

The Economist, "How lego Become the World's Hottest Toy Company," *Business Insider,* accessed November 13, 2019, https://www.

businessinsider.com/how-lego-become-the-worlds-hottest-toy-company-2014-3.

Richard Milne, "LEGO Suffers First Drop in Revenues in a Decade," *Financial Times*, September 5, 2017, https://www.ft.com/content/d5e0b6b0-9211-11e7-a9e6-11d2foebb7fo.

"Chronology of Defining Events in NASA History," accessed November 13, 2019, https://history.nasa.gov/40thann/define.htm.

Geoffrey Moore, *Crossing the Chasm*, 3rd ed. (New York: Collins Business Essentials, 2014), 80–81.

Andrew Wray, "Former Apple Manager Tells How the Original iPhone Was Developed, Why It Went with Gorilla Glass," February 4, 2012, https://www.imore.com/apple-manager-tells-original-iphone-born.

"Marc Benioff: A Brand Is Not Just a Logo—It's Your Most Important Asset," *Salesforce* blog, accessed November 13, 2019, https://blogs.salesforce.com/company/2013/07/marc-benioff-logo-brand-advice.html.

Diane Gage Lofgren and Debbie Cantu, "Five Lessons from Kaiser Permanente's Thrive Campaign," *Marketing Health Services*, 2010.

Dave Hamilton, "Why *did* Apple Create the iTunes Music Store?" *The Mac Observer*, accessed November 13, 2019, https://www.macobserver.com/tmo/article/why_did_apple_create_the_itunes_music_store.

Erik Sherman, "What It Was Like to Work at Amazon 20 Years Ago," *Fortune*, July 15, 2015, https://fortune.com/2015/07/15/amazon-startup-employees/.

Guy Kawasaki, "Guy Kawasaki—The Art of Evangelism," *Guy Kawasaki* (blog), April 29, 2014, https://guykawasaki.com/the-art-of-evangelism/.

"Recipients of the Bernard M. Gordon Prize for Innovation in Engineering and Technology Education," NAE, accessed November 13, 2019, https://nae.edu/55293/GordonWinners.

Chris Beard, "Safeguarding Choice and Control Online," *The Mozilla Blog*, July 30, 2015, https://blog.mozilla.org/blog/2015/07/30/safeguarding-choice-and-control-online.

Fred R. Ricker and Ravi Kalakota, "Order Fulfillment: The Hidden Key to e-Commerce Success," *Supply Chain Management Review*, 1999, http://www.pearsoned.ca/highered/divisions/text/cyr/readings/Ricker_KalakotaT3P1R2.pdf.

"Amazon's Competitive Advantage Tied to Fulfillment | JOC.Com," November 16, 2015, https://www.joc.com/international-logistics/

distribution-centers/amazon%e2%80%99s-competitive-advantage-tied-fulfillment-operations_20151116.html.

Grove, *Only the Paranoid Survive*, 68.

CHAPTER 4

Business Insider, LEGO.

Brian Merchant, "The Secret Origin Story of the iPhone," *The Verge*, June 13, 2017, https://www.theverge.com/2017/6/13/15782200/one-device-secret-history-iphone-brian-merchant-book-excerpt.

CHAPTER 5

"Memo from President John F. Kennedy to Vice President Lyndon Johnson," April 20, 1961, https://www.visitthecapitol.gov/exhibitions/artifact/memo-president-john-f-kennedy-vice-president-lyndon-johnson-april-20-1961.

Martin Eberhard, "Lessons from the Electric Roadster," *Entrepreneurial Thought Leaders*, Stanford eCorner, October 10, 2007, https://ecorner.stanford.edu/podcasts/lessons-from-the-electric-roadster/.

Faith Storey, "The Early Days at Salesforce—From Salesforce First Investor (Video)", 2018, https://www.saastr.com/how-customers-saves-salesforce/.

Dr. Kathy Fields, Phone Interview with Theresa Lina, March 20, 1998.

John M. Logsdon, *John F. Kennedy and the Race to the Moon* (New York: Palgrave Macmillan, 2010), 80–118.

"Strategic Plan," *Alzheimer's Association*, accessed November 17, 2019, https://www.alz.org/about/strategic-plan.

"Our Vision," Stanford University, accessed November 17, 2019, https://ourvision.stanford.edu/.

"REI Is Creating Some Great Marketing That Capitalizes on Black Friday," Brand Culture, October 30, 2015, https://brandculture.com/insights/black-friday-good-marketing-for-rei/.

Roger Launius, "NASA and Its Interagency, Academic, Industry and International Partners," accessed November 17, 2019, https://www.nasa.gov/50th/50th_magazine/partners.html.

"Airbnb: The Growth Story You Didn't Know," GrowthHackers, accessed November 17, 2019, https://growthhackers.com/growth-studies/airbnb.

CHAPTER 6

Karen Breslau, "The Resurrection of Al Gore," *Wired*, May 1, 2006, https://www.wired.com/2006/05/gore-2/.

David Parker, "Let's Talk about the Elephant in the Room," *A Changemaker in the Making* (blog), February 10, 2010, https://davidparker9.wordpress.com/tag/social-media/.

Nicholas Confessore and Karen Yourish, "$2 Billion Worth of Free Media for Donald Trump," *The New York Times*, March 15, 2016, https://www.nytimes.com/2016/03/16/upshot/measuring-donald-trumps-mammoth-advantage-in-free-media.html.

Malcolm Gladwell, *The Tipping Point: How Little Things Can Make a Big Difference* (New York: Bay Back Books, 2002), 12.

James Kauffman, *Selling Outer Space: Kennedy, the Media, and Funding for Project Apollo, 1961–1963* (Tuscaloosa: University of Alabama Press, 2009).

David Scott and Richard Jurek, *Marketing the Moon: The Selling of the Apollo Lunar Program* (Cambridge, MA: MIT Press, 2014), 113.

Susan Strasser, "Opinion | What's in Your Microwave Oven?" *The New York Times*, April 14, 2017, https://www.nytimes.com/2017/04/14/opinion/whats-in-your-microwave-oven.html.

Brittany Spanos, "Lady Gaga's 'The Fame' at 10: How Her Debut Was a Self-Fulfilling Prophecy," *Rolling Stone* (blog), August 19, 2018, https://www.rollingstone.com/music/music-news/lady-gagas-the-fame-at-10-how-her-debut-was-a-self-fulfilling-prophecy-711142/.

"Lady Gaga's Social Media Strategist on How She Helped Build an Empire," *Business News Daily*, June 8, 2012, https://mashable.com/2012/06/08/lady-gaga-strategist/.

Scott and Jurek, *Marketing the Moon*, 17–44.

Richard Jurek, Phone Interview with Theresa Lina, July 3, 2019.

"Apollo Press Kits: The David Meerman Scott Collection," Cover image used with permission, accessed November 22, 2019, https://www.apollopresskits.com/.

Everett M. Rogers, *Diffusion of Innovations*, 5th ed. (New York: Free Press, 2003).

Bob Sorokanich, "Elon Musk Admits to Shareholders That the Tesla Roadster Was a Disaster," *Road & Track*, June 1, 2016, https://www.roadandtrack.com/new-cars/news/a29378/elon-musk-admits-to-shareholders-that-the-tesla-roadster-was-a-disaster/.

Jocelyn McClurg, "John Gray Looks Back at 'Men Are from Mars,'" *USA Today*, October 30, 2013, https://www.usatoday.com/story/life/books/2013/10/30/men-are-from-mars-women-are-from-venus/3297375/.

Stephanie Buck, "Fear of Nuclear Annihilation Scarred Children Growing Up in the Cold War, Studies Later Showed," *Timeline*, August 29, 2017, https://timeline.com/nuclear-war-child-psychology-d1ff491b5fe0.

"Who Are Your Centers of Influence?" *CUInsight*, March 26, 2013, https://www.cuinsight.com/who-are-your-centers-of-influence.html.

Tom Kosnik, Text Message to Author, July 1, 2019.

Elizabeth Lesly Stevens, "The Power Broker," *Washington Monthly*, July 7, 2012, https://washingtonmonthly.com/magazine/julyaugust-2012/the-power-broker/.

Eugene Kim, "The Epic 30-Year Bromance of Billionaire CEOs Larry Ellison and Marc Benioff," *Business Insider*, accessed November 22, 2019, https://www.businessinsider.com/larry-ellison-marc-benioff-relationship-2015-8.

Megan Garber, "Astro Mad Men: NASA's 1960s Campaign to Win America's Heart," *The Atlantic*, July 31, 2013, https://www.theatlantic.com/technology/archive/2013/07/astro-mad-men-nasas-1960s-campaign-to-win-americas-heart/278233/.

Scott and Jurek, *Marketing the Moon*, 8.

"Harley-Davidson History Timeline | Harley-Davidson USA," Harley-Davidson, accessed November 22, 2019, https://www.harley-davidson.com/us/en/museum/explore/hd-timeline.html.

"Collaborating for Good," REI, accessed November 22, 2019, https://www.rei.com/stewardship/outdoor-industry-collaboration.

Sarah Leary, "Celebrating Lorelei, America's First Nextdoor Neighborhood," *Nextdoor Blog*, May 22, 2017, https://blog.nextdoor.com/2017/05/22/celebrating-lorelei-americas-first-nextdoor-neighborhood/.

CHAPTER 7

Betsy Mason, "The Incredible Things NASA Did to Train Apollo Astronauts," *Wired*, July 20, 2011, https://www.wired.com/2011/07/moon-landing-gallery/.

Elon Musk, "Elon Musk's Vision for the Future," interview by Steve Jurvetson, Stanford, October 7th, 2015, https://stvp-static-prod.s3.amazonaws.com/uploads/sites/2/2015/10/3620.pdf.

Ed Catmull, "Creativity, Inc.," interview by Bob Sutton, Stanford, April 30, 2014, https://stvp-static-prod.s3.amazonaws.com/uploads/sites/2/2014/04/3321.pdf.

Emily Petsko, "11 Secrets of Butterball's Turkey Talk-Line Operators," November 16, 2018, https://www.mentalfloss.com/article/563246/butterball-turkey-hotline-secrets.

Jerry Seelig, Phone Interview with Theresa Lina, August 31, 2019.

"Dollar Shave Club | Look, Feel, & Smell Your Best," Dollar Shave Club, accessed November 27, 2019. https://www.dollarshaveclub.com.

Mark Fidelman, "How Vitamix Serves Up a Unique Blend of Customer Experiences To Cope With Explosive Growth | CustomerThink," August 3, 2017, http://customerthink.com/how-vitamix-serves-up-a-unique-blend-of-customer-experiences-to-cope-with-explosive-growth/.

Jason Del Rey, "The Making of Amazon Prime, the Internet's Most Successful and Devastating Membership Program," *Vox*, May 3, 2019, https://www.vox.com/recode/2019/5/3/18511544/amazon-prime-oral-history-jeff-bezos-one-day-shipping.

"How to Train an Animator, by Walt Disney," June 15, 2010, http://www.lettersofnote.com/2010/06/how-to-train-animator-by-walt-disney.html.

Scott and Jurek, *Marketing the Moon*, 49–52.

James Marcus, *Amazonia: Five Years at the Epicenter of the Dot.com Juggernaut* (New York: The New Press, 2004), 52.

CHAPTER 8

Megan O'Neill, "How Netflix Bankrupted and Destroyed Blockbuster," *Business Insider*, March 1, 2011, https://www.businessinsider.com/how-netflix-bankrupted-and-destroyed-blockbuster-infographic-2011-3.

"iinnovate Presents Barry McCarthy, Chief Financial Officer of Netflix," *The Unofficial Stanford Blog*, accessed November 27, 2019, http://tusb.stanford.edu/2008/01/barry_mccarthy_chief_financial.html.

Don Reisinger, "Blockbuster Streaming: Too Late," CNET, March 28, 2009, https://www.cnet.com/news/blockbuster-streaming-too-late/.

"After Apollo, Budget Realities Limit NASA Options," *Houston Chronicle*, June 27, 2019, https://www.houstonchronicle.com/local/space/mission-moon/article/After-Apollo-budget-realities-limit-NASA-options-14045367.php.

David Portree, "Ending Apollo (1968)," *Wired*, September 22, 2013, https://www.wired.com/2013/09/ending-apollo-1968/.

John T. Correll, "From a Bucket and a Rope," *Airman*, July 1975.

Timothy B. Lee, "How Apple Became the World's Most Valuable Company," *Vox*, November 17, 2014, https://www.vox.com/2014/11/17/18076360/apple.

Josh Lowensohn, "MobileMe, a Rare Apple Screwup, Finally Bites the Dust," *CNET*, June 29, 2012, https://www.cnet.com/news/mobileme-a-rare-apple-screwup-finally-bites-the-dust/.

"2 Years of Losses at Harley-Davidson," *The New York Times*, January 26, 1983, https://www.nytimes.com/1983/01/26/business/2-years-of-losses-at-harley-davidson.html.

Alyson Shontell, "The Greatest Comeback Story of All Time: How Apple Went from Near Bankruptcy to Billions in 13 Years," *Business Insider*, October 26, 2010, https://www.businessinsider.com/apple-comeback-story-2010-10.

"Harley-Davidson Struggling as Millennials Seek Easy Transportation, Not Flashy Motorcycles," *Washington Examiner*, January 30, 2019, https://www.washingtonexaminer.com/red-alert-politics/harley-davidson-struggling-as-millennials-seek-easy-transportation-not-flashy-motorcycles.

"Harley-Davidson Accelerates Strategy to Build Next Generation of Riders Globally," July 30, 2018, https://www.harley-davidson.com.

Bruce Cleveland, "Lessons from the Death of a Tech Goliath," *Fortune*, January 23, 2014, https://fortune.com/2014/01/23/lessons-from-the-death-of-a-tech-goliath/.

Julie Bort, "Amazon's Cloud Is Now a Profitable $7 Billion+ Business," *Business Insider*, July 23, 2015, https://www.businessinsider.com/amazon-cloud-grows-even-bigger-2015-7.

"Tenneco History | Tenneco Inc," accessed November 27, 2019, https://www.tenneco.com/careers/tenneco_history/.

"Tenneco Wins 2006 Automotive Shareholder Value Award | Tenneco Inc," January 20, 2005, https://www.tenneco.com/tenneco_wins_2006_automotive_shareholder_value_award/.

Reuben Gregg Brewer, "Why Tenneco Stock Plummeted 36% in March," *The Motley Fool*, April 4, 2019, https://www.fool.com/investing/2019/04/04/why-tenneco-stock-plummeted-36-in-march.aspx.

"What Is Jeff Bezos's 'Day 1' Philosophy?" *Forbes*, April 21, 2017, https://www.forbes.com/sites/quora/2017/04/21/what-is-jeff-bezos-day-1-philosophy/.

CHAPTER 9

Paul Festa, "'Click of Death' Strikes Iomega," CNET, January 30, 1998,
    https://www.cnet.com/news/click-of-death-strikes-iomega/.

Kimberly Amadeo, "This Bailout Made Bernanke Angrier than Anything
    Else in the Recession," *The Balance*, November 20, 2019, https://www.
    thebalance.com/aig-bailout-cost-timeline-bonuses-causes-effects-
    3305693.

Megan Ritter, "5 Businesses That Survived the Recession and Why," January
    27, 2015, https://www.business2community.com/finance/5-businesses-
    survived-recession-01137706.

"Unrecognized Apple II Employees Exit," *Infoworld*, April 15, 1985, 35.

ABOUT THE AUTHOR

Theresa M. Lina has over twenty years of experience as a recognized Silicon Valley thought leader and strategist. She is the CEO of Lina Group, Inc., which specializes in market dominance strategy, and has been involved at Stanford University since 2006. She has served as chief strategy and marketing officer for several technology start-ups, has advised hundreds of companies, and began her career at Accenture, where she helped found, lead, and grow the firm's communications industry group, now a multibillion-dollar business unit. Theresa is a frequent speaker and workshop leader on strategy, market leadership, innovation, and technology topics.

Made in United States
Orlando, FL
17 September 2022

22497135R00232